High Skills

High Skills

Globalization, Competitiveness, and Skill Formation

PHILLIP BROWN
ANDY GREEN
HUGH LAUDER

OXFORD

UNIVERSITY PRESS

Great Clarendon Street, Oxford OX2 6DP

Oxford University Press is a department of the University of Oxford.
It furthers the University's objective of excellence in research,
scholarship, and education by publishing worldwide in

Oxford New York

Athens Auckland Bangkok Bogotá Buenos Aires Cape Town Chennai
Dar es Salaam Delhi Florence Hong Kong Istanbul Karachi Kolkata
Kuala Lumpur Madrid Melbourne Mexico City Mumbai Nairobi Paris
São Paulo Shanghai Singapore Taipei Tokyo Toronto Warsaw

with associated companies in Berlin Ibadan

Oxford is a registered trade mark of Oxford University Press

in the UK and certain other countries

Published in the United States
by Oxford University Press Inc., New York

© Phillip Brown, Andy Green, Hugh Lauder 2001

The moral rights of the authors have been asserted

Database right Oxford University Press (maker)

First published 2001

British Library Cataloguing in Publication Data

Data available

Library of Congress Cataloging in Publication Data

Brown, Phillip, 1957–
    High skills : globalization, competitiveness, and skill formation /
    Phillip Brown, Andy Green, Hugh Lauder.
        p. cm.
    Includes bibliographical references.
    1. Employment forecasting.   2. Skilled labor—Supply and
    demand—Forecasting.
    I. Green, Andy, 1954– II. Lauder, Hugh. III. Title.
    HD5701.55 .B77 2001   331.11'422—dc21   2001032922

ISBN 0–19–924418–9
ISBN 0–19–924420–0 (pbk.)

10 9 8 7 6 5 4 3 2 1

Typeset by Florence Production, Stoodleigh, Devon
Printed in Great Britain
on acid-free paper by
T. J. International Ltd., Padstow, Cornwall

CONTENTS

LIST OF FIGURES

LIST OF TABLES

PREFACE

The debate over the nature of competitiveness, which has now raged
for nearly a decade, is central to questions of economic survival and
welfare. The focal point for these debates concerns the question of
national routes to a high skills economy. The view that human capabilities are more central than ever to economic and social welfare has been
seized on by politicians throughout the world. Recent US presidents
have claimed themselves 'education presidents', while in the UK Tony
Blair placed education at the centre of his 2001 election manifesto. In
Australia, the Hawke government of the 1980s wanted to create a 'clever
country'. Politicians have reason to make a skills strategy central to their
political platforms in an era when the financial structure of the global
economy has limited their economic powers. In the post-war era, full
employment could be achieved by the Keynesian expedient of manip-
ulating demand. At times of economic downturn, governments could
inject funds into the economy, thereby maintaining the demand for
goods and services which, in turn, sustained full employment. This
strategy met its nemesis in the early 1980s. Confronted with rising
unemployment, the French government sought to spend its way out of
the problem only to find a *run* on the franc as global investors pulled
out of France. Overseas financiers feared inflation would result from
pumping money into the economy devaluing their investments. Global
financial institutions had flexed their muscles and nations took note.

Thereafter, a subtle change occurred in political rhetoric from
promises of full employment to full employability. Full employability
signalled a shift from demand side policies to promote employment to
supply-side policies which emphasized individuals' education and
skills. Several factors served to make the rhetoric plausible. The development of the IT revolution demanded higher basic skills for even
factory work. Murnane and Levy (1996) calculate that someone working

at Fords in Detroit now requires the equivalent of schooling to the age of 14 as a minimum, where once more skill was exercised driving a Ford than assembling it. At the same time, the demand for professional work has risen with managerial and professional occupations expanding in all the advanced economies. As the new global economy has developed, it has been argued that labour markets have become more perfectly competitive (Reich, 1991). Consequently, many of the factors which had served to bid up the wages of the unskilled in the Western world such as trade union power and state forms of social insurance have been stripped away. This view is controversial (P. Brown and Lauder, 2001a), for the decline of union and state protection of workers can be seen as either a cause of the global economy or as an ideological response to it by some of the advanced economies.

Whether the removal of workers' protection from the vagaries of the capitalist economy are cause or effect, politicians have seen the development of skills as workers' primary, and sometimes only, resource in the intensified global competition for work and income. A highly skilled workforce is seen to bring many benefits: the economic benefits come from creating a more competitive workforce as brainpower is substituted for brawn. In a global economy where brawn is plentiful, brainpower generates a premium in terms of value added. As Reich has noted, 'in 1920, more than 85 per cent of the cost of an automobile went to pay routine labourers and investors. By 1990, these two groups received less than 60 per cent with the remainder going to designers, engineers, stylists, planners. . . . More than 85 per cent of [the price of semiconductor chip] is for specialised design and engineering services' Reich 1991: 104).

The social advantages are seen to be no less significant. As incomes have polarized in some of the advanced economies and social disintegration has threatened, so the raising of workforce skills is intended to reduce the gap between rich and poor and re-create a middle class with the virtues of thrift and discipline to hold nations together. Similarly, providing the unskilled with skills is seen as an antidote to unemployment, thereby eradicating poverty. Finally, work in the twenty-first century is most likely to be unstable. Most can expect to change jobs many times. Providing workers with skills is, therefore, an insurance against the caprice of the labour market, giving them a greater chance of market power and hence employability.

The aim of a high skills policy is not, therefore, just economic. Education and skill development are as central to social policy as they are to competitiveness strategies. In this sense we can view politicians' rhetoric as being as much about a high skills *society* as a high skills economy.

The High Skills project, on which this book is based, is an attempt to interrogate the assumptions underlying the rhetoric of 'high skills'. It is a comparative study of high skills strategies in Britain, Germany, Japan, Korea, Singapore, Germany, and the United States funded by the Economic and Social Science Research Council (UK).[1] From the outset the project was conceived as multidisciplinary, for the study of skill development and formation must take into account a nation's history, culture, and politics as well as its economic trajectory. It has been a fundamental failing of the economic theory of human capital, as argued in Chapter 1, that it has not been able to comprehend the broader historical and social dimensions contributing to skill formation. The study was comparative because we wanted to see what differences and similarities there were between nations' approaches to economic development. We chose, therefore, nations like Britain and the United States where economic development is governed by the market, Germany where there is a strong emphasis on social consensus underwriting market mechanisms, and the Asian tiger nations of Japan, Korea, and Singapore in which the state has taken a leading role in governing the market. Given these radically different approaches to skill formation and economic development, the study enabled us to ask six key questions. These were:

(1) To what extent is the dominant theory used to explain skill formation and guide skill formation policy adequate to the task? (Chapter 1)

(2) Do nations need a similar kind of skill profile in order to be economically competitive? (Chapter 2)

(3) Given the speed of change of knowledge and skills required how do different nations diffuse skills? Is one national system of skill diffusion more effective than another? What are the barriers which exclude groups from acquiring new skills? (Chapter 3)

(4) What is the impact of globalization on national systems of skill formation and diffusion? Is globalization likely to lead to a convergence in systems of skill formation? (Chapter 4)

(5) What are the major pressure points that nations now confront in seeking to develop a high skills economy and society? To what extent is the aim of a high skills society feasible in any of the nations studied? (Chapter 5)

[1] Award No: R000236664.

Underlying these questions is the sixth and most general:

(6) To what extent can high skills strategies achieve politicians' aspirations for a high skills society?

In seeking to answer these questions, we have sought to address current debates about the nature of competitiveness, the impact of education and training systems and labour markets on skill formation and diffusion, the role of multinational companies in transferring skills, and the methodological issue of how best to compare the skill formation strategies of nations with radically different histories and cultures.

This research took us to the six countries included in this study where senior politicians, state officials, trade unionists, educationists, academics, and the senior management of some of the world's largest multinationals gave generously of their time. We completed over 240 interviews in seeking to find out key stakeholders' visions of a high skill economy and how it might be achieved for their country. By triangulating the views of the major interest groups in each country, we could assess the degree to which there was consensus or possible conflict between the means and the ends of achieving a high skills economy and society. We owe all those we interviewed our gratitude. While we can name the organizations that collaborated with us (see Appendix), we cannot for obvious reasons name individuals.

If there is one conclusion we would foreshadow, it is that, to borrow the title of a recent book (Hutton and Giddens 2000), each of the nations in our study is in some sense 'on the edge'. Their aim of achieving a high skills economy is very much in the balance in which the coming years will tell whether the decisions being made now will bring them closer to or further away from the ideal of a high skills society.

ACKNOWLEDGEMENTS

This book could not have been written without the support of the Social and Economic Research Council (ESRC) of Great Britain. We are extremely grateful for being given the resources to undertake this project. We are also greatly indebted to all those in government departments, companies, and not-for-profit organizations who gave time to meet with us. We hope that this book goes some way towards repaying them for their contributions.

We received help and advice from a large number of people, including David Ashton, Saravanan Gopinathan, Chon-Sun Ihm, Zoe Fearnley, Hilary Fleming, Chelly Halsey, Teruhisa Horio, Hyun-Suk Yu, Ewert Keep, Lee Byung Jin, Lee Seong-Gyu, Linda Low, Park In-Sub, Seizaburo Sato, Carmel Smith, Miri Song, Hilary Steedman, Tadahiro Takeno, Matthew Williams, and Joan Wills.

Finally, we would like to thank David Musson, Sarah Dobson, and Lynn Childress from Oxford University Press.

P.B.
A.G.
H.L.

1

Skill Formation in the Twenty-First Century

PHILLIP BROWN

INTRODUCTION

It is widely argued that global economic competitiveness rests on the knowledge and skills of the workforce. Such ideas have led developed nations to find ways of upgrading the skills of the many rather than limiting the opportunity for high skilled work to an elite of executives, managers, and professionals. The US summit report *21st Century Skills for 21st Century Jobs*, noted that 'America's competitiveness and the prosperity of our people in a changing economy depend increasingly on high-skill, high-wage jobs. Realizing our potential will require investing in education and learning for all of our people throughout their lifetimes' (Department of Commerce 1999). The same recognition that the future depends on lifting the skills of all, led Tony Blair to depict the challenge for New Labour in Britain as one of liberating people from the bondage of low skills and low expectations, 'People are born with talent and everywhere it is in chains. Fail to develop the talents of any one person, we fail Britain. Talent is 21st century wealth' (T. Blair 1999). The implications for skill formation policies are clear—if the developed nations are to fully benefit from the impact of a global labour market, significant efforts need to be made to lift the skill base, otherwise those who have failed to learn and acquire marketable skills are destined to fall into the 'black holes' of the information society (Castells 1998: 345).

In the Anglo-Saxon economies such views are premissed on human capital assumptions of an evolutionary process of technological progression from a low skill to a high skill economy. It follows that skill formation policies will need to focus on how to improve the *supply* of intermediate and high skilled workers to meet the growing demand for professional, technical, and managerial jobs that are seen to exist (DfEE 2000). This approach is bolstered by the idea that knowledge-driven capitalism has created a global labour market, in which it is those countries that can succeed in upgrading the quality of their workforce who will become the 'magnet' economies for high skilled work (P. Brown and Lauder 1996; 2001a).

In this introductory chapter we examine human capital theory and how it has been extended to explain global economic trends and the scope for skill formation policies in the new economic competition (Best 1990). Human capital theory will be contrasted with a *new political economy* of skill formation that draws on economic sociology and the new institutionalism (Swedberg 1996; Crouch and Streeck 1997). The new political economy represents a different approach to skill formation issues in the twenty-first century, although we concur on the increased significance of human talents, knowledge, and skills as a factor in raising productivity that is the source of wealth. Porter, Takeuchi, and Sakakibara note that:

Productivity ... defines competitiveness for a nation. Productivity, rightly understood, encompasses both the value (prices) that a nation's products command in the marketplace and the efficiency with which they are produced. Improving efficiency alone, or producing more units per unit of labor or capital, does not necessarily elevate wages and profits unless the prices to the products or services are stable or rising. As global competition places greater pressure on the prices of standard goods, efficiency alone is insufficient. Advanced nations improve their standard of living more by driving up the value of their products and services (because of better technology, marketing, and associated services, for example) and moving into new fields through innovation than by producing standardized products at lower cost. (2000: 100–1)

We suggest that the nature of skill and its relationship to productivity is changing. We also offer a different understanding of the role of the nation state under conditions of global capitalism. It will be argued that smart economies require smart government. Globalization has changed the context in which nation states manoeuvre but, if anything, it has made their strategic role more, rather than less, important.

Our analysis is informed by a detailed study of skill formation strategies and policies in Britain, Germany, Japan, Singapore, South Korea, and the United States. This analysis has led us to reject the idea of a global convergence leading all the developed nations to address skill formation issues in the same way. Globalization presents important challenges to all these countries in their common commitment to generate 'high skill' societies, but this is understood in different ways that reflect the historical, cultural, social, political, and economic conditions in each country. An important 'societal effect' is discernible that will shape the direction of skill formation policies and the prospects for 'success' in each country.

Throughout the book we use the term 'high skills society' to highlight the fact that high skill formation depends on building 'societal capacity' that points to the importance of studying the social foundations on which high skills formation is achieved (or otherwise). Equally, the emphasis on 'society' rather than a narrower focus on the national 'economy' also reflects the importance we attach to the study of political economy. It is not only the social foundations of skill formation that require our attention but also the social purposes or goals which they address. A high skills society is not an inevitable feature of knowledge-driven economies, but a social and political aspiration that involves a national commitment to its creation. This view will be extended in subsequent chapters, but our immediate purpose is to outline a conceptual framework for the analysis of skill formation that avoid the flaws associated with human capital theory.

HUMAN CAPITAL THEORY

For the best part of 200 years after Adam Smith's *Wealth of Nations* (1776), 'labour' was treated as a homogeneous category. What counted was the numbers of workers or the size of the workforce, akin to the area of land for agricultural production or the number of machines in a factory. The possibility that differences in the skills of workers could have a significant impact on productivity and economic growth was largely ignored. This blatant disregard of human 'capital' was less surprising when one considers Adam Smith's account of the division of labour. In his enquiry into the nature and causes of the wealth of nations, he argued that the most 'civilized' nations of the time had the most complex division of labour. It was the detailed division of labour characterized by splitting work tasks into simple operations that he saw as the driving force for economic growth.

Here the role of education assumed importance. But this was not required to prepare the working masses for their place in the division of labour, but rather to compensate for the 'almost entire corruption and degeneracy of the great body of the people' that would result from this model of economic progress (Smith 1976: 781). State funding of education was also viewed as necessary to ensure an acceptance of the divine authority of their superiors. While Smith recognized that the dexterity and productivity of the worker was enhanced by 'reducing every man's business to some one simple operation' by making this the 'sole employment of his life' (781), he also recognized that the division of labour dulled the intelligence of the mass of workers.

In the progress of the division of labour, the employment of the far greater part of those who live by labour, that is, of the great body of the people, comes to be confined to a few very simple operations; frequently to one or two. . . . The man whose whole life is spent in performing a few simple operations . . . has no occasion to exert his understanding, or to exercise his invention in finding out expedients for removing difficulties which never occur. He naturally loses . . . the habit of such exertion, and generally becomes as *stupid and ignorant as it is possible for a human creature to become.* (Smith 1976: 781–2, emphasis added)

Karl Marx was later to argue that it was not the division of labour per se that limited the intellectual, social, and moral development of workers but its organization according to the principles of capitalism (Marx 1976). The ownership and control of the means of production in the hands of a few inevitably involved the subjugation and exploitation of the mass of workers. Indeed the development of industrial capitalism was seen to destroy the long tradition of craft production and the reproduction of skills across the generations (Thompson 1968). The longevity of these ideas has been impressive. Harry Braverman (1974) wrote an influential sociological account of the degradation of work in the twentieth century that was subject to extensive academic debate. This was based on the argument that white-collar jobs were being subjected to the same processes of 'deskilling' that had destroyed the skill content of craft employment throughout the nineteenth and early part of the twentieth century (Bendix 1956; Sabel 1982).[1] Moreover, much of industry in Britain and the United States was based on a model of economic efficiency inherited from Adam Smith and ably assisted on its historical mission by Charles Babbage and Frederick Winslow Taylor. It was not until the 1980s that the detailed division of labour based on low skilled, low trust relation (Fordism) was successfully challenged in Britain and the United States as the principal paradigm of economic efficiency.

---

[1] This argument has also been applied to the future of knowledge workers, see Aronowitz and DiFazio (1994).

The idea that the quality and skills of workers may have a direct impact on productivity and economic growth also remained heretical within mainstream economics until the development of human capital theory in the 1960s (Becker 1964; Schultz 1971). Human capital theorists rejected the contention that labour could be treated as a homogeneous category inherent in classical political economy. They asserted the need for a broader concept of capital that included the skills, knowledge, and know-how of workers. Moreover, the knowledge and skills that increase the capital yields of human labour are believed to result from system-atic investment as the 'price of learning from trial and error is high' (Schultz 1971: 2; Becker 1964).[2] Consequently, education and other forms of work preparation were defined as forms of investment rather than consumption. Economists distinguish between investments that involve expenditure on assets that will produce income in the future and money spent on consumption that produces immediate satisfac-tion or benefits, but does not contribute to future income potential (Woodhall 1997: 219).

Human capital theorists argued that much of the unexplained increase in productivity, wages, and economic growth recognized by economists could be explained by investments in human capital. Therefore, by investing in themselves through education and training individuals are able to increase their lifetime earnings. Equally, govern-ments could use such investments as a way of enhancing economic growth (Psacharopoulos 1987; OECD 1998b).

It is notoriously difficult to measure the contribution of human capital to productivity and economic growth as we will argue, but various attempts have been made to take such measurements (Healy 1998; M. Blair and Kochan 2000). In the United States, for instance, the output per production worker has virtually tripled since 1930 from a value of $22,000 to $60,000. Over the same period, the proportion of the workforce directly engaged in production has declined from 27 per cent to 15 per cent. Moreover, for every production worker there are another 21 non-production workers who are employed in sales, marketing, cler-ical, technical, managerial, and professional activities. Most of these non-production workers have received some form of tertiary education (Carnevale and Porro 1994: 31). Indeed, the expansion of higher educa-tion from an elite to a mass provider is explained in terms of the

---

[2] Schultz goes on to say, 'This knowledge and skill are in great part the product of investment and, combined with other human investment, predominantly account for the productive superiority of the technically advanced countries. To omit them in studying economic growth is like trying to explain Soviet ideology without Marx' (Schultz 1971: 28).

exponential increase in scientific and technical knowledge, which has led to greater investment in human capital to supply the technical, professional, and managerial workers required in the shift to post-industrial societies (Bell 1973; Neef 1998).

Other commentators have suggested that human capital has increased in economic significance to the point where it has become as important to contemporary society as land was to feudal society and financial capital to the industrial revolution. Between 1948 and 1973 almost one-fifth of the increase in GNP has been attributed to the expansion of the American education system. Subsequently, when productivity growth began to falter in the United States, between 1973 and 1981 the contribution of education to productivity rose from 25 per cent to more than 30 per cent (Carnevale and Porro 1994: 10). In Britain it has been estimated that in 1867 the returns to skilled labour accounted for between 5 and 25 per cent of national income, whereas by 1967 they amounted to between 46 and 58 per cent of pre-tax household income. Today, that figure will have increased significantly as the wage differentials between educated and unskilled workers have dramatically polarized, especially in America (Department of Commerce 1999; Auerbach and Belous 1998).

From a human capital perspective the technological upgrading of employment, coupled to the increasing value of labour, also involves a power shift that transforms not only class antagonisms but the relationship between capital and labour. This view imbues most of contemporary thinking about occupations and careers in a knowledge-driven economy. Peter Drucker, for example, suggests that the dominant wealth-creating activities no longer result from the allocation of capital to productive use nor 'labour' (in its physical unskilled form), but productivity and innovation achieved through the application of knowledge to work. Accordingly, the economy is driven by knowledge executives, professionals, and employees, 'Yet unlike the employees under capitalism they own both the "means of production" and the "tools of production"—the former through their pension funds which are rapidly emerging in all developed countries as the only real ownership, the latter because knowledge workers own their knowledge and can take it with them wherever they go' (Drucker 1993: 7).[3]

---

[3] Drucker is less sanguine about the possibilities of high skilled employment for all when he suggests that 'the social challenge of the post-capitalist society will, however, be the dignity of the second class in post-capitalist society: the service workers. Service workers, as a rule, lack the necessary education to be knowledge workers. And in every country, even the most highly advanced ones, they will constitute a majority' (1993: 7).

It is individual 'employability' (that determines the value of one's human capital) that is now seen as the source of economic opportunity, choice, and occupational status. As Schultz has suggested, 'by investing in themselves, people can enlarge the range of choice available to them. It is one way free men can enhance their welfare' (Schultz 1971: 26). Such ideas fit well with Western individualism and principles of democratic participation. Prosperity, power, and control are no longer seen as the preserve of a small elite of capitalist owners, but have been extended to those who can successfully convert themselves into invaluable economic assets in their own right, freed from Marx's 'dull compulsion' of low skilled toil in order to make a living.

The efficient development and utilization of human capital is also furthered through the widespread application of meritocratic rules of achievement. It is argued that individual employability should reflect the talent, efforts, and achievements of individuals rather than ascribed characteristics such as socio-economic background, gender, religion, or race. Indeed as the economy becomes more complex and based on high skilled work, it becomes more important to ensure that the most able people are allocated to skilled and important occupational positions based on achievement (Davis and Moore 1945). Yet as Schultz acknowledged, 'there are many hindrances to the free choice of professions. Racial discrimination and religious discrimination are still widespread. Professional associations also hinder entry, for example, into medicine. Such purposeful interference keeps the investment in this form of human capital substantially below its optimum' (Schulz 1971: 36; R. Collins 1979).

Such caveats remain submerged under a wave of technocratic optimism. The creation of a high skills economy is seen as an evolutionary process of technological upgrading, compelling national governments and companies to invest in the workforce, and individuals to invest in themselves, as the demand for technical, managerial, and professional 'knowledge' workers increases and the demand for low skilled jobs declines (Clark 1962; Kerr et al. 1973). The assessment that returns to human capital increase over time also offers a solution to the enduring question of how income should be distributed throughout the population. There is, so the argument goes, little need to agonize over issues of distribution because if societies make the necessary investments in human capital few need be excluded from the prosperity these investments will generate. Finally, human capital theory is seen to have general applicability to developing as well as developed nations. It is indifferent to national history, culture, and identities because it conforms to the universal laws of economic development (Becker 1964).

Globalization, Nation States, and Human Capital

The significance of human capital ideas has not only increased with the view that the quality of human resources stands at the heart of future economic competitiveness, but as a result of economic globalization (Spring 1998). For most of the twentieth century, skill formation issues were couched in the context of 'walled' economies. These walls were built around national economies that served to limit international competition through tight controls over national currencies, trade barriers, and tariffs on imported goods and services. The rise of multi-national companies took the form of 'national champions' with overseas operations that now seem almost parochial when compared to the global ambitions of multinationals at the beginning of the twenty-first century. In the post-war period, the leading economies of North America and Europe were able, in albeit different ways, to develop Keynesian (or Fordism) settlements between the dominant interests of employers, trade unions, and government. These settlements, based on prosperity, security, and opportunity (P. Brown and Lauder 2001a), were underpinned by the mass production of standardized goods and services that brought within reach of the general population 'white goods' such as refrigerators, freezers, and washing machines; radio, television, and record players; along with motor cars. The combination of mass production and mass consumption depended on wage levels that enabled the majority to engage in the emerging consumer culture. This maintained corporate profitability at the same time as paying relatively high wages to low skilled workers. In this context human capital theory was restricted to providing an argument for why further investments should be made in education and training as the technological complexity of consumer goods and services increased.

Economic globalization has greatly expanded the policy significance of human capital theory, as neo-classical ideas about economic competitiveness came to the fore in the 1980s. Global market forces were believed to expose economic inefficiencies in politically negotiated settlements between capital and labour due to 'artificial' increases in wages that were not tied to improvements in productivity. The consequences of such inefficiencies it was argued were high unemployment, inflation, and sluggish economic growth. The application of human capital theory to global economic trends added weight to the assertion that income should reflect the market value of labour judged by international, rather than domestic, standards. Failure to make wages globally competitive would, it is argued, lead multinational companies to transfer operations to countries with more 'realistic' wage rates and lower social overheads. Adrian Woods has calculated that up to 1990 changes in global trade had reduced the demand for unskilled labour by approximately 20 per cent due to the transfer of low skilled jobs to newly industrializing countries (NICs) (Wood 1994: 11). However, the impact of the scale of globalization on low skilled workers has been challenged (Esping-Andersen 1999).

These ideas are elaborated in Robert Reich's (1991) *The Work of Nations*. Reich, who served as President Clinton's first Labour Secretary, observed that there is a global labour market in which job seekers from different countries have to compete. In the United States the increasing income polarization in the 1980s is explained in terms of the relative ability of workers to acquire and sell their skills, knowledge, and insights in the global labour market (Frank and Cook 1996).

The winners in this competition are those who have acquired human capital with global appeal. Reich calls these the 'symbolic analysts' who are engaged in problem-identifying, problem-solving, and strategic-brokering activities in the global knowledge economy (Reich 1991: 177). The symbolic analysts represent approximately 20 per cent of the work-force, including design, software, civil and biotechnology engineers; management, financial, tax, legal and energy consultants; advertising, marketing, and publishing executives, as well as research scientists (177–8). If income potential depends on the ability of workers, whether as employees or self-employed consultants, to make a 'value added' contribution on a global scale, the converse of this argument is that those who remain tied to local or national labour markets due to a failure to acquire the necessary skills and credentials to compete successfully in the global labour market will see their incomes stagnate or decline (Murnane and Levy 1993).

National skill formation policies, therefore, need to focus on creating a world-class labour force. This rests on the idea that the developed nations can act as 'magnet' economies attracting high skilled and high waged investment capital from MNCs, and offering high value added services to the rest of the world, if they can win a competitive advantage in the global 'knowledge wars' (P. Brown and Lauder 1996). There is, therefore, no reason why the vast majority of the workforce in Britain and America cannot be in high skilled and high waged jobs. The main policy objective is to outsmart other countries in the development of the nation's human resources. As the quality of a nation's human resources are being subjected to global benchmarking, upon which companies will make their investment decisions, the key priority is to lift the skills base of the entire population, rather than get side-tracked by debates about equalizing life chances, which will be resolved by the new miracle drug of global 'human' capitalism.

There is a further dimension to this discussion that relates to the future of skill formation policy. This is the view that the nation state is virtually powerless to intervene in global markets in ways that were previously used to support the 'national' interest of companies and workers. As Tony Blair told the *Financial Times*, 'The determining context of economic policy is the new global market. That imposes huge limitations of a practical nature . . . on macro economic policies.'[4] A sign of this weakness is the way that the major Western nations have establish free trade agreements aimed at increasing economic cooperation and trade with neighbouring countries. These include the North American Free Trade Agreement (NAFTA) incorporating the United States, Canada, and Mexico, and in Europe, the single market embracing fifteen member countries (soon to be expanded) is part of a European Economic Area of 360 million consumers across 19 nations. Such agreements are taken to signal the declining power of individual nation states to control the economic forces that determine their growth rates, unemployment figures, and whether incumbent governments are likely to get re-elected (Elliott and Atkinson 1998).

This decline in the governing competence of states is also related to the availability of new technologies, as Yergin and Stanislaw have noted in their account of why governments are losing power to the market-place:

Information technology—through computers—is creating a 'woven world' by promoting communication, coordination, integration, and contact at a pace and scale of change that far outrun the ability of any government to manage. The accelerating connections make national borders increasingly porous—and, in terms of some forms of control, increasingly irrelevant. (1998: 14)

Such interpretations of the impact of globalization on the role of national states are central to human capital theory because neo-liberal economic ideas (from which it draws) are not only presented as a virtue but a necessity. The logic of globalization, so the argument goes, is forcing all governments to adopt neo-liberal market policies.

Robert Wade (1990: 11) identifies six features of the neo-liberal view of the economic functions of government:

---

[4] Tony Blair, Reported in the *Financial Times*, 22 May 1995, p. 6.

(1) maintain macroeconomic stability;
(2) provide physical infrastructure, including harbours, railways, roads, sewers;
(3) supply 'public goods' including education, basic research, market information, defence and national security, environmental protection;
(4) facilitate the markets for labour, finance, technology, etc;
(5) offset or eliminate price distortions which arise in cases of demonstrable market failure;
(6) redistribute income to meet the basic needs of the poorest members of society.

The implications of the neo-liberal approach to skill formation are that governments should not (and cannot due to globalization) attempt to intervene in economic matters that are better left to the market: industrial policies are assumed to lead to market rigidities and inefficiency because governments lack the information they require to make informed judgements; labour markets need to be as 'flexible' as possible, as this enables the economy to respond rapidly to changes in the global market for goods and services, and lead to lower unemployment because wage rates will reflect the 'true' value of human capital; vocational training should be driven by employers because they are best placed to make judgements about the demand for specific kinds of skill; and the role of the welfare state should be limited to encourage individual enterprise and incentives for people to invest in their human capital and to find employment.

From a neo-liberal view questions of skill formation are limited to 'supply side' policies that place schools, colleges, universities, and training organizations at the frontline in the battle for economic competitiveness. This represents a major problem in countries such as Britain and the United States where their educational systems are consistently outperformed in international attainment tests (Green 1997a). The solution from a neo-classical approach rests on exposing educational institutions to market competition believed to raise standards for all (Marginson 1993; Lauder et al. 1999).

There are two conclusions to be drawn from this part of our analysis. First, the new settlement between the individual and the state is increasingly based on a *skills nexus*. The state is responsible for giving people the opportunity to gain education and training necessary to develop marketable skills, and the individual is responsible for their employability demonstrated through continuous employment. Taken to its logical conclusion the skills nexus pays no attention to building indigenous economic capacity as industrial policies are the purview of business. Ultimately, the state is indifferent to whether the skills nexus leads to employment within the domestic economy or in another country. This view is captured in Richard Rosecrance's account of the rise of the virtual state:

political and economic decision-makers have begun to recast their horizons, but middle managers and workers lag behind. They expect too much and give and learn too little. That is why the dawn of the virtual state must also be the sunrise of international education and training. The virtual state cannot satisfy all its citizens. The possibility of commanding economic power in the sense of effective state control has greatly declined. Displaced workers and businesspeople must be willing to look abroad for opportunities. In the United States, they can do this only if American education prepares the way. (1998: 45–6, 1999)

Secondly, if the scope for government involvement in skill formation is limited to the 'supply side', the move towards a global convergence in policy is inevitable. We should expect to find governments abandoning any commitment to a 'social partnership' based on tight labour market regulation as in Germany, or 'developmental' state action in industrial policies as found in Japan, Korea, and Singapore. The financial crisis in Asia in the late 1990s, for instance, was interpreted by some commentators as a manifestation of mounting pressure towards policy convergence based on neo-liberal economics (Wade and Veneroso 1998; C. Johnson 1998). Likewise, the performance of the American economy for much of the 1990s and at the beginning of the 2000s has also been taken to confirm the superior performance of neo-liberal economies in a context of global knowledge-driven capitalism (Jasinowski 1998).

There is little doubt that the policy appeal of investment in human capital will remain irresistible to national governments around the world. It offers a win–win scenario, as the economic benefits from investments in education and training are seen to lead to improvements in productivity and wealth creation, at the same time that individuals can expect a return on their investment of time, effort, and financial resource through greater earning potential as more opportunities exist for skilled work. But this 'win–win' scenario is challenged in this book, as we will show that national economies can remain competitive without upgrading the skills of large sections of the workforce. It will also be argued that the routes to a high skills formation and the policies required for its achievement are subject to considerable variation between countries (Ashton and Green 1996).

WHAT'S WRONG WITH HUMAN CAPITAL THEORY?

Human capital theory casts a long shadow over debates about global-ization and economic competitiveness. There has been almost universal recognition that the human side of enterprise is a key feature of rising productivity and that the demand for skilled labour has increased in all the developed economies (OECD 1998*b*). Moreover, the radical assertion in the 1960s that education was an 'investment' for governments and individuals (rather than something one consumes for immediate grati-fication) has become a truism. Nations, businesses, and individuals around the world have been willing to spend substantial and increasing sums on the economic value attached to education and training. But at the very time that human capital theory has taken centre-stage in debates about economic competitiveness, widely acknowledged prob-lems associated with its ideas have become more pronounced in a context of post-industrial change (Block 1990). A brief discussion of some of these problems are outlined here as a way of moving towards an alternative conceptual model for the study of skill formation in the early decades of the twenty-first century.

The Supply Side

Human capital theory reduces individual workers to a bundle of tech-nical skills that are fed into the economy. Therefore, while it successfully challenges the limited understanding of 'capital' in classical eco-nomics, it perpetuates a 'mechanistic' view of the individual worker.[5] Disciplinary boundaries between economics and other social sciences led human capital theorists away from analyses of how skills are socially constructed, to extend the definition of technology to deliver 'an all-inclusive concept . . . including the innate abilities of man' (Schultz 1971: 10).[6] Hence, despite recognizing the importance of human intelli-gence and skills to productivity growth, their view of human beings has changed little from Adam Smith's view that they were 'expensive

---

[5] As Galbraith observed, when the economy is viewed as a machine, 'raw materials are fed into it; the workers turn it; the capitalist owns it; the state, the landlords, the capitalists and workers share its product, usually in an egregiously unequal way' (1977: 12).

[6] There are some exceptions, perhaps most notably Paul Romer (1994). Also see the discus-sion in Dasgupta and Serageldin (2000).

machines' (Smith 1976). Investments in human beings are treated as no different from investments in land or machines, as they all represent part of the technological upgrading of the economy.

The limitations of this approach are captured by Fred Block:

in treating the major inputs into production—labor, capital, and raw materials—in a parallel fashion, economists tend to analyze labor in isolation from the social relations in which individuals are embedded. It is not actual human beings who are an input into the production process, but one of their characteristics—their capacity to do work. But this is an inherently paradoxical strategy since the individual's capacity to do work is not innate; it is socially created and sustained. (1990: 75)

Moreover, as the economy becomes 'knowledge' based rather than driven by the production of widgets and Wendy burgers, the more social and cultural issues of identity, motivation, and high trust have become central to skill, productivity, and economic competitiveness.

The issue of 'motivation', for instance, is addressed by human capital theorists mainly as a question of getting the 'incentives' right, between rewards (increased pay, promotion, status) and punishments (pay cuts, unemployment, stigma), based on a model of economic rationality (Becker 1964). However, the assumption that human beings are driven by self-interest and individual optimization has led to sustained criticisms, for amongst other things, its one-dimensional view of human nature (Ashton and Green 1996; Fevre, Rees, and Gorrard 1999). Equally, motivation to learn and acquire skills are only partially explained in terms of economic incentives. Research on working-class youth in Britain has shown how cultural understandings of 'being' and 'becoming' can lead young people to restrict their commitment to education and training, irrespective of a cost-benefit analysis of whether it is in their self-interest. Such self-assessments are not made in social isolation (P. Brown 1987; G. Rees et al. 1997). Post-modernist concerns about cultural identities also show how ethnic, gender, and class influence attitudes and approaches to learning. It is recognized that investments in human capital involve making investments in the self, rather than simply a pecuniary calculation made by rational self-seeking economic agents (Rose 1989).

The weight of evidence suggests that issues of motivation and commitment are tied to social and cultural questions of economic involvement and to what Goleman calls 'emotional intelligence' (1996).[7]

---

[7] Goleman includes in his definition of emotional intelligence self-control, zeal and persistence, and the ability to motivate oneself (p. xii).

To put it crudely, if people do not share a sense of involvement or commitment in what they do, they may be able to fulfil a mechanical task such as attaching components onto television sets on an assembly line under close supervision, but they will not use their creative powers or work effectively in a team. This represents both the old problem of how to convert labour power into labour that was achieved by having vast armies of supervisors and line managers, and the new problem of how to harness the emotional and creative energies of a large proportion of the workforce to innovate and produce quality goods and services.

The failure to understand the social context of motivation has accentuated other problems inherent in human capital approaches since routine job performance under the watchful eye of a supervisor is no longer enough to raise productivity in many workplaces today. Employers have to win the commitment of employees to do a good job through the internalization of corporate culture, or minimally a pride in the job or commitment to a work team (Peters and Waterman 1982). As Landes (1998) argues:

This is symbolized by the new Japanese approach to quality: quality ... is no longer simply the assurance of durability and reliability (the product works); that was the old way of thinking about it. Quality today is change, that is, ceaseless improvement, the continuing incorporation of new features that redefine the product and its uses and, so doing, make the consumer feel he wants it. Quality is the invention of needs. (1998a: 64)

This requires something fundamentally different from the workforce than that of leaving their brains at the factory gates (P. Brown and Lauder 2001a). But equally the pace of change has also transformed the nature of individual 'skill'.

Skill is not simply a question of acquired technical competences through formal education and training, it also includes an ability to 'learn how to learn' as a lifelong activity. The short life cycle of knowledge and skills make the ability to grasp new information and acquire new skills an inherent feature of skill formation in post-industrial societies. This is true for all categories of workers including executive, managers, technicians, clerical workers, and factory operatives. Some jobs become obsolete or stripped of their skill content, whilst new jobs are created or require increasing levels of skill. It is estimated that the average American worker has more than ten jobs in a lifetime, and even if you exclude those who move within the same company, 10 per cent change jobs each year. A European Commission report into *Living and Working in the Information Society* further suggests that in Europe an average of 10 per cent of all jobs disappear each year and 'are replaced by different jobs in new processes, in new enterprises, generally requiring new, higher, or broader skills' (European Commission 1996: 194).

Innovation in high-performance workplaces puts 'learning' at the heart of companies and of what is means to be 'skilled' (Appelbaum et al. 2000). Shoshana Zuboff observed in her study of the introduction of computer-based technologies in a range of work settings,

Learning is no longer a separate activity that occurs either before one enters the workplace or in remote classroom settings. Nor is it an activity preserved for a management group. The behavior that defines learning and the behavior that defines being productive are one and the same. Learning is not something that requires time out from being engaged in productive activity; learning is the heart of productive activity. To put it simply, learning is the new form of labor. (1988: 395)

As the skill content of many jobs changes, the preparation of future workers also assumes greater significance. This not only requires more investment in education, training, and lifelong learning, but new ways of thinking about skill formation that recognize that it is no longer helpful to think of skills as an appendage to the person who possesses them. Skill acquisition is not a technical formality. The embodiment of what it means to be skilled including its cognitive, emotional, and cultural facets, also leads to a better understanding of how these are socially constructed. As individuals, we possess only the potential to become 'skilled', such as an ability to acquire and interpret information; to solve problems; to think critically and systematically; to communicate ideas to others; and to apply new skills and techniques. It is developments in the social world including technological advances, models of organizational efficiency, and changes in political purpose, that stimulates individual potential to develop new skills, ways of feeling, understanding, and learning (P. Brown and Lauder 2000, 2001*a*). As the human facets of economic activity are being recognized so the disembodied nature of skill inherent in human capital theory inhibits our understanding of skill formation and the social relations of productivity growth in post-industrial societies. This is an issue we will return to shortly, but there are other concerns that require elaboration.

The Demand Side

As suggested, human capital theory assumes a model of technological progression from low to high skilled work. It also harbours an assumption that investments in human capital will create its own demand as employers will readily upgrade their skills base when well qualified labour is available (Kuttner 2000). This explanation of the demand for high skilled employment is inadequate, as it ignores the complexities of the empirical world in which many factors, including existing management practices, attitudes to women, or industrial relations, shape the skill content of particular jobs.

This is not to say that technological innovation has little direct impact on the demand for skills. But the centrality of capitalism as the driving force for change must not be forgotten. New technologies may permit the integration of global business, but it is capitalism that shapes its application. As Manuel Castells has observed, for the first time the whole planet is organized according to the same set of economic rules (1998: 338). But the nature of capitalism has also changed in terms of the importance now attached to knowledge and information.

It is informational capitalism, relying on innovation-induced productivity, and globalization-oriented competitiveness to generate wealth, and to appropriate it selectively. It is, more than ever, embedded in culture and tooled by technology. But this time, both culture and technology depend on the ability of knowledge and information to act upon knowledge and information, in a recurrent network of globally connected exchanges. (1998: 338–9)

These tools of technology can be appropriated in different ways in the pursuit of profits and financial returns to shareholders. They offer greater flexibility and discretion to senior managers in deciding how to organize production or in service delivery. This 'flexibility' can have a profound impact on the level of skill requirements, especially when presented in the global context; as Harvey observed, 'The revival of sweatshops in New York and Los Angeles, of home work and "telecommuting", as well as the burgeoning growth of informal sector labour practices through the advanced capitalist world, does indeed represent a rather sobering vision of capitalism's supposedly progressive history' (1989: 187).

The evidence suggests that the impact of technology on employment skills is uneven (Crouch, Finegold, and Sako 1999). Changes in workplace design invariably have a mixed impact on skill. Some jobs become deskilled or eliminated, others present the opportunity for re-skilling or upskilling (Gallie et al. 1998; Ashton, Felstead, and Green 2000). The shift from manufacturing to service sector employment also reflects the impact of technology on increasing productivity in the manufacturing sector (Appelbaum et al. 2000). Far fewer people are required to meet the demand for consumer goods such as cars, phones, computers, and video-recorders.

Table 1.1. Distribution of the total labour force by sector (percentage)

	Agriculture total[a]		Industry total[b]		Manufacturing		Services total[c]	
	1980	1997	1980	1997	1980	1997	1980	1997
Germany	6.9	1.4	45.4	31.7	36.8	25.1	47.7	67.0
Japan	11.0	4.3	34.6	33.9	24.1	24.0	54.4	61.8
S. Korea	37.1	5.7	26.5	41.1	20.9	31.0	36.4	53.2
Singapore	1.6	−0.3	41.7	32.2	26.0	30.0	56.8	68.1
United Kingdom	2.6	1.8	38.0	21.2	26.8	14.5	59.5	77.0
United States	3.5	2.3	31.1	22.0	22.3	14.1	65.4	75.6

[a] Agriculture includes: agriculture, hunting, forestry, and fishing.
[b] Industry includes: mining and quarrying; electricity, gas, and water; construction and manufacturing. The overall per cent for manufacturing is given separately.
[c] Services include: wholesale and retail trade; restaurants and hotels; transport, storage, and communication; financing, insurance, real estate and business services; community, social, and personal services.

Source: ILO 1998.

Table 1.1 shows that in all these countries the shift from manufacturing to service sector employment is unequivocal. However, this does not mean that manufacturing is becoming irrelevant to the economy as a whole. Indeed, manufacturing remains an essential part of the economy even if the numbers employed continue to decline in all the developed economies. Eileen Appelbaum and colleagues have shown that in the United States where many see the future economy as based on information technologies and the Internet,

It may come as something of a shock . . . to learn that it is still manufacturing and goods production, not information-age knowledge production, that fuels productivity growth. The United States continues to depend on its manufacturing sector for increases in its wealth, improvements in its living standards, and the competitiveness of its companies in global markets. Although manufacturing accounts for just 18 per cent of real GDP, it remains overwhelmingly the main source of U.S. productivity growth. (2000: 2)

It would also be a mistake to assume that the shift to the service sector mirrors a rise in the level of skills. In a survey of these issues Gosta Esping-Andersen (1999) has shown that not only does the scale of the expansion of service sector employment vary between countries, but that rapid expansion is primarily based on increasing the numbers of low skill, low waged jobs. In Germany, for instance, the service sector is largely composed of professional and other skilled workers, whereas

Sweden and the United States have larger service sectors but also a large proportion of these workers are low skilled. Esping-Andersen explains this in the following terms:

substantial employment expansion requires heavy growth in consumer and social services, both characteristic of a large unskilled quotient the more they grow—hence an apparent trade-off between either joblessness or a mass of inferior jobs ... [but] ... it makes a notable difference whether inferior jobs provide inferior welfare. In Sweden, they are relatively well-paid and secure welfare state jobs; indeed, private sector 'Macjobs' hardly exist. . . . In the United States, the low-end service workers are mainly in the private sector, typically poorly paid and excluded from occupational welfare entitlements and basic job security. (1999: 110–11)

Other ·evidence supports the view that despite the increasing importance of technology, knowledge, and information, along with a

Table 1.2. The bases of post-industrial employment: The distribution of occupations and the size of the outsider population (percentage change, 1960–1980s, in parentheses)

	Germany 1985	Sweden 1985	United States 1988
'Industrial' society			
Unskilled manual	16.5(–0)	12.4 (–42)	14.4 (–33)
Skilled manual	17.3 (–32)	15.2 (–18)	8.7 (–34)
Clerical and sales	29.6 (+30)	18.6 (+16)	28.3 (+21)
Managers[a]	4.5 (+36)	4.0 (–15)	9.1 (+17)
TOTAL	67.9 (–0)	50.2 (–18)	60.4 (–8)
'Servicing' society			
Unskilled service	4.5 (–48)	16.9 (+78)	11.7 (–0)
Skilled service	5.0 (+194)	4.4 (–0)	6.6 (+57)
Professional-technical	17.3 (+121)	21.9 (+89)	18.1 (+56)
TOTAL	26.8 (+47)	43.2 (+70)	36.4 (+31)
'Outsider' society			
Not employed	35.2	16.7	29.5
Long-term unemployment[b]	46.3	5.0	5.6

[a] Includes also self-employed (non-professional).

[b] As a percentage of all unemployed (1990).

Note: The table excluded primary sector occupations.

Sources: Esping-Anderson 1999: 109.

significant increase in the demand for professional workers as predicted in Daniel Bell's (1973) *The Rise of Post-Industrial Society*, none of the countries that are the focus of this book have more than 40 per cent of their workforce in professional, managerial, and technical occupations. There has not been an end to low skilled employment (or unemployment), although its extent varies between countries (see Table 1.3).

The linear model—technological change → education and training → high skills → high wages—is inadequate as a description of the route to a high skills economy. A prominent slogan in the United States is 'the more you learn the more you earn', following the script of human capital theory. Evidence in the United States shows that in one respect this is indeed true. Earnings not only reflect level of education, but returns to education have become more pronounced. Figure 1.1 shows that the discrepancy between those with an associate's degree and high school drop-outs is less than that between those with an associate's degree (two-year community college) and those with a Bachelor's Degree.

However, much of the difference in financial returns from investments in education does not stem from differential increases in income that conform to the human capital idea that learning pays, but due to the decline in the earning power of non-university graduates, especially in the 1980s. Figure 1.2 shows that while educational levels have been improving in the United States, many students at the end of the 1990s were earning little (or no) more than they did in the 1970s.

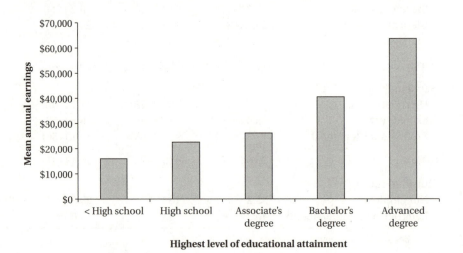

Fig. 1.1. Mean annual earnings by educational attainment, 1997

Source: Department of Commerce 1999.

Table 1.3. Changes in total employment by occupational sector, 1985–1998

Occupational sector	Singapore			Japan			Germany			USA			UK*			Korea*		
	1985	1997	% +/-	1985	1997	% +/-	1985	1997	% +/-	1985	1997	% +/-	1991	1997	% +/-	1993	1998	% +/-
Administrative and Managerial	7.6	13.0	5.4	3.6	3.4	-0.2	3.8	5.9	2.1	11.4	14.2	2.8	17.5	18.7	1.2	2.7	2.6	-0.1
Professional and Technical	14.4	27.4	13.0	9.3	12.6	3.3	15.0	32.8	17.8	15.6	18.1	2.5	19.5	21.0	1.5	12.3	16.3	4.0
Clerical, Sales, and Services	29.8	28.7	-1.1	45.0	47.4	2.4	40.1	32.5	-7.6	41.6	39.9	-1.7	35.6	35.7	0.1	44.4	46.4	2.0
Production and Related	43.4	30.9	-12.5	37.7	36.6	-1.1	38.8	28.8	-10.0	31.4	27.8	-3.6	27.4	24.6	-2.8	40.6	34.7	-5.9
TOTAL	95.2	100		95.6	100		97.7	100		100	100		100	100		100	100	

Notes: [a] Data for 1985 is not available. Percentage change figures represent the increase or decrease in each occupational sector between 1985 and 1997.

Germany: Figures for Germany exclude workers not classified by occupation. Data up to 1991 only includes data on West Germany, post-1991 data pertains to the whole of Germany. Only the 1991 figures include Armed Forces. Figures for 1995 and 1997 comprise of a different occupational breakdown which has been altered to enable comparison—the only noteworthy alteration is that clerical, sales, and services includes the elementary occupational group, which comprises of transport workers and the like.
Figures for non-classifiable occupations: Germany 91: 3%, 95: 1.5%, 97: 1.4%; UK 91: 8.8%, 95: 9.4%, 97: 7.3%.

Korea: Figures for clerical, sales, and services also include the 'elementary occupational group'. Figures for 1985 are in a non-comparable format, they are as follows: pro., tech., admin., and managerial workers 5.8%; administrative 1.6%; official 11.5%; sales workers 15.5%; services workers 10.8%; agri., forestry, hunters, fishermen and related 24.6%; production and rel., transport, operators, labourers 34.8%.

Sources: Singapore: Singapore Dept. of Statistics; Japan: Statistics Bureau, Management and Co-ordination Agency; Germany: Statistics Bureau; USA: Bureau of Labour Statistics; UK: Institute for Employment Research; S. Korea: National Statistics Office.

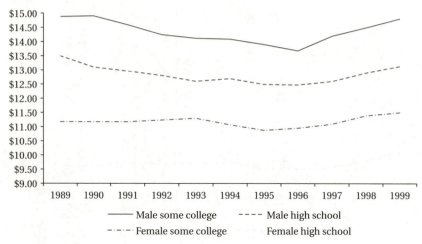

Fig. 1.2. The changing relationship between education and income, 1989–1999 (1998 dollars).

Source: Bernstein et al. 1999: 7.

A further issue is that the categories used to relate education to income, such as four-year college, two-year college, high school diploma, etc., are not disaggregated. If they were, it may suggest a pattern that is far from uniform. The study of one subject rather than another at a four-year college may lead to significant differences in returns to education. Equally, studying in an elite rather than a less prestigious university may also lead to significant differences in future remuneration. Levin and Kelly (1997) also point out that calculations of educational investments on future earnings are usually based on 'cross-sectional' analyses that are invalid. Previous returns may not be an accurate guide to future returns.

Figure 1.2 also shows an important gender difference in returns to education. This reflects broader problems with the way gender (and racial) discrimination have often been ignored by human capital theories. Feminist writers have clearly shown how gender dictates the way male employers and trade union representatives have sometimes conspired to define women's work as less skilled than men's, even in circumstances where men and women are performing essentially the same job tasks (Blackmore 1997; Rees 1998). This is evident in gender inequalities in wages and career prospects that reflect the power relations that shape our understanding of skill (see Table 1.4). A recent report on science and research within the European Community has shown that

Table 1.4. Female labour force and wage gap

	Females as % of labour force		Female Wage Gap[a] (%)
	1980	1998	
Germany	40	42	25
Japan	38	41	41
S. Korea	39	41	42
Singapore	35	39	—
United Kingdom	39	44	26
United States	41	46	24

[a] Difference between female and male full-time earnings, 1997.

Source: World Bank 2000.

while women constitute half the undergraduate population there is a brain drain of female talent from physics, engineering and technology, mathematical sciences, chemistry, and even biological sciences. As this report highlights, 'while the presence of women in science has been increasing, extraordinarily few have an equal opportunity to make a contribution and enjoy the benefits of a scientific career. This is both unjust and inefficient' (Osborn et al. 2000: 1). Unless there is active intervention in the way schools, university, and research establishments are organized, female talent will remain underutilized. It cannot be left to the 'enlightened' self-interest of employers (see Figure 1.3).

Measuring Skill

'Skill' is a notoriously difficult concept to define, let alone measure (Department of Labor 1999). These problems are not restricted to human capital theorists, but they confront particular problems because of their assertion that skills can be accurately measured in quantitative terms. Skill is variously defined as the expertise, ability, or competence to undertake specific activities often acquired through formal instruction or work experience.[8] An obvious problem is how to measure the skill levels of different jobs. What should be included or left out of any classification of skill? A taxi driver has a number of 'skills' to master in

[8] The importance of non-formal learning in the acquisition of skills is now receiving more attention (see Eraut 1997; Coffield 2000*b*).

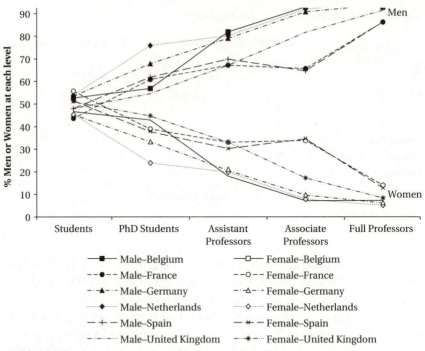

Fig. 1.3. Women and men in science in six European member states
Source: Osborn, et al. 2000: 13.

order to drive a car safely, he or she must also have a good knowledge of the area to minimize the time and distance of the journey, and be able to keep a simple account of fares. But it is also advantageous to the driver (and his of her employer) to have good conversational skills to maximize the income from 'tips'. Should these communication skills be counted as part of the skills required of the taxi driver, and if so, how should they be measured? Such problems of definition and measurement have been compounded by the importance employers now attach to teamwork, creativity, and self-management skills. Human capital theorists have either ignored the importance of 'key' skills because they are difficult to quantify or treated them as technical competences to be taught, learnt, and assessed in a formal way.

A further problem is that skill is defined at the level of the individual. This typically involves measuring the skill levels of national economies as the sum total of individual skills measured by the stocks and flows of qualifications, the proportion of students in some form of tertiary education, or the extent of workplace training. Countries can then be delineated as low, medium, or high skilled based on these measures. This is not a fruitless activity, as it is important to have data on, for instance, participation rates in education and training. But such measures need to be complemented by others of both a quantitative and qualitative kind in order to improve our understanding of comparative skill formation (see below). Again, there are inevitable boundary problems over what constitutes a high or low skill society. Any absolute criteria, for example, where high skills societies are defined as those with 80 per cent of the age cohort in tertiary education and at least half the workforce in professional, managerial, or technical occupations are inevitably arbitrary. But a recognition of these problems of definition need not lead to the wholesale rejection of attempts to distinguish high skilled as opposed to low skilled societies as long as the same definition is applied to different national contexts.

A related problem of measurement is the assumption that wages reflect the productivity of labour: some people are paid more because their human capital is more valuable. We have seen how this argument has been extended to include global as opposed to domestic issues of wage negotiation. There are a number of cogent critiques of this view that point to differences in the power of individuals and occupational groups to hike up their income (Hirsch 1977; R. Collins 1979), along with cultural differences in what constitutes an appropriate level of remuneration for different categories of workers. A stark example is that in 1965 the average pay packages of CEOs in US corporations were forty-four times those of factory workers, this increased to 419 times in 1998 (Lazonick and O'Sullivan 2000). The wages of CEOs in US corporations are also 34 per cent higher than in Britain, 106 per cent higher than in France, 155 per cent higher than in Japan, and 169 per cent above those in Germany (Thurow 1999: 43). It is difficult to imagine that these differences reflect the superior management skills of American CEOs, even the very good ones!

But perhaps the most serious weakness of human capital approaches is that the obsession with measurable outcomes has led them to ignore the *process* of skill formation. This has remained a 'black box' revealing precious little about skill formation in motion. The importance of process has become more important because of the pace of economic innovation and changing skill requirements in knowledge-driven economies. Moreover, in respect to national skill formation policies the emphasis on process is not only a question of the social construction of individual skills, but of building *societal capacity* that includes the collective (as well as individual) dimensions of skill formation.

Myth of the Global Labour Market

The view that workers now have to operate in a global rather than a national market is also a simplification of existing realities for most workers. This is because the global labour market does not operate as a 'free' market (Castells 1996; Held et al. 1999). Nationality continues to operate as a vital tool for restricting the competition for jobs by excluding millions of well qualified workers from other parts of the world, such as skilled software engineers from India competing for IT jobs within the European Community or North America (Kobrin 2000). These restrictions are sometimes loosened when there are national labour or skill shortages, such as the current use of H1B visas in the United States for IT workers, or the foreign talent scheme in Singapore. This also applies at the other end of the labour market for those who are willing to work as 'guest' workers to undertake the jobs that the indigenous workforce are unwilling to consider given the long hours, poor remuneration, and bad conditions involved in a lot of this work.

Moreover, there are already a number of bilateral agreements that extend labour market opportunities (and risks), but these by definition are intended to limit the competition for human capital rather than to make it global in scope. The free movement of labour is enshrined in the statutes of the European Community, where people are assumed to be judged on the basis of their knowledge, skills, and experience. Graduates from Britain, France, Germany, and the Netherlands may find themselves in increasing competition for technical, managerial, and professional jobs in international agencies and MNCs (P. Brown 2000). But these graduates are largely sheltered from direct competition from graduates from Moscow, Lahore, and Beijing.

For most workers, most of the time, where they are born and grow up continues to structure their labour market opportunities within local or national contexts. But this does not mean that limitations on the physical movement of labour undermines the importance attached to global economic trends. It is capital that is mobile rather than workers. Workers from different countries come into competition based on *market* rules of inclusion and exclusion, when companies make decisions about where to invest in new plants, offices, or research capability. These decisions will include a number of considerations such as proximity to markets, political stability, transportation networks, social overheads, wage costs, incentives in the form of cheap rents, tax holidays, government grants, as well as skill levels and the quality of education and training.

Workers from different parts of the world also come into competition as a collective resource rather than as individuals, not only in situations where companies are deciding where to inwardly invest, but also in circumstances where companies may be deciding to relocate to another part of the world. The fact that these decisions will be made on market rules is exemplified by the problem confronting low skilled workers. In capitalist markets a successful strategy to lift the skills base of the whole population may lead to low skilled jobs disappearing as the workforce is seen as too expensive or 'over educated' relative to workers in developing nations (Wood 1994). However, as the recent surge in jobs growth in the United States exemplifies, a large proportion of low skilled jobs in the service sector are no more subject to the rules of international trade than the services they produce, given that they are highly localized (Esping-Andersen 1999).

Finally, there is little evidence to support the claim that income polarization reflects the operation of a global labour market (P. Brown and Lauder 1996; Freeman 1997). This is because the comparative evidence is very weak. In a global context it is to be expected that all the leading economies would reveal the same pattern of income polarization, but in Germany, for instance, income inequality during the 1980s actually narrowed. A more plausible explanation is that it is those countries that have adopted a neo-liberal agenda of social, political, and economic reforms including Britain and the United States, that have experienced the race to inequality. Polarization is therefore to be explained in terms of how countries have responded to globalization rather than in terms of a convergence based on the global value of human capital (P. Brown and Lauder 2001*a*).

The End of the Nation State?

There is no doubt that national governments have lost some of their executive powers in the new global economy (Hutton and Giddens 2000). They cannot control market forces in areas such as exchange rates, but even the most cursory examination of differences in the organization of European states and the factors that led to the economic success of leading East Asian economies suggests that national governments maintain more clout than is often supposed. National governments will continue to play a decisive role in developing strategies for high skill formation. We must avoid conflating the deregulation of world markets with those of how nations are responding to these changing rules of international competition. In effect, market individualism in Britain and the United States is a political rather than an inevitable response to the deregulation of global markets. The deregulation of national markets is part of a political project extolling the sovereignty of the market both at home and overseas. The nation state is not powerless, but rather the linkage between the 'nation' and the 'state' should not be taken for granted. Within the walled economies of the past, it was assumed that 'by definition' the state acted as the protagonist of a nation's citizens. Some got more out of this arrangement than others, but nevertheless the 'hidden' hand of the market was helped by the 'visible' hand of the state. Whereas in the context of the global economy, when the state acts to introduce widespread market reforms, the impact in terms of educational, social, and economic polarization is exaggerated by the operation of the global economy.

This negates the idea that investments by governments and by individuals work as a win–win combination, because the 'hidden hand' of the market often fails to work in the common interest (Polanyi 1944). It is assumed, for example, that when individuals decide to invest in a postgraduate university course this will increase the value of their human capital because they will become more skilled and therefore more productive. This greater productivity leads companies to improve their profitability and wages will rise, feeding more money into national accounts through taxation (direct and indirect). What this ignores is the fact that investments in human capital can take the form of a zero-sum game. An example is where elite groups attempt to preserve entry into the most prestigious educational institutions through the exclusion of children from less privileged social backgrounds. It will be argued that 'positional competition' (Hirsch 1977; Brown 2000) is an inevitable feature of national skill formation. How governments seek to structure it—through, for instance, meritocratic or market competition—is an important issue that offers an invaluable insight into national strategies for high skill formation.

The different ways in which national states intervene in public and economic policy remain vital to understanding variation in national strategies for a high skilled economy, as will be explained below. Indeed, the success of Japan and the Asian tiger economies in the 1970s and 1980s can be explained by the role of government agencies operating in a 'developmental' capacity to achieve rapid industrialization and international competitiveness (C. Johnson 1982; Castells 1998). As Wade has observed, East Asian economic performance is due to a number of related facts but, 'using incentives, controls, and mechanisms to spread risk' is a key part, as it 'enabled the government to guide—or govern—market processes of resource allocation so as to produce different production and investment outcomes than would have occurred with . . . free market . . . policies' (1990: 26–7). The argument that these ideas ignore the new rules of economic competition is not supported by our national surveys. Indeed, Singapore has the highest proportion of any workforce in the world working for foreign MNCs, but there is a major government involvement in economic planning (Ashton, Green, et al. 1999).

Contrary to proclamations of the end of the nation state (Ohmae 1995), the economic competitiveness that benefits the many rather than the few will depend on the way national governments respond to competitive pressures from 'foreign' countries, companies, and workers. In other words, nations must confront new problems that threaten the living standards of workers and their families. Globalization has made it more important to have a democratic political voice that serves the 'national' interest. What is more, there is no other institution apart from the nation state that has the power and moral authority to balance the interests of individuals and social groups. This is reflected in the fact that at least half the spending of modern states is concerned with income redistribution in forms including taxation, universal education, and health care. Such internal income transfers are as much as fifty times larger than international ones in the form of economic, technological, or other aid programmes (Kennedy 1993).[9]

THE POLITICAL ECONOMY OF HIGH SKILLS

Here we propose an alternative *new political economy* of skill formation. This approach has its roots in economic sociology (Granovetter and

---

[9] There may, therefore, be nothing intrinsically worthy in nation states as such, they are for the most part a recent historical creation and they have their dark side—jingoism and imperialism. But the fact remains that it is the national framework of social, cultural, legal, and economic institutions which will determine the well-being of workers, families, and communities (P. Brown and Lauder 2001a).

Swedberg 1992) and the 'new institutionalism' (Dore 1986; Best 1990; Streeck 1992). It shares the contention that issues of skill formation and economic performance are socially constructed and experienced within social institutions such as schools, offices, or factories, that can be organized in different ways even if 'capitalism' is the overarching system of economic organization (Ashton and Green 1996; Crouch, Finegold, and Sako 1999). Within capitalist economies we find variations in historical and economic conditions; cultural, political, and social mores; constellations of political interest groups and classes; and in labour markets, that shape skill formation policies. These differences may not only give rise to variations in productivity and economic growth but also lead to differences in the distribution of income, employment opportunities, and life chances.

Economic globalization has exposed all nation states to new challenges that are yet to be resolved, for instance, it is unclear what form a new settlement (if any) will take between the government, employers, and the trade unions in Korea following the demand for structural adjustment by the IMF as a condition for financial support following the Asian financial crisis in the late 1990s. The government is attempting to increase labour market flexibility, rationalize the operations of the large Korean multinational companies, and restructure the financial sector making it easier for foreign companies to invest (takeover) in indigenous businesses. The trade unions have actively resisted these changes, as they see it increasing unemployment, poverty, and inequality. Whatever the outcome in Korea, the organization of 'national' economies will continue to shape the future direction of skill formation. This is true for all countries which is why we reject the idea of a global convergence of national economies based on free market principles. There are a number of related points that mark out the new political economy of skill formation.

First, skills upgrading is as much a political as an economic goal. In political dialogue the commitment to a high skills economy is wrapped in the political safety blanket of 'competitiveness'. Whether the argument is couched in terms of global competition from low waged competitors, technological innovation, or as a solution to income inequality, we are told that high skills are a necessary basis for competitiveness. For some firms there is a genuine commitment to upgrade their skills base as a means of improving productive performance, but there remains more than one way to make profits especially in the short term (Keep 1999). Competitiveness can also be secured by downsizing in an attempt to lower labour costs, reduce spending on training, or investments in R & D. If this is true for companies, it is also true for national economies. At the beginning of the twenty-first century, the United States was judged one of the most 'competitive' economies in the world. This should serve as an important caveat to those who see the creation of high skill economies as a logical outcome to technological based, knowledge-driven capitalism. The US economy has vast armies of low skilled, low waged workers, one-third of children living in poverty, and 2 per cent of Americans in prison (Freeman 1997).

Secondly, a recasting of the way we think about skill formation issues involves recapturing the long tradition of political economy that dates back to Adam Smith. The 'drying out' of social facets of skill formation represents the remarkable achievement of neo-classical economics in the 1980s. But the founding fathers of political economy did not make such a sharp distinction between the social, political, and economic (Smith 1976). The importance of political economy was a major concern of Alfred Marshall in the late nineteenth and early twentieth century (1925, 1961). Contrary to Adam Smith, he believed that technological change in the early twentieth century would increase the skill levels of the working class. This he believed to be of major social importance, as these changes in the nature of economic opportunity offered the prospect of a cultural revolution where all men can become 'gentlemen' [sic]. 'The question is not whether all men will ultimately be equal—that they will certainly not—but whether progress may not go on steadily if slowly till the official distinction between working men and gentlemen has passed away; till, by occupation at least, every man is a gentleman' (1925: 102). Marshall blurred the distinction between the economic and the social given his concern with issues of social order and poverty at the turn of the twentieth century, 'the study of the causes of poverty is the study of the causes of the degradation of a large part of mankind' (1961: 3). For Marshall, economic policies were an instrument of social progress.

Concerns about economic inequality and poverty have resurfaced, especially in Anglo-Saxon nations, as economic prosperity has left a significant minority bereft of its benefits. The political economy of skill formation, therefore, raises fundamental issues about inequality, social justice, and economic opportunities. It leads us to consider who are the beneficiaries of gains in productivity and innovation? Is the circle of prosperity drawn in a way that is inclusive or in a way that excludes a large minority from its fruits? The scale of income inequality in the United Kingdom and the United States suggests that a return to a broader notion of political economy is vital given the wastage of talent, inefficiency, and threat to social welfare that it poses. It also leads to questions about the value of economic measures such as GDP or per capita income. Two economies may have similar GDP per capita incomes, but in one country there may be huge disparities in income between the top 5 per cent and the bottom 20 per cent, whereas in the other countries incomes gravitate around the mean. GNP measures of economic performance obscure significant national differences in educational performance; who gets 'skilled' and who does not; the demand for different kinds of workers; how much they earn and the overall scale of economic opportunity for high skilled work. The study of skill formation is never a simple matter of raising productivity and economic competitiveness because these issues are deeply implicated in the psychological, legal, and social contracts between the individual and society. Therefore, the political economy of nations remains vital in shaping national settlements in terms of skill development, economic opportunity, and social welfare.

Thirdly, in classical political economy it was generally assumed that economic change led to social advancement, but there was little sense in which inequality, democracy, and social justice could impact on economic productivity and wealth creation.[10] However, in the *new* polit-ical economy issues of income distribution, opportunity, democratic participation, and the ways people come together in pursuit of their individual interests and collective goals, are seen to have a decisive impact on national skill formation strategies. In part, this explains why the centre-left have focused on the polarization of income and wealth. The centre-left have championed 'high skills' as a way of reuniting the principles of social justice and economic efficiency. Social inequality and polarization are seen as an impediment to the creation of a high skills society. The idea that social health leads to economic wealth is based on the view that 'egalitarian countries are more socially cohe-sive. They have a stronger community life and suffer fewer of the corrosive effects of inequality. The public arena becomes a source of supportive social networks rather than of stress and potential conflict' (Wilkinson 1996).[11]

---

[10] This is reflected in the growing interest in the concept of social capital. However, much of the debate about social capital conflates a number of key dimensions, such as the relationship between social inequality, democracy, and civic participation. For an interesting review of these issues, see Baron, Schuller, and Field (2000).

[11] This emphasis on the economic benefits of social justice reflects a political climate in which there is little hope of maintaining, let alone expanding, public provision unless it is underpinned by an economic rationale. A condition of funding is to show how public services will contribute

If societies are characterized by social polarization, it is extremely difficult to build a society that furnishes all with the material, cultural, and employment opportunities in which current skill levels can be significantly increased. Equally, the distribution of skills will be shaped by the social groups to which an individual belongs and the cultural, economic, and political fabric of society more generally. In low trust societies, for instance, education, knowledge, and learning are restricted to a minority, where extending opportunities to less privileged groups is seen as a threat to the positional advantage of social elites (P. Brown 2000). Rising productivity in the twenty-first century not only depends on new technologies, research and development, or the level of funding devoted to education and training, but how these are embedded in 'institutional' relations of high or low trust. Politicians, employers, and trade unions may talk about their commitment to building high skilled economies, but issues of trust relations are more than a matter of attitude, even if we accept the sincerity of such pronouncements. Trust relations are more than a question of how we treat each other at home, school, or work, because these sentiments are reflected in social and economic institutions. As Alan Fox has noted we must look not only at the principles by which people 'act and treat each other within the existing social institutions, patterns, and processes, but more fundamentally at those which are embodied in the institutions, patterns, and processes themselves, for these, too, are devised, supported, and operated by men [and women] who are capable of choosing differently' (1974: 15).

Industrial production in the United Kingdom and America has been based on low trust relations that severely limited the discretion of all but a small cadre of managers and executives (Fox 1974; Sabel 1982). The image of workers as cogs in the proverbial machine was not without empirical foundation. But the more workplace learning, innovation, and productivity are seen to depend on technical, interpersonal, and self-management skills of a large proportion of the workforce, the more the discretionary commitment to acquire skills, to be innovative and creative, to work constructively with others, matters in terms of the overall performance of the economy. This will require more than

to economic priorities. Another inevitable consequence is that the potential of education and training to solve social and economic problems is greatly exaggerated. The collusion between those who work in the public sector and the spin-doctors of economic competitiveness is, however, not restricted to public servants. The more volatile global markets have become, the more the economy and employment prospects are 'talked up' as an aid to bolstering share prices on global financial markets.

the technical upgrading of individual skills, it will require a social transformation (P. Brown and Lauder 2001*a*).

Fourthly, the neo-classical model of the state outlined above, is highly circumscribed in terms of its sphere of competence and governance, but this is far removed from the ways states have shaped national economies in all manner of explicit (including legal frameworks, strategic investments, taxation, training budgets) and implicit (including relationships with employer organizations and trade unions) ways. A feature of our analysis is to get beyond distinctions between the market versus the state. Here we find the debate based on the assumption that markets exist prior to, or independent of, states or society. It is assumed that markets work best when they are 'free' of government interference. This leads neo-classical economists to portray 'stakeholder', 'social partnership', or 'developmental state' models of economic organization as forms of bastardized capitalism, given life through political expedience rather than on the grounds of economic rationality. Despite the obvious implausibility of this view (Marquand 1988), it has served to obscure the much more important question of how to reform social and economic institutions for high skill formation. This requires a holistic approach that reconnects enduring questions about the relationship between the economy, politics, and society to those of globalization and the changing nature of work.

THE SEVEN C'S OF HIGH SKILL FORMATION

How does our approach to skill formation policy diverge from human capital models? Our policy framework centres on the question of how to build the *societal capacity* for high skills. This emphasis on societal capacity rather than simply the stock of individual skills is intended to highlight the dynamic nature of skill formation as noted above. It also reflects the need for a conceptual framework that is sensitive to both issues of supply and demand for skills and how these mesh (or otherwise) in an innovative process of skill upgrading. Building societal capacity depends on the creation of a number of 'complementary conditions' (Levin and Kelly 1997) that embrace the institutional foundations of high skill formation. It also reflects our contention that skill acquisition and utilization are social acts which represent more than the sum total of individual action, but are predicated on relations of trust (high or low) which are themselves embedded (or disembedded) in a historical context (Streeck 1992). To aid understanding we will outline an 'ideal type' of the *seven C's of high skills*. This represents a holistic approach aimed at sketching the main ingredients of national agendas for high skill societies.

1. Consensus

Consensus is the extent to which the major stakeholders, government, employers, and trade unions are signed up to a commitment to upgrade the skills of the workforce.

High skill societies exist by design not evolution. They depend on a national *consensus* that binds together the major stakeholders of employers, workers, and government in a commitment to skill upgrading throughout the economy. The extent to which competing vested interest groups coalesce around the idea of 'high skills' will not only influence the policy commitment to skills upgrading but the prospects of policy implementation leading to progressive institutional change in education and training systems, the labour market, industrial relations, and business organization. Hence, the greater the level of trust between government, employers, and trade unions the more likely they are to view themselves as stakeholders in the change process (Streeck 1992; Green with Sakamoto, Chapter 2 in this volume).

We reject the view that knowledge-driven economies will inevitably lead to the exploitation of the intelligence, skills, and abilities of all. Capitalism is based on profit maximization rather than universal skills upgrading. It is naive to assume that economic competitiveness will lead employers to invest in upgrading of skills throughout the economy. This is at best a partial truth as Hugh Lauder (1999) has argued, Britain and America have remained economically competitive with a dual-equilibrium with high and low skilled sectors, and there appears to be little incentive for employers to move low skilled, low waged jobs up the value chain, especially in the service sector (Esping-Andersen 1999).

Economies where skilled work is widespread rather than restricted to managerial or professional enclaves, require a national political commitment to a specific 'model' of competitiveness based on developing the productive capacity of all. What this also recognizes is that issues of skill formation are inextricably linked to social and political questions about social cohesion and social justice. In Singapore, for instance, a commitment to skills upgrading through the economy has been used to ensure that all sections of this ethnically diverse society benefit from rising prosperity to maintain the political legitimacy of Singapore as an independent city state and the legitimate political authority of the Peoples' Action Party that has been in power since the 1960s. Whereas in Germany the development of the productive capacity of all is at the core of the 'social partnership' (Streek 1992). It is our contention that the prospects for high skill formation will depend on building national settlements based on a commitment to the upgrading and utilization of the skills of the workforce, although these will take different forms depending on the historical, political, social, and economic circumstances.

2. Competitive Capacity

Competitive capacity refers to the potential for productive innovation and change. A high skills society depends on entrepreneurial and risk-taking activities whether in terms of new business ventures or through innovation within existing enterprises, linked to new technologies, R & D, and the upgrading of skills. This is best achieved in a context of 'value added' rivalry between companies rather than its 'zero-sum' variety that leads to cost cutting, downsizing, and loss of competitive innovation.

High skill formation depends on developing *competitive capacity* within the world economy. Without a viable strategy for creating 'value added' companies based on quality, it will be difficult to increase investment in education, training, research, and technological innovation. There will be little scope or incentive to increase the demand for skilled workers. In knowledge-driven economies this depends on nations improving productivity based on research and development linked to strategic investments that look to be medium term (Archibugi and Michie 1997; Thurow 1999). In turn, the supply of intermediate and highly skilled jobs depends on companies that can engineer 'customized' niches in the global marketplace because it is more difficult for competitors to mass produce the same goods or to offer customers tailored services (Schumpeter 1961; Blackwell and Eilon 1991). In high-performance organizations it is equally recognized that improvements in productivity depend on the 'organic' integration of applied knowledge, technological innovation, free-flow information networks, and high trust relations between multi-skilled managers, professionals, and technicians.

Again, it is worth remembering that the competitive capacity of companies may not coincide with building national capacity for high skills. In stark terms, the competitive capacity of companies can be based on cost-cutting *or* productive innovation. The former may meet the short-term demands of stock markets and shareholders but does little to build competitive capacity for a high skills society. It does little to contribute to the skills base of the workforce, where corporate investment is restricted to those activities that hold the prospect of a rapid return on capital investment (Lazonick and O'Sullivan 2000). It is only through productive innovation that there is the incentive to upgrade skills.

Productive innovation requires a mixer of blue-skies research and incremental improvements in areas such as product development, design, service delivery, reliability, marketing, production techniques, or after-sales service. The key being the application of knowledge to products and services that add value to companies and skills to workers.

There has been a tendency to treat R & D as basic research having little immediate relevance to skills, employment, or company profits. This view is outdated as a great deal of activity that goes under the rubric of R & D is dedicated to the application of knowledge to create new products and processes. In Japan, almost all of its R & D resources have a strong emphasis on 'development' and market application. And a study of industrial patents found that almost three-quarters of all such patents were derived from basic research funded by government agencies or other non-profit organizations (Osborn, Rees, et al. 2000).

Lester Thurow (1999) suggests that advancing knowledge is rather like drilling for oil as big scientific breakthroughs are invariably expensive team efforts, which few companies want to run the risk of funding, especially when the returns are uncertain. However, when companies introduce innovative new products they are keen to emphasize the 'in house' brains behind the brand, but what is rarely acknowledged is that the platform breakthroughs on which such developments rely, are often publicly funded over many years. Some of the best examples of this come from the United States—the archetype of neo-liberalism. The US government ploughed massive sums into military research in the Cold War era and beyond, that contributed to the microelectronics revolution and the advent of the Internet. It has also been the main funding source of the Human Genome Project. Private biotechnology companies are now queuing to exploit its commercial potential.

The cost of R & D suggests that public funding of basic research is essential to complement the R & D activities of private firms. But creating ideas is only part of a process, as their development and market application are just as important. Indeed, while what is known may not be that different, how it is exploited lies at the heart of competitive capacity (R. Collins 1986; Lauder, Chapter 3 in this volume). This is because the extent to which competitive capacity leads to the creation of high skilled jobs depends on the market application of basic research. However, it is unrealistic for all the advanced economies to adopt comprehensive programmes of basic research where the costs would be prohibitive for small countries. There are obvious advantages to being at the forefront of scientific developments, but access to knowledge has become globally networked giving greater scope to engage in the market application of new knowledge, even when a country has little involvement in the initial research. There is also considerable scope for nations as well as multinational corporations to form strategic alliances for research and development, which is exactly what many companies are doing today.

Competitive capacity requires the existence of large firms with the resources to engage in product and service development, and despite much talk about global companies most multinationals continue to develop or repatriate knowledge to the home base (Hood and Young 2000). It also depends on having entrepreneurs who are able to challenge existing barriers to markets or established mindsets that are institutionally blind to new opportunities. A classic example was IBM's failure to recognize that the future was in creating the industrial standard for computer software rather than putting all its efforts into the development of the hardware. This gave Bill Gates's company Microsoft the opportunity to establish Windows as the world standard. Equally, as Thurow has pointed out, despite being aware of advances in microbiology 'none of the world's leading pharmaceutical companies played a leading role in the development of biotechnology' (1999: 94). When entrepreneurial activities are based on science and new technologies, there is enormous scope for productive innovation as the microelectronics industry testifies in the Unites States. This not only gave rise to Silicon Valley in California but also in Boston, the Massachusetts Institute of Technology (MIT) was reported to have 4,000 MIT-related companies, employing 1.1 million people and annual sales of US$232 billion (BankBoston 1997). These examples suggest that competitive capacity depends on competition as a spur to improve productivity and the ability to compete in international markets. But competition can frequently lead to downsizing, cost-cutting, and low skilled, low waged jobs. It has to be balanced with cooperation and commitment to upgrade skills (Best 1990).

A synergy is required between basic research and market application. The priority is to have clusters of well trained people who can 'do the science' and apply scientific knowledge to market applications. In Singapore they use the term 'technopreneur' to signify the importance of technical and scientific knowledge, along with a strong emphasis on innovation within existing businesses. It is also intended to encourage knowledge workers to be more entrepreneurial in developing business start-ups.

Productive innovation is not restricted to the realm of highly specialized expertise but needs to be defused throughout the economy, but this cannot be achieved when employers adopt a 'plug-in-and-play' model of human resource management (Lauder 1999). In most circumstances a *flat-pack* rather than a *plug-in-and-play* model of skills training is more appropriate, as the skills of employees need to be 'built up' and supplemented over time within a work context. This is because vocational education and training (VET), although having an important role in preparing people for employment, including theoretical development and reflection, is no substitute for systematic 'on-the-job' training (Ashton and Green 1996). This is because of the need for training using state of the art technologies that are often prohibitively expensive for colleges, universities, and training centres. But also because training involves preparing people to flourish in the social context of work which will vary according to such things as company ethos, culture, organization, size, and industrial sector. As Stasz (1997) observed, work context matters in the consideration of skills. While communication, problem-solving, and teamworking skills are identifiable in all jobs, their nature and importance vary depending on the company. These contextual differences are a vital part of what it means to be productive and can only be learnt on the job. Hence companies play a vital role in developing the individual and collective intelligence on which competitive capacity depends (P. Brown and Lauder 2001*a*; ILO 1998).

3. Capability

Capability refers to the dominant model of human capability that informs the way people think about their abilities and those of others. In Western nations this has been premissed on a 'dim view' of intelligence, that assumes that only a minority are capable of high skilled work and that the education system must be organized in order to identify and cultivate this limited pool of talent. Alternatively, the development of a high skills society clearly depends on a model of human capability based on an assertion that all have the potential to benefit from skills upgrading and lifelong learning. It depends on an inclusive system of education and training that achieves comparatively high standards for all social groups irrespective of social class, gender, race, or ethnicity. It also depends on teaching the new basic skills to all.

This refers to the need to develop a high level of human *capability* through education, training, and lifelong learning. It depends on the provision of quality ET provision that is geared to lifting both generic educational standards and training to meet the specific needs of individual employers. It is, for instance, difficult to see how educational standards for all can be raised if school buildings are in desperate need of repair; teachers are poorly trained or where their morale is low; where there are insufficient books or poor access to information technologies in the delivery of the curriculum; where there is a shortage of state-of-the-art equipment in colleges and universities for training and research purposes; where relatively low levels of remuneration make it difficult to recruit talented teachers, college lecturers, and university researchers. Education in the school of hard knocks is cheap, education for lifelong learning requires significant investments of hard cash.

The new 'basic' skills, including communication, collaborative, information technology, and lifelong learning skills, rest on a different set of assumptions from those that have informed the understanding of human capability in virtually all the developed economies. The overriding view has been to prepare people for their future occupational and adult roles. Most of these roles were clearly prescribed which led to an emphasis on discipline, routine, and reliability necessary to 'fit' people into their appropriate pigeonhole within the existing division of labour. For white-collar workers this typically involved the development of a bureaucratic personality. As Merton described in his classic essay on this subject,

The bureaucrat's official life is planned for him [or her] in terms of a graded career, through the organizational device of promotion by seniority, pensions, incremental salaries, etc., all of which are designed to provide incentives for disciplined action and conformity to the official regulations. The official is tacitly expected to and largely does adapt his [or her] thoughts, feelings and actions to the prospect of this career. (Merton 1949: 200–1)

The bureaucratic personality in many organizations has become a source of 'trained incapacity' that disables people from working effectively in more 'flexible' organizational structures. Facets of 'charismatic' personality have come to the fore, including interpersonal, communication, teamworking, and creative skills (P. Brown and Scase 1994). The charismatic personality seeks to challenge routine actions and rule-following behaviour, to replace it with patterns of innovative and creative activity. Therefore, the charismatic personality is the creator of a new order as well as the breaker of routine order (Shils 1965).[12] In high skills economies it is not only those in technical, managerial, and professional employment that need to develop good interpersonal, communication, and teamworking skills. Manufacturing production has also been transformed over the last two decades in all the developed economies drawing on just-in-time systems of lean production developed in Japan. On our visits to various factories we were struck by the emphasis placed on the so-called 'soft' skills, including teamworking, communication, problem-solving, and interpersonal and self-management skills, rather than by the upgrading of technical competence. Employers were unanimous in the view that if technical upgrading was a requirement it could be provided by the company without great difficulty, but developing a culture of personal responsibility, teamworking, and learning was more difficult.

When these changes are coupled to changes in the labour market that require people to remain employable through upgrading skills, and to changes within society more generally that have led to increasing 'individualization' where there is more scope for people to make decisions about their lives and to become more reflexive (Beck 1992; Giddens 1991), the new basic skills (Murnane and Levy 1996) involve the development of new 'model' workers aimed at enhancing individual employability and empowerment. In this context education has little to do with teaching students the specific skills that employers state they need because these are subject to rapid change, as previously noted. Education for a high skills society involves cultivating 'multiple' intelligence

---

[12] Edward Shils (1965, 1968) has questioned Weber's restricted use of charisma to refer to extraordinarily gifted individuals engaged in intense, concentrated, and innovative action. Shils suggests that the 'normal' form of charisma is more attenuated and dispersed. Indeed, Weber clearly recognized that charisma invariably became 'routinized' into traditionalism or into bureaucratization: 'The routinization of charisma, in quite essential respects, is identical with adjustment to the conditions of the economy, that is, to the continuously effective routines of workaday life' (in Gerth and Mills 1967: 54). What is being suggested here, is that many of the features which Weber associated with the charismatic personality are becoming part of a changing ideology of symbolic control in an attempt to resolve command and control problems in 'flexible' organizations (P. Brown 1995).

(Gardner 1993) that enables people to develop the cognitive, emotional, and collective intelligence required in flexible labour markets, high-performance work systems, and for a general improvement in the overall quality of life.

Change in all facets of everyday life has reinvigorated the old cliché of 'learning how to learn'. In important respects these include schools and colleges doing what they have done for decades in developing the literacy, numeracy, and problem-solving skills of students, but doing it better. These now need to be taught to all students to a higher standard of attainment. A familiarity with computers, email, and the Internet have become part of the new basic skills because they contribute to the power tools that enable communication and learning beyond face-to-face interactions, as more of what they will learn in the future will not take place in a classroom or workshop, but in informal settings increasingly via a computer terminal. Wherever possible the focus needs to be placed on knowledge and information that is enduring rather than ephemeral: 'transferable' and 'extendable' to new circumstances. This needs to be combined with a critical and creative ethos that helps people reflect on how existing practices can be modified to new conditions or when new ways of doing things are called for.

The new basic skills also involve 'learning how to learn with others'. This extends beyond the development of teamworking that encourages cooperation, tolerance, and mutual respect. The idea of teamworking tends to focus on discrete projects or activities. But learning how to learn with others also refers to broader relationships between the individual and society. This is what Brown and Lauder call 'collective intelligence' (Brown and Lauder 2001a). The more societies are characterized by processes of individualization, the more important it becomes to educate people about their mutual dependence and how to live and learn together. It is for this reason that virtually all the advanced economies are thinking afresh about moral and citizenship education. A major problem is that the education system is based on individual forms of assessment that make group activities peripheral to the real action of gaining marketable qualifications, only to arrive in jobs that expect people to work and learn with others.

Since the inception of mass schooling there has been a contradiction between the principles of a liberal education and vocational preparation, which for many students involved an early exit from formal education with only a basic grasp of numbers, reading, and writing. Vocational education has typically been regarded as 'second class' relative to academic study, largely because it led to inferior qualifications and exclusion from the real vocational prizes in the labour market reserved for those who went to university. The new basic skills undermine the academic/ vocational distinction because much of what is taught and learnt conforms to what may be regarded as a generic education as well as a vocational preparation (Young 1998; Green 1998). In other words the skills required at work significantly overlap with those required in everyday life. But this should not obscure the importance of attracting motivated and talented people entering technical and scientific studies that are at the sharp end of a knowledge-driven economy. It is easier to train an engineer to become a manager, than a manager to become an engineer.

Finally, we require a transformation in the way we understand human capability. In Western societies it is assumed as limited by natural endowment rather than a reflection of the societies in which people live (Holloway 1988). Charles Sabel has noted that 'it is often social hierarchy and the world views associated with it that restrict the unfolding of human capacity, and not the limitations of natural endowment' (1982: 224). If we are serious about developing the capability of all rather than a few, we must rid ourselves of the dim view of intelligence. This dim view leads to low expectations about the capability of the bottom 30 per cent of the population and leads employers to see little point in investing in the training of those in easy entry jobs because they are not seen to have the potential to develop their skills. The dim view of intelligence equally infects the self-confidence of individuals who do not feel they 'have the brains' to undertake post-compulsory education or training.

4. Coordination

This refers to the coordination of the supply and demand for labour. It recognizes that there is often an over-emphasis on supply-side issues of education, training, and employability. This ignores the need to foster the demand for skilled employment that cannot be left solely to market forces. A key issue here is how national governments try to tailor their education and training systems to the perceived 'needs' of the economy, and how they seek to incorporate the expanding numbers in higher education into high skilled jobs.

While issues of *capability* have dominated debates about skill formation given its focus on the supply of 'skills' to the labour market, *coordination* refers to how this supply is coordinated (or otherwise) with the demand for skilled workers. Skill formation does not end when labour market entrants log onto 'whatjob.com'. Coordination involves more than having an effective way of meshing supply and demand that can be achieved on the basis of a low skilled equilibrium (Finegold and Soskice 1988). It refers to whether 'supply and demand' are geared towards the upgrading of skills throughout the economy. This cannot be left to investments in education and training systems, in the hope that in combination with new technological breakthroughs, it will lead the market to soak up the supply of 'knowledge' workers now leaving tertiary education in large numbers in all the major economies. Ways have to be found to stimulate the demand for high skilled workers. Equally, attempts need to be made to help employers attract talented students to pursue careers in key areas of knowledge-driven economies, especially in science and engineering.

It is those countries that can successfully develop 'joined up' policies involving different government departments, regional assemblies, employer organizations, trade unions, and local communities, that are most likely to achieve a significant upgrading of skills (Cooke and Morgan 1998; Ashton, Green, et al. 1999). This is not only true with respect to policy formation but also their implementation at the local level, for instance, in schools, universities, training centres, and small and medium-sized enterprises.

Therefore, the familiar distinction between state knowledge and market knowledge should be rejected.[13] In saying that the state has a key role to play in the creation of a high skills society is not to say that the state should try to monopolize knowledge of new technologies, innovations, or market opportunities. Rather it is based on an understanding that markets can be organized in different ways and with different consequences for the supply of, and demand for, skills. Coordination is not based on nation states trying to 'govern' markets. The globalization of markets and advances in information technologies, exponentially increased the amount of market knowledge that governments would need to 'govern'. But it is precisely because of this growing complexity that coordination needs to become more systematic. It now, for instance, includes identifying key areas of knowledge-driven economic development through indigenous investment and inward investment, where efforts can be made to create new employment and increase the skill content of jobs, such as in high-performance

---

[13] The classic statement of this distinction is to be found in the work of Friedrich A. Hayek (1944, 1960). For a recent example of a similar argument, see Daniel Yergin and Joseph Stanislaw (1998).

manufacturing and exportable service clusters, including telecommunications, wafer fabrication, biotechnology, precision engineering, international business services, health, and education. This will require sophisticated foresight planning, which will include the coordination of regional economic development through networks of local stakeholders, national strategists, research institutes, technopoles, and global companies.

It is small and medium-sized enterprises (SMEs) that are expected to generate the majority of new employment opportunities, but because of their size and limited resources they are restricted in their scope to upgrade products and services, along with the skills of their workforce. They do not have the resources to engage in information gathering whether it concerns new technologies, international markets, or production techniques; the time to build domestic, let alone international networks; access to cheap investment capital to help them compete in national and international markets; or provide skills training in anticipation of business expansion. Rosebeth Moss Kanter has observed that 'the independence of entrepreneurs and small businesses is often stressed in popular lore, but the truth is that small businesses gain competitive advantage through collaborative advantage' (1998: 95). Here the need for a coordinated partnership between the municipal authorities, local business, trade unions, and communities can play a key role in overcoming the problem of innovation, training, and skill upgrading in SMEs.

Thus, the role of government—national or local—is not to direct but to inform, facilitate, and coordinate networks of stakeholders for innovation and upskilling. In this context, subsidiarity—encouraging those affected by policy decisions to make their own decisions in collaboration with other stakeholders—is important because we have learnt that old forms of central state economic policies are likely to be inefficient in post-industrial economies. The federal state does have a key role to play in coordinating industrial foresight, but the whole point of the exercise is not to make decisions in isolation but to facilitate decision-making at the lowest possible level, involving as many stakeholders as possible. In economic terms, subsidiarity is desirable because the knowledge to make sound investment decisions linked to skills upgrading require a detailed understanding of local companies, labour market conditions, and training provision at the local level. In effect regional economies should aim to integrate both local and transnational firms in partnerships subject to democratic forms of accountability, whilst conforming to a national strategy of skills upgrading.

5. Circulation

Circulation focuses our attention on the way nations, regions, and industrial clusters diffuse skills upgrading beyond 'beacon' companies, R & D institutes, research centres, and universities. In a high skill society we would expect to find a high level of circulation or diffusion of high skills throughout the workforce.

This refers to the 'diffusion' of high skills throughout the economy. In circumstances where information, knowledge, and skills change rapidly the question of the circulation of skills, knowledge, and new technologies, assumes added importance. Competitive advantage depends in significant part on the nature and speed at which skills can be upgraded and circulate throughout the economy. If they cannot be diffused rapidly and effectively, the opportunities for innovation and skills upgrading will be limited.

Circulation depends on lifting the skills base for the workforce to benefit from opportunities for skills upgrading. The larger the skills gap between existing skill levels and those in leading-edge companies the more difficult it becomes to overcome this gap, partly because employers will perceive that the investment in training will be too great, both financially and in the time required for training. This is why the circulation of high skills is best achieved within a culture of learning that is not restricted to leading-edge companies (Coffield 2000a, b). Skill diffusion depends on a major expansion of high skilled employment opportunities. All developed economies have clusters or enclaves of high skilled workers, but vary in the extent to which high skills are found more generally throughout the working population. This relates to the question of how nations try to overcome the problem of a low skill equilibrium. Finegold and Soskice define the term 'equilibrium' '*to connote a self-reinforcing network of societal and state institutions which interact to stifle the demand for improvement in skills levels*' (1988: 22). This recognizes that there may be a mismatch between the rhetoric of 'high skills' and the realities of policy implementation, unless the institutional mechanisms, along with the ethos of skills upgrading, are put in place. If large numbers of employers are reluctant to invest in new technologies or to upgrade the skills of the workforce, given a concern with price competition rather than product or service innovation, the circulation of skills will be extremely limited.

The circulation of high skills depends on reducing information, labour market, and social rigidities (P. Brown and Lauder 2001a). Where there is intense competition between local companies or suspicion between large corporations and local suppliers or subcontractors, the spread of 'best practice' on which skills upgrading depends cannot be developed as a key element of high skill formation. If labour markets are structured in ways that close off opportunities for intermediate or advanced training because it is reserved for those employed in leading-edge companies, skill diffusion is equally restricted. These issues relate to the need to limit social rigidities that limit education, training, and employment opportunities for high skill work to high socio-economic groups, men, or dominant ethnic groups. This is dealt with in our discussion of *closure* that addresses issues of social inclusion and exclusion.

Finally, the circulation or diffusion of high skills also refers to a dynamic process that can be analysed in terms of how successful national economies have succeeded in creating the infrastructure of ET, labour market, employment, and economic institutions that shape the societal capacity for skills upgrading. There is no single model of how this can be achieved because of national differences in historical development, culture, and political economy, but what is abundantly clear is that claims that inward investment from multinational companies can diffuse skills through the economy have been exaggerated. Such a strategy must be balanced with policies aimed at growing indigenous small and medium-sized companies in clusters offering high skilled employment (Cooke and Morgan 1998). This is turn will depend on building institutional relations of high trust.

6. Cooperation

Cooperation is a feature of all forms of economic organization on a large scale. The more productivity depends on 'brains' rather than 'brawn', the more important cooperation based on high trust becomes. The extent to which high trust relations are woven into the fabric of society will tell us a great deal about the degree of individual discretion and individual empowerment as well as collective commitment to skills upgrading.

Cooperation refers to the trust relations that are embedded in the institutional fabric of society including the education and training system, labour market, industrial relations, and social welfare. This emphasis on cooperation may initially appear surprising given that capitalist economies are typically characterized in terms of economic conflict between competing classes or interest groups, or else in terms of a competition between rational self-seeking individuals. Competition and conflict are inherent features of post-industrial societies, but they can be woven into the social fabric in different ways that can lead them to be exaggerated as in Mrs Thatcher's (in)famous remark that there is no such thing as society only families and individuals, or as a constant reminder of the importance of building a social partnership in which common interests are given precedence over individual or sectional interests (these are often defined as mutually compatible such as the idea that you can have economic efficiency and social justice espoused in much of the rhetoric about the knowledge economy).

Interestingly, even Karl Marx recognized that all forms of large-scale work organization involve aspects of social cooperation (Marx 1976). It is impossible to run factories without people being willing to turn up for work at regular hours and to fulfil routine tasks even if these were reinforced by a method of paying people for what they produce, employing armies of supervisors, or placing them under the constant threat of being sacked. Throughout the twentieth century the adoption of Fordist methods of production continued to limit the scope for cooperation at work. Indeed, low trust relations of suspicion, ill will, and conflicting interests were built into the techniques of production (Noble 1977).

If the advanced economies are to reap the potential for high skill formation, the model of human cooperation will need to be premissed on high trust relations for the simple reason that the more people cooperate, communicate, and share common goals the more they are able to learn and achieve (Fox 1974; P. Brown and Lauder 2000). High trust relations are pivotal to raising productivity linked to skills upgrading. But as high trust relations assume greater importance their institutional character must also change. When we talk about high trust, it is not simply an issue of giving workers a greater share of the spoils or financial stake in the company, but changing the nature of organizational involvement, including scope for individual initiative, problem-solving, creativity, teamwork, and innovation. Gains in productivity not only depend on a workforce that is committed, disciplined, hardworking, and able to accurately learn and copy routine ways of doing things, but on employees who are creative problem-solvers, self-managers, enterprising, and lifelong learners. Cooperation offers people the 'power' tools to work in new and more productive ways (Appelbaum et al. 2000).

The importance of cooperation is not limited to the workplace as we have shown. It is integral to building the societal capacity for high skills.

If cooperation is a source of increasing individual and collective intelligence, nations will require far-reaching changes in their social and political institutions to cultivate the 'skilled' workforce of the future. The nature of such changes will depend on the country in question. The problem this poses for Asian countries such as Singapore is that creativity, self-reliance, and empowerment are seen to go together with Western individualism. This may seriously weaken the social cement that has been judged to be crucial to any adequate explanation of the economic success of Japan and the Asian tigers (World Bank 1993). Alternatively, the question of creativity and individual commitment takes a different form in Britain and North America where the focus has been on increasing teamworking skills, strengthening corporate cultures, and citizenship education.

Cooperation for high skill formation also depends on building social solidarity that can no longer narrowly focus on contributions within waged work, but on a political commitment to develop the individual and collective intelligence of all (P. Brown and Lauder 2001a).

7. Closure

Closure addresses social inclusion and exclusion in education, training, and the labour market. In a high skills society we would expect to find inclusive skill formation policies aimed at reducing the social closure that has traditionally confronted women, ethnic minorities, and those from lower socio-economic backgrounds. It highlights the problem of developing policies for a high skills society that are socially inclusive, as it is relatively easy for all of the advanced nations to develop an elite of high skills workers.

Closure refers to issues of social inclusion and exclusion. It addresses the question of whether the opportunities to enter a good job are open to all rather than restricted to social elites, to men rather than women, or to dominant ethnic groups. The definition of social closure in terms of opportunity structure is valid as long as we avoid the fallacy of composition. That is, the idea that if some people are able to find managerial or professional jobs everyone can, and conversely if they cannot they must look to their personal failing for an explanation. In a high skills society we would expect to find at least 50 per cent of occupations categorized as technical, managerial, or professional. The vast majority of the remainder would require formal skills training.

No existing economy has attained this rather modest target. Thus, even in 'high skills' societies, a large minority of the workforce will not be in high skilled jobs. It is also difficult to avoid a trade-off between *skill* and *employment*. In other words, the greater the skill content of jobs throughout the economy, the greater the risk of exclusion through unemployment. Conversely, an emphasis on full-employment, irrespective of skill levels, can lead to skill and income polarization. Such problems are inherent in post-industrial societies. The trade-off between skill and employment may be eased by declining birth rates in the developed economies that are likely to create labour short-ages (assuming that there will not be a major recession) that may encourage employers to increase investments in training as a way of improving productivity (the alternative is to increase immigration in areas of labour shortage which are likely to be for both high and low skilled jobs).

Equally, the focus on social closure leads to the question of how work is defined and rewarded. There seems little doubt that the idea that social worth is reflected in the market value of one's employment must be transformed in post-industrial societies. There is no reason why unemployment should be associated with enforced idleness, loss of self-respect, and dependence on the state. There is no shortage of work, only waged work. We need new ways of thinking about the relationship between learning, work, and employment. If, for example, the skills of the future workforce are now at a premium, it is time for us to start rewarding those who add to the individual and collective intelligence of others, such as currently unpaid carers (Brown and Lauder 2001*a*).

With these caveats in mind we can proceed with our definition of social exclusion. Opportunity is increasing based on the competition for credentials (Collins 1979; Offe 1976), as employers use them to screen out unsuitable applicants (Bourdieu and Baltanski 1978). Although quali-fying for specific kinds of employment is not enough, as tough entry jobs usually involve an extensive recruitment process, including a detailed assessment of the candidates' communication, interpersonal, and groupwork skills.

This competition is inevitable because of the need to have people with the appropriate education and training to enter employment for which they are qualified and suited (although this remains an ideal rather than a reality). From the individual's point of view, the primary goal of the game is to finish with better qualifications than other people in order to improve one's chances of getting access to the best jobs, but as a national strategy for high skill formation the primary goal is to create a culture of learning based on the new basic skills.[14]

This reminds us of the importance of the absolute quality of education and job opportunities, on the one hand, and the relative issue of whether it gives everyone an equal chance to get the credentials required to enter high skilled employment. We have seen how greater significance has been attached to positional competition in a context of economic globalization, as the prosperity of individuals and nations are seen to depend on the skills, knowledge, and abilities of the workforce. Such arguments have led some governments to redefine the problem of equality of opportunity based on class, gender, or race, as one of raising absolute standards of achievement to enable all to take advantage of new opportunities for skilled work which the globalization of labour markets is seen to present (Reich 1991). Positional competition is a question of how to outsmart other nations as previously noted (P. Brown and Lauder 1996, 2001a).

It was also noted that this account of the globalization of positional competition should be rejected. First, the assumption that domestic positional competitions have declined in significance is based on an erroneous understanding of the consequences of globalization on labour market opportunities. Equally, the competition for credentials continues to be organized at the local or national level, although there is some evidence of an internationalization of higher education and the prospects of social elites opting to study for an international baccalaureate rather than for 'national' certificates (P. Brown 2000).

Secondly, there are important national differences in the way positional competitions are organized, which may have major implications for the life chances of fellow contestants. Credential competition, for instance, can be organized as a zero-sum or positive-sum game (Hirsch 1977: 52). A zero-sum game is characterized by 'winner-takes-all-markets' (Frank and Cook 1996) where high skilled, high waged work is restricted to a small proportion of the population. 'The contrast is with competition that improves performance and enjoyment all round, so that winners gain more than losers lose, and all may come out

---

[14] Hirsch defines 'positional' competition in terms of how one stands relative to others within an implicit or explicit hierarchy. If, for instance, everyone is able to improve their academic performance by 50%, it would do little to alter the relative position of contestants. Hirsch writes, 'The "quality" of schooling, in effect, exists in two dimensions. There is an absolute dimension, in which quality is added by receptive students, good teachers, good facilities, and so on; but there is also a relative dimension, in which quality consists of the differential over the educational level attained by others' (1977: 6).

winners—the positive-sum game' (Hirsch 1977: 52). In the positive-sum game some students may gain more credentials than others, but all gain a good education that, for instance, prepares them as skilled employees or as empowered citizens. Whether positional competition takes the form of a zero-sum or positive-sum game is important because the skills, knowledge, and insights of a growing proportion of employees have become a key aspect of economic competitiveness, even though credentials will inevitably be used as a screening device by employers (Collins 1979).[15]

High skill formation depends on the creation of a positive-sum game that offers the educational foundation required for high skilled employment to all rather than a few. This is best achieved based on 'meritocratic' rather than 'market' models of educational competition, as it is the children from socially advantaged families who are able to unfairly benefit from financial investments in their education which are not available to those from less affluent backgrounds (Lauder et al. 1999). Moreover, even if positional competition is based on meritocratic criteria, it will fail to widen educational achievement and occupational opportunities unless child poverty is eliminated. Decades of research have shown how children living in poverty lack material resources at home such as books, computers, or the space to do homework, as well as the cultural capital attuned to the demands and expectation of the school system (Bourdieu and Passeron 1977). Issues of poverty are sometimes compounded by gender and racial discrimination that also need to be overcome if social inclusion is to be achieved.

A NOTE ON COMPARATIVE METHOD

A theory of skill formation that can advance our understanding of the societal capacity for high skills remains in its infancy. While there are a lot of excellent studies on different features of skill formation such as on vocational education and training, the labour market, economic development, state formation, and welfare regimes, these studies frequently lack the 'joined up thinking' required to further the study of the societal capacity for high skills. There is also a surprising lack of research on the process of skills upgrading, with notable exceptions

---

[15] There is obviously more to the competition for a livelihood than the pursuit of credentials. Paper qualifications enable an individual to stay in the competition, but it does not guarantee success in the labour market (Heath and McMahon 1997; Brown and Scase 1997).

(Ashton, Green, et al. 1999). Little headway will be made unless there is a greater willingness to cross disciplinary boundaries between economics, sociology, social policy, education, politics, history, business, and management studies. A holistic understanding of societal capacity depends on developing insights from all these disciplines within an overarching social science approach.

The comparative study of skill formation also throws up a major methodological challenge of how to broaden the range of quantitative data typically collected by human capital theorists. The level of income inequalities, child poverty, and occupational trend data need to be combined with attitude surveys that seek to examine the degree of consensus about the economic and social goals of society, along with measures of societal trust. This is important given the above analysis that suggests that the societal capacity for high skill formation is much more than the sum total of individual skills even if these could be accurately measured. It reflects the quality of the social and economic institutions that shape the relations of trust between government, employers, and employees. Therefore the methodological challenge is to capture issues of process, coordination, and trust relations which will determine whether societies will succeed in re-engineering their social and economic institution in ways that exploit the post-industrial possibilities for high skills. We have argued that the qualitative dimensions of capacity building have become central to skill formation. This will require detailed case studies of how skill formation policy-making takes place, how it informs (or otherwise) the way companies approach the training of their workforce, and how questions of skill, employability, and lifelong learning are understood by individuals and groups from different socio-economic backgrounds, ethnicity, race, and gender. A major task will be the creation of a comparative *Skill Formation Index*, similar to the Human Development Index sponsored by the United Nations.

Our approach also continues to recognize the importance of 'society' at a national level. This is not to suggest that global networks, supranational organization, and intergovernmental agreements (such as within the European Community) are unimportant, but differences in national contexts hold the key to understanding the future of skill formation. It calls for a detailed analysis of the societal capacity for skill formation in each country. This is because the study of skill formation must always include an analysis of the historical, institutional, cultural, political, and economic context.

A common problem with cross-national studies is a failure to develop methodologies that offer comparative purchase. What gets presented is a series of country case studies that make it difficult to identify similarities and differences between them. For purposes of comparative analysis we did not impose a definition of high skills (as a benchmark to assess differences in national performance) but rather investigated how key stakeholders in different countries understood 'high skills'. In the social sciences some of the concepts that we subject to systematic definition are also used in a variety of ways within everyday social, cultural, and spatial contexts. These include concepts such as social class, intelligence, and democracy. This is also true of 'high skills'. It has the advantage of being understood in different national contexts, but in a variety of ways, such as in terms of the quality of employment, training opportunities, and the abilities of individuals.[16]

When it is recognized that the discourse of high skills in each country represents a study of political economy *par excellence*, it can become an invaluable research tool for comparative analysis. At the level of national political discourse, it can be used to examine how key stakeholders (politicians, civil servants, trade unions, employer organizations, MNCs) interpret and represent issues such as global competition, economic change, changing skill requirements, skill formation strategies, social justice, and the management of economic risk. It offers the researcher an insight into how key stakeholders define their social, economic, and political goals and how these serve as a 'guide to action' that makes some policy reforms possible whilst ruling out others. What is 'strategic pragmatism' (Schein 1996) in Singapore, for example, may be defined as politically unacceptable in other countries such as universal wage cuts to maintain price competitiveness.

A comparative study of skill formation can be achieved by focusing the analysis around common post-industrial 'pressure points' which expose the challenges, tensions, and conflicts in national skill formation systems. This focus is intended to facilitate an analysis of the possibilities and limitations of future skill formation in a way that connects to

[16] On the basis of official reports and interviews with stakeholders in different countries, it is possible to identify a number of competing definitions including the following:

  (a) that all jobs are highly skilled, e.g. professional, managerial, technical;
  (b) that jobs can become high skilled through a linear progress which takes all jobs in a high skills direction;
  (c) that a growing proportion of jobs are high skilled, but that some will inevitably remain low skilled;
  (d) that more jobs require higher skills levels than before;
  (e) that every employee will have a job which requires formal training;
  (f) that people will be trained for jobs which fulfil their human capabilities;
  (g) universal tertiary and lifelong learning.

macro issues of post-industrial change. The study of these pressure points also facilitates a comparison of how common problems are defined and 'managed' in each country. In the final part of this book we will outline each of the key pressure points as a way of thinking through the prospects for high skill formation in each country. But we begin our comparative analysis with national differences in the meaning of competitiveness and how these relate to national systems of education and training.

2

Models of High Skills in National Competition Strategies

ANDY GREEN, WITH AKIKO SAKAMOTO

POLICY ARGUMENTS FOR HIGH SKILLS

The high skills, high wage economy has become a common aspiration across many of the world's developed and developing nations. Business leaders talk about the growing importance of knowledge and skills, economists about generating higher 'value added', and policy-makers about the virtues of the so-called 'knowledge-driven economy'. Their arguments are by now familiar (see Chapter 1).

The broad argument for skills is compelling, but there is often little precision in debates about what is actually meant by a 'high skills economy'. Does it mean an economy which has highly skilled creative elites—the so-called 'symbolic analysts' whose high priced labour in international markets Robert Reich (1991) claims generate most of the national value added? Does it mean an economy with a wide distribution of skills throughout its workforce and relative equality of income distribution? Does it imply high levels of technical skills and knowledge specialization? Or does it mean, rather, a wide spread of generic competences (such as in IT, communications, and problem-solving) and the broad general education which provides the basis for future learning and civic participation for all? How far does a high skills economy rest on 'social capital' (Putnam 1993) and the capacity for trust and cooperation? To what extent does it involve the inculcation of attitudes and values conducive to social order and work discipline? In different national contexts these aspects of skill all rank as important constituents of the skills regime. Which version of high skills are we striving for?

National Competitiveness Strategies, Productivity, and Skills

The reference point for most policy discussions about high skills, particularly in the English-speaking world, is 'national economic competitiveness'. However, what this term actually means is debatable, and some economists—notably Paul Krugman—dismiss the concept entirely.[1] There is no universally agreed way of defining and measuring national competitiveness, nor any consensus about how to achieve it. Globalization may lead to integration of world markets and increasing convergence in technologies in advanced economies, but it has not yet thrown up one best strategy for national competitiveness and is unlikely to do so (Gray 1997; Berger and Dore 1996).

The World Economic Forum (WEF) and the OECD argue that 'national competitiveness' refers broadly to the abilities of a country's economic (and social) institutions to compete internationally in a way that leads to sustained national growth and high average incomes for national citizens (Tan Kong Yam and Toh Mun Heng 1998). In Michael Porter's classic definition, it is 'the degree to which a nation can, under free and fair market conditions, produce goods and services that meet the test of international markets while simultaneously maintaining or expanding the real incomes of citizens' (1990: 4). The definitions, however, beg a number of questions. What are 'free and fair market conditions'? Is competitiveness best measured by sustained growth or high national income?[2] How far does high national income translate into high average living standards? How equally is income distributed? Depending on the criteria used, different national economies rank highest in competitiveness. On measures of GNP per capita, the United States outperforms most countries, but its post-war record of growth

---

[1] Krugman (1996) argues that the term 'national competitiveness' is meaningless because only firms can be competitive, since countries do not have a bottom line in the same way as firms. They do not usually go bankrupt.

[2] Wealthy countries may raise national incomes less rapidly than successful developing countries, but still be regarded as equally or even more competitive. The USA tops the competitiveness league tables of both the WEF and the International Institute of Management Development (IMD) despite having had substantially lower rates of growth in real per capita income than other less developed countries that come further down the list.

has been low to moderate and its income distribution is amongst the most unequal of the advanced countries (Luttwak 1999). On a measure of sustained growth (say over thirty-five years), Singapore far outranks the Unites States, but trails the latter in terms of national income per capita, and has wider income differentials than either Germany or Japan. Until the last decade, Germany and Japan were high income *and* high growth countries with relatively low income differentials. They still rank relatively highly on the latter two measures, but Germany now has only moderate growth and Japan is still in recession at the time of writing.

Productivity as a measure can be more precisely defined than 'national competitiveness' and is often taken as the best indicator of underlying or 'structural competitiveness' in an economy, acting as a strong predictor for wages and standards of living (Gough 1999). However, there are a number of different definitions of productivity, each one measuring different facets of competitiveness and each one subject to numerous measurement difficulties, particularly as concerns the output of service industries.

Total Factor Productivity (TFP) is the best overall measure, according to economists, because it includes both capital productivity and labour productivity, both of which contribute towards national income and which are likely to contribute towards growth and personal incomes. However, high TFP does not automatically translate into either high growth or high average personal income, since other factors are involved. It is also difficult to analyse the contribution of skills to the capital productivity component of TFP, as opposed to the labour productivity component.

Labour productivity can be measured in different ways: as output per worker, output per hour worked, and output per head of population. The proper measure of productivity per se is output per hour worked, which is a function of technology, organizational efficiency, the skills and knowledge employed in given inputs of labour, and the capital invested in the plant and equipment which the labour sets to work (some of which constitutes the so-called residual which TFP seeks to incorporate) (see Abramovitz 1989). These can be at least proximately measured. Output per hour worked is also generally a good indicator of income levels and one aspect of quality of life since, other things being equal, where it is high, wages are likely to be higher and hours shorter.

However, 'national competitiveness', as the term is commonly used, refers to a range of national economic characteristics and indicators which may derive from other factors and from other forms (and measures) of productivity. Competitive advantage in terms of economic growth may accrue from comparatively low labour costs, or from the existence of other conditions which attract foreign investment, such as predictable business environment, high levels of social order, and good infrastructures (as is still the case in Singapore amongst our comparator countries). Other forms of productivity may also contribute towards national competitiveness. Competitiveness can be improved through increases in output per worker achieved through longer working hours (as in Japan and probably recently in the United Kingdom) or through increased output per head and concomitant reductions in social costs achieved through higher employment rates (as true for many years in Japan and Singapore and also currently in the United Kingdom).

National competitiveness measures thus confound a number of characteristics which may be considered aspects of aggregate economic success, whilst saying relatively little about such things as personal incomes and living standards and the way these are distributed across populations. Skills are only one amongst a range of factors which influence each of these different outcomes at the national level. The way in which skills contribute to competitiveness in different countries varies depending on the dominant types of competitiveness pursued in each of these countries, and, more specifically, on the dominant types of competitiveness pursued in the different sectors of each national economy.

National economies compete in the world market in different ways. Within any given national economy, some sectors will be more competitive than others, and each sector's productivity will depend on a different mix of factors. The role of skills in generating productivity and competitiveness will vary in each organization and sector. National competitiveness is the aggregate of the productivity in the different sectors to which skills have in each case made quite different contributions. The overall contribution of human capital to the competitiveness of national economies will therefore vary in terms of the types, levels, and distributions of skills employed through them. Different national skills profiles map onto the different national configurations of company competition strategies.

Regini (1995), for instance, argues that there are at least four dominant types of the latter in Europe, based on different product market strategies. In the Diversified Quality Production model (e.g. in Baden-Württemberg), firms compete mainly on quality and to some extent on diversification; in the Flexible Mass Production model (e.g. in Rhône Alps), they compete on variety, scale, and cost. Flexible Specialization

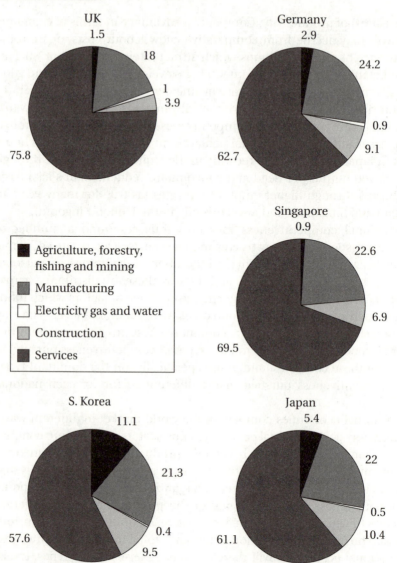

Fig. 2.1. Structure of employment by country and industry

ᵃ Figure for manufacturing includes mining.

Sources: UK: Office for National Statistics, *Labour Market Trends*, Oct. 1998; Germany: Federal Statistics Office, Dec. 1998: S. Korea: National Statistical Office, Republic of Korea: *Annual Report on the Economically Active Population Survey*, 1997; Singapore: Research and Statistics Department, Ministry of Labour, *Report on the Labour Force Survey of Singapore*, 1997; Japan: Management and Coordination Agency, Statistics Bureau, Government of Japan, *Monthly Statistics of Japan*, Aug. 1998.

Systems (Lombardia) compete on rapid response to demand through enterprise flexibility; and Traditional Small Firms Systems (e.g. Catalonia) compete not on scale but on low wages and prices.

At the aggregate national level we may suggest the following generalizations about our comparator countries using a range of the above indicators.

The Unites States has the highest Total Factor Productivity (TFP) in the world because capital productivity is high and because labour is highly productive in most sectors of the economy. In the market sector during the 1994–6 period, TFP was higher than in leading European economies (benchmarked at 126 compared to 114 in west Germany, 113 in France, and 100 in the United Kingdom).[3] The Unites States produces the highest skilled elites in the world which keep the economy at the leading edge in dynamic areas such as financial services, entertainment, aero-engineering, biotechnology, and software development. Its skills distribution is relatively poor and society lacks a strong base of social capital but it has still managed to remain 'competitive', even in the lower skill service sector, through labour flexibility (if often in casualized low paid jobs) (see Castells 1998; Luttwak 1999; Thurow 1996).

Germany has relatively low capital productivity (its financial sector is relatively underdeveloped), but high labour productivity, particularly in the still substantial manufacturing sector. Output per head of population and output per worker have remained high, despite short average working hours and recently high levels of unemployment, because output per work hour is high, due to high capital investment, intensive R & D activity, and worker skills (see Figures 2.2 and 2.3). Germany is widely considered to be a 'high skills economy' (see Albert 1993; Dore 2000; Gray 1997; Hutton 1995; Streeck 1992, 1997). It has highly expert elites, particularly in basic and applied science and in engineering, and a broad distribution of general education and technical skills. It is also considered a 'high trust' society, with a propensity for workforce co-operation and professionalism, although this takes a different form in Japan (Fukuyama 1996; Streeck 1997).

Japan has moderately high overall labour productivity, mainly due to the productivity of its manufacturing sector (the service sector, aside from banking, is less developed). But productivity is often measured as higher on output per worker measures than in terms of output per hour worked (see Figure 2.3). Japan has high capital investment and 'high

[3] Labour productivity (output per hour worked): UK (100); France (126); W. Germany (126); USA (137). Capital productivity (output per capital services): UK (100); France (92); W. Germany (93); USA (110). Figures for market sector for 1994–6 in McKinsey Global Institute 1998: exhibit 2.

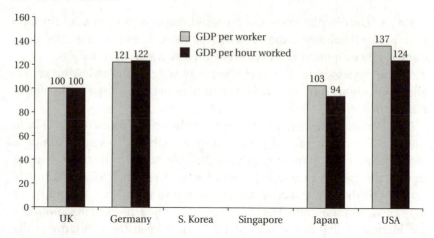

Fig. 2.2. Labour productivity by country, 1996 (UK = 100)

Source: DTI 1998.

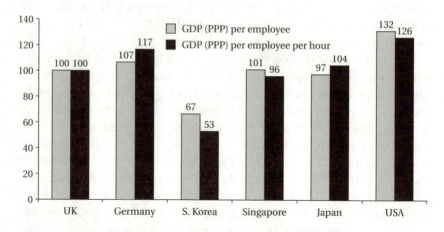

Fig. 2.3. Labour productivity by country, 1998 (UK = 100)

Source: IMD 1999.

skills', but people also work long hours. The Japanese workforce has a wide distribution of general education and generalist skills; and a heavy concentration of engineering expertise. There is also a strong propensity for cooperation and teamwork, based on high levels of social capital and trust (Perkin 1996). Organizational capacity for learning is high and values strongly reinforce the work ethic (Hampden-Turner and Trompenaars 1993) (although this may be beginning to erode).

Singapore ranks high in international competitiveness league tables and its productivity levels are higher than those in other tiger economies (see Figure 2.2 and Castells 1998). However, labour productivity still lags substantially behind Japan, Germany, and the Unites States, which suggests that it is competing on factors other than value added through workforce skills. The Singaporean skills base has improved rapidly over the past twenty years. The workforce has a strong work ethic, substantial capacity for cooperation relative to UK and US workforces, and the younger generation of workers have a sound basis in general education (Green 2000b). However, overall levels of knowledge and skills within the workforce are still low by comparison with leading countries.

The United Kingdom lagged behind the Unites States, west Germany, and France on TFP over the 1994–6 period, but less so than it would have done had its capital productivity (indexed at 100) not been higher than both west Germany (93) and France (92). Labour productivity in 1996, however, was substantially lower than in major competitor countries on both GDP per worker and per hour measures (see Figure 2.3).[4] Relatively high employment rates and long working hours act to raise per capita income, but this remains significantly below the levels in France, Germany, Japan, Singapore, and the Unites States (see GNP per capita at PPP in Figure 2.4).

Lower productivity in the United Kingdom has been due in part to lower capital investment in plant and equipment, which trailed the average for the United States, France, Germany, and Japan by over 30 per cent in the 1983–93 period. However this only accounts for a small part of the difference compared with the effects of lower investment in R & D and human skills.[5] The United Kingdom has highly skilled elites, particularly in basic science, finance, design, and the creative professions. However, its distribution of general education and technical skills at intermediate levels is, as in the United States, poor by comparison with Germany and Japan. Neither is it an obvious example of a 'high trust' society.

[4] In 1996 GDP per hour was benchmarked at 100 against 122 in Germany, 94 in Japan, and 134 in the USA. In 1998 according to a more recent set of OECD figures (Scarpetta et al., 2000), GDP per hour worked was 100 compared with the USA (122), France (124), Germany (110), and Japan (83). International Institute for Management Development (IMP 1999) figures for manufacturing only in 1999 show output per hour in Purchasing Power Parity (PPP) $ at: USA 31.28; Germany 28.94; Japan 25.73; UK 24.84. The USA had a world ranking of 6, Germany of 7, Japan of 15, and the UK of 19.

[5] For every £100 per worker invested in the UK between 1983 and 1993, Germany and the USA invested nearly £140, France almost £150, and Japan over £160. See DTI 1997: 7, chart 1.5. McKinsey Global Institute (1998) argue that only 5% of the lower labour productivity can be explained by lower capital investment.

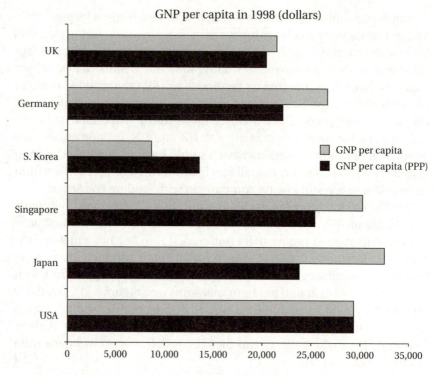

GNP per capita in 1998 (dollars)

Fig. 2.4. GNP per capita and world ranking by country
Source: IBRD/WB 2000.

Which of these should be classified as high skills society in terms of national competitiveness depends on which competitiveness criteria are used and how one estimates the contribution of skills towards these.

The High Skills Economy and its Variants

The classic political economy model of the 'high skills, high value added' economy, familiar from the work of Albert (1993), Finegold and Soskice (1988), Hutton (1995), Streeck (1992, 1997), and others, addresses both social and economic consequences of high skills. A high skills economy is defined as an economy with a wide distribution of work-force skills where these are fully utilized to achieve high productivity across a wide range of sectors, at the same time producing high wage rates and relative income equality. A high level of workforce cooperation supported by civic trust and social capital is seen as an important part of the model (Streeck 1997).

The most frequently studied example of this kind of model is west Germany, whose high wage/high skills economy is based on successful competition in quality global markets. High labour productivity is achieved on all measures, despite short working hours (and now relatively low employment rates), through the wide distribution and high utilization of worker skills and it is this which has enabled the relative income equality which has generated much of the admiration for the model (Streeck 1997). However, the so-called 'Rhine model' has not been the only example of this phenomenon. Until 1990 at least, Japan also matched the main criteria albeit with some crucial differences.

Like Germany, Japan has a wide distribution of skills throughout its workforce and relative equality in income distribution (see Table 2.1 and Castells 1998). High labour productivity in the manufacturing sector has produced the competitively priced quality products which have dominated the world markets and which drove Japan's exceptional rates of growth until the last decade. However, the Japanese high skills economy differs in crucial ways from that of Germany. In the first place, its high productivity is largely confined to the manufacturing sector. Its service sector, with the possible exception for awhile of banking and finance, had rather low levels of productivity compared with leading Western economies. Secondly, the smaller enterprises in Japan have often been much less productive than the larger firms, which is not generally the case in Germany. Thirdly, the skills mix used to achieve high productivity in Japan is rather different from that in Germany.

Productivity in Japanese manufacturing relies on high levels of R & D and capital investment as in Germany but also on the unique forms of labour organization achieved through so-called Japanese management systems. These require long working hours and high levels of workforce

Table 2.1. Wage spread across a range of countries, 1980s and 1990s

	Ninth decile of income over fifth decile		First decile over fifth decile	
	Early 1980s	Early 1990s	Early 1980s	Early 1990s
Germany	1.63	1.64	0.61	0.65
UK	1.72	1.99	0.68	0.59
Japan	1.63	1.73	0.63	0.61
USA	2.16	2.22	0.45	0.4

Source: Streeck 1997: 239.

cooperation and teamworking. The workforce skills required for this thus involve not only specialist technical expertise and the high levels of general education which allow flexible working practices but also the sets of values and attitudes which are compatible with long working hours and low levels of individual autonomy (Dore 2000; Dore and Sako 1989; Perkin 1996). Any account of the contributions of high skills to productivity in Japan must therefore take account of the strong emphasis placed on the forming of values and attitudes in work social-ization processes. Whereas Germany has placed a high premium on the wide diffusion of technical, professional, and creative skills, requiring an inclusive system of apprentice-style occupational training, Japan (and Singapore) have tended to place more stress on attitude and value formation, achieved through a wide diffusion of general education, followed by on-the-job, company-specific training.

The United Kingdom, it is often argued, presents another picture entirely from both the United States and German/Japanese models. United Kingdom national economic competitiveness rests heavily on the profitability of its financial sector and the efficiency of its capital markets. Labour productivity in manufacturing is not contributing as much as it should to competitiveness, and this relates both to low capital investment and low skills (see Figures 2.2 and 2.3). One conclu-sion from this which has frequently been drawn is that the United Kingdom is not really a 'high skills economy', in that high skills are not the main foundation of its competitiveness. Indeed, other aspects of competitiveness, like high capital productivity and flexible labour markets, may impede high skills formation (Albert 1993). Because of flexible labour markets, economic underperformance does not neces-sarily translate into lower employment. Rather, as the McKinsey Global Institute argues, 'employers simply tolerate lower productivity, rewarding it with lower wages' (1998: 6). The apparent neglect of skills formation in the United Kingdom is thus partly related to the finance-driven, capital-productivity-maximizing nature of the competition strategy amongst firms and in the national economy generally. Profit is often made through mergers and acquisitions, and company competi-tiveness often rests on flexible employment practices and cost reduction, rather than value added through skills as in Germany. This is part of what has often been referred to as the 'low skills equilibrium' (Finegold and Soskice 1988).

This traditional portrait of national underperformance may now need some redrafting, however, since it focuses unduly on the problems of the manufacturing sector and pays too little attention to the service sector which includes many highly successful industries competing primarily on skills. Taking the full picture, the United Kingdom might be considered an uneven or 'patchy' high skills economy in the same way as Japan, excepting that it retains a very high level of wage and educational inequality. In terms of its narrow distribution of skills and high income differentials, the United Kingdom still remains closer to the United States than to our model of a high skills society.

In each of these cases the place and nature of skills in the national economy and in competitiveness strategies has varied widely. We may broadly hypothesize four types of high skills strategies character-ized primarily by a predominance of (a) high skilled elites and skills polarization (United States and United Kingdom); (b) high skilled elites, wide skills distribution, and relative income equality (Germany); (c) wide skills distribution, relative income equality, and labour intensity and cooperation (Japan); and (d) rapid but uneven skills formation but with high labour intensity and discipline (Singapore). The following sections analyse these models country by country.

GERMANY—THE HIGH SKILLS SOCIETY MODEL

Germany is often taken as the paradigm case of the high skills society, combining high levels of workforce skills with high wages and high labour productivity (see Figures 2.2 and 2.3 and Streeck 1997; Albert 1993). In contrast with economies characterized predominantly by high skills elites, Germany exhibits a relatively even dispersal of skills through-out labour market sectors. The latter, though highly segmented, are accorded relative equality of status and pay. The drive towards 'equality of productive capacity', supported by all the social partners, has been seen as an essential basis of social solidarity and competitiveness.[6]

Wide distribution of skills throughout the German workforce has been underpinned by a solid foundation of 'trust' in a civil society (Fukuyama 1996) and a training system embedded in social partnership institutions based on dense associational networks (Cooke and Morgan 1998) and complex neo-corporatist forms of interest group bargaining (Streeck 1992). A long history of societal respect for technical skills and knowledge and for professional autonomy, encoded in the uniquely German concept of the *Beruf* (profession/occupation), has been

---

[6] Wolfgang Streeck in an interview talked about the importance of 'equality of productive capacity' as the basis for social solidarity and low wage inequality.

comprehensively institutionalized in the Dual System of occupational training which prepares two-thirds of German youth for working life and serves to transform the majority of paid jobs into skilled occupations. Concerted sectoral bargaining between the social partners, which fixes wage and skills levels for different jobs, also drives up levels of skills and pay, forcing German employers to maximize the productivity returns on skills. This has resulted in one of the lowest levels of wage inequality in the advanced industrial world, again forcing companies to compete on quality rather than price in low wage sectors and encouraging the wide dispersion and utilization of skills (Streeck 1997) (see Table 2.1).

The German economy is driven primarily by the manufacturing sector, which is highly diversified and specialized and which combines high levels of capital concentration in large firms with a dynamic small firms sector. Germany has maintained a relatively large manufacturing sector employing 24.2 per cent of the workforce in 1997, compared with 22.6 per cent in Singapore, 22 per cent in Japan, 21.3 per cent in Korea, and only 18 per cent in the United Kingdom (see Figure 2.1). The sector is characterized by an exceptional diversity of deep industrial clusters (Porter 1990) related by a common dominance of chemicals and machinery. Despite high wages and social costs, firms have managed to compete in high value international markets with an incomparable range of quality products (Porter 1990), most notably through the large firms in autos and chemical production, and a range of large and smaller firms in machine tools. Despite the strains of unification, Germany continues to be seen as the premier exemplar of what has become known as 'diversified, quality production' (Streeck 1997).

The indices of the historic success of the German high skills society are manifest. Between 1953 and 1973 it grew by an average of 5.5 per cent per annum, lower than Japan at 8 per cent but above France and the United Kingdom at 5.3 per cent and 3 per cent, respectively. By 1991 united Germany, despite the high cost of unification, had by far the strongest economy in the EU and the third largest GDP in the world, after the United States and Japan. Before unification, Germany was the major exporting economy in the world. By 1993 its visible exports had slipped from 12 per cent of total world exports (in 1988) to 10.1 per cent, compared with 12.3 per cent for the United States, 9.6 per cent for Japan, and 4.8 per cent for the United Kingdom (Streeck 1997: 238). However, in relation to its GDP Germany maintained a better exporting performance than any of the other major economies. Despite substantially lower productivity in the new *Länder*—barely one-third of western levels in 1991—Germany retains high levels of productivity and relatively high per capita national income (GNP per head in PPP in 1998 was $22,026 compared with $29,240 in the United States, $25,295 in Singapore, $23,592 in Japan, $20,314 in the United Kingdom, and $13,286 in Korea, see Figure 2.4). The growth rate declined to 2.8 per cent by 1998 (Economic Intelligence Unit, 1998) but was still respectable by European standards.

The Institutional Basis of the German High Skills Society

Of all the European economies, Germany was most successful in converting the costs of war into the gains of peace in the post-war democratic world. In the early nineteenth century, Prussia represented, arguably, the first example of state developmental industrial modernization (Moore 1967; Green 1990) and became the leading force in the new Germany. After unification under Bismarck in 1871, Germany developed its own brand of economic nationalism after the principles of its formerly exiled political economist, Friedrich List, adopting a permissive attitude towards cartels, and building up its large national firms. By 1913 Siemensstadt was the most extensive industrial complex in the world and the merger of chemicals companies in 1925 produced the giant IG Farbenindustrie, the world's largest chemical industry (Fukuyama 1996).

The post-war settlement ensured a transformation of the German economy along acceptably open market lines. The large cartels were broken up and replaced by powerful trade associations (*Verbände*) (Fukuyama 1996) and the power of the central state under the new Federal Constitution was strictly curbed. However, this did not signal the adoption of a laissez-faire market model. Some features of the national economy were to carry through into the post-war world—most notably the solidaristic national training and social insurance systems, inaugurated by Bismarck, and the preference for national finance through domestic banks rather than foreign capitalization. Market and non-market principles were combined.

The post-war 'Ordo-Liberal' school, associated with intellectuals at the University of Frieburg, argued that the state had to intervene to set strict rules for the regulation of the market and for the protection of the interests of the groups participating in it. Liberal capitalism had to be combined with a strong welfare state, regulated labour-management

relations, and protection for traditional status groups such as the arti-
sanal farmers, smaller employers (*Mittelstand*), and the civil servants
(*Beamten*) (Streeck 1997). What emerged was the distinctive form of
social market (*Socialmarketwirtschaft*) which underpinned the post-war
economic miracle first associated with the finance ministry of Ludwig
Erhard.[7] A number of institutional features have characterized the social
market form of the German high skills society.

The polity developed in post-war Germany is best described as a
complex form of neo-corporatism, which eschews both the *étatism*
traditional in continental powers like France and the neo-liberal model
of the Anglo-Saxon countries. Markets are highly regulated within a
centrally determined framework, but powers are distributed widely
between different tiers of government, independent agencies, and the
social partner organizations, according to their legally constituted roles.
Interest group intermediation is highly concerted and formalized, with
encompassing and legally empowered representative bodies negotiating binding settlements which regulate economic activity. The Federal
Government in Germany, according to the Constitution, delegates
many of its powers to *Land* governments and the social partners, and
performs an enabling rather than interventionist role in the economy
(Streeck 1997). Its strategic role in economic policy-making is
constrained both by the federal system and by the typically centrist
drift of coalition politics, so that, for instance, it has less capacity for
developing a selective industrial policy than the individual *Land* governments, which, in some cases, do this. In the absence of this, what the
central state can and does do is to empower and define the roles of the
social partner organizations, to regulate standards, and to ensure a wide
range of infrastructural supports for the economy. Federal Government
constitutes and regulates the apprentice training system (through the
Bundes Institut für Berufsbildung (BIBB)), and invests heavily in
research and development, not least through intermediate technology
transfer organizations like the Max Planck, Fraunhofer and An
Institutes, and the Steinbeis Foundation (Cooke and Morgan 1998).

The social partner organizations play the major roles in economic
policy determination and concertation in many areas, at national,
sectoral, regional, and firm levels. Peak organizations of employers and
employees are legally empowered within specific spheres, have encompassing representation and the ability to bind their members, and this

---

[7] The term was actually coined by Alfred Müller-Armack, Erhard's chief civil servant (Perkin
1996).

allows them to negotiate and implement policy within their designated fields of competence. At the sectoral level, employer and employee organizations set product standards and negotiate wage and skills agreements which have an effect throughout their sectors. At the region/local level, there are Chambers of Commerce (*Kammern*) with compulsory membership and covering most sectors, and these play an important economic role, not least in overseeing the Dual System of apprentice training. At the company level, co-determination laws (*Mitbestimmung*) give employee representatives rights alongside managers, shareholders, and other stakeholders. This *Mitbestimmung* system goes back to the 1922 Works Council Law which gave elected workers in large companies a role in overseeing collective agreements and in nominating, along with shareholders, the members of the supervisory board. The latter became part of a two-tier system of control over the corporation, with supervisory boards (*Aufsichtsrat*), on which workers are represented alongside management, shareholders, and major creditors, to oversee the managerial executive (*Vorstand*). Now, according to the 1972 Law, all firms employing over five people must have works councils which must approve all hirings, dismissals, transfers, work allocations, and alterations in the scale and speed of production. Legislation in 1976 gave workers equal representation on supervisory boards of all companies with over 2,000 workers, with the shareholder's chairperson exercising the casting vote (Perkin 1996).

These social partnership arrangements have had significant positive effects on German economic performance, despite the sometimes unwieldy processes they involve. They have helped to maintain reasonably peaceful industrial relations, giving workers and their organizations a stake in decision-making and a broad view of their collective interests. They have helped to promote company stability and long-term loyalty amongst employees which has been beneficial for skills development. They have also helped to encourage a degree of cooperation between firms in relation to product standards and research and development. Above all they have allowed German companies to overcome some of the collective goods problems which have beset firms in countries like the United Kingdom. Sectoral agreements on wages and skills, for instance, can set challenging standards for workforce qualification and prevent employers from poaching employees trained by other firms with enhanced pay offers. Generally, they have had the effect of deterring company strategies of price competition through low pay and low skills labour, and, alternatively, of encouraging high levels of training. Co-determination and labour market regulation also encourage skills enhancing behaviour on the part of the employees. Despite the system of occupational labour markets, job tenure in Germany is typically longer than in most advanced countries with a median period of 7.5 years compared with 8.2 in Japan and 3 in the United States (Streeck 1996: 144), which allows time for employee skills development. Relative employment security and co-determined decision-making also encourage worker flexibility and multi-skilling. Many German firms are notable for their relatively flat hierarchies, which encourage the distribution of responsibility and skills.

Company law in Germany encourages long-term investment and also reinforces a climate conducive to high skills development. Companies are legally bound to represent the interests of various stakeholders over and above the shareholders. Banks often hold the major part in the equity of firms, either on their own behalf or on the behalf of their investors, and tend to take a long-term perspective on company development.[8] Given the predominance of bank finance, the exercise of voting rights by banks on behalf of the holders of shares that they manage, and the frequent company practice of issuing non-voting shares, private shareholder influence over company policy is limited, which reduces the pressures for short-term profit. Mergers and takeovers are also discouraged by company law and practices in Germany. About one-third of German companies issue registered shares that may not be sold or transferred without the express authorization of the company (Albert 1993: 89). By law, a takeover requires a 75 per cent shareholder majority to go through. As a result takeovers have been rare in Germany, particularly when resisted by management and the major owners.[9] 'Patient' capital investment and the relative absence of takeover threats have both helped to promote a long-termism in companies that favour investment in R & D and training.

Most important, perhaps, of all the institutional foundations of Germany's high skills society has been the much celebrated Dual System of apprentice training. Based on an elaborate system of social partnership and distributed control, this is one of the most impressive historical products of German neo-corporatism (Streeck 1987) and has played the major part in developing the high skills base of the German economy. Typically, the Dual System apprenticeship involves a three

---

[8] Banks control about 50% of the shares in large companies. About 80% of corporate capital is long-term capital and less than 19% stock market equity, compared with 51% in Britain (Perkin 1996: 116).

[9] Although the final, hard-fought, capitulation of Mannesmann to the Vodaphone takeover suggests the changing trend.

and a half year contract,[10] according to the ordinances and regulations determined centrally by the BIBB. Apprentices will normally undergo three days a week in the company, receiving a structured programme of training under the supervision of a technically and pedagogically qualified *Meister*, and two days in the *Berufsschule* studying general education and the theoretical foundations of their profession or occupation. Some two-thirds of young people go through this programme and the vast majority (around 90 per cent) subsequently qualify as skilled workers (*Facharbeiter*), with a solid grounding in occupational theory and skills as well as general education.

The system has become comprehensive in scope, to a degree unmatched in other countries, through the delicate balancing and concerting of the interests and responsibilities of the different parties concerned. Employers generally support the Dual System because it provides a pool of skilled, occupationally socialized, and relatively flexible labour at acceptable costs. Legal incentives play a part, since *Land* laws frequently require firms employing young people in classified occupations to provide training according to the regulations. However, the major incentives for firms are internal. They want the skills which the system delivers and the costs of training have been generally acceptable, since they are offset by savings accruing through trainee productivity, enhanced flexibility in labour deployment, and the reduction of costs for future employee selection, induction, and training (Wagner 1999). Sectoral agreements reduce the risks of poaching[11] and reinforce company predispositions to regard training investment as both in their self-interest and as a collective good worthy of support. Young people are motivated to train because the apprentice qualification gives access to a range of skilled jobs from which they would otherwise be excluded: federal law requires skilled qualifications for the practice of a wide range of occupations and sectoral agreements also tend to credentialize access to jobs. Legal compulsion also plays a part in that young school leavers in many *Länder* are obliged to undertake continuing part-time education anyway. However, the incentives are, again, primarily non-coercive. Apprenticeships involve relatively low wages for several years, but the long-term benefits of the generally good quality training apprentices receive make this a worthwhile sacrifice.

The Dual System has been successful not only because of its broad coverage of most sectors of employment, but also because of

---

[10] Only 5% of apprenticeships are less than three years.

[11] Two-thirds of apprentices are retained by their employers after completion and 36% after five years (Reuling interview).

its generally high quality. This is ensured by the tight specification of national standards through the tripartite BIBB and through the close monitoring of the process by Chambers of Commerce at the local level and by works councils at the firm level. Even the assessment system rests on joint social partner action, with training committees and teams of apprenticeship jurors at the *Kammern* representing different interests. Ubiquity and quality in the Dual System result in over 65 per cent of young people qualifying as skilled workers, with sound vocational skills and a solid foundation of general education. Having undergone a broad occupational training, they have the technical skills and knowledge and the general professional socialization which will equip them to work in their chosen *Beruf* or in an allied occupation. They also have an educational foundation which prepares them for further training. Indeed some 20 per cent of apprentices go on later to qualify as *Meisters* (Wagner 1999). The Dual System as a whole not only thus serves the immediate skills needs of employers; it also acts to drive up levels of skills by converting most jobs into skilled occupations and creating a surplus of skills available for companies upgrading their work processes.

The German Skills Profile

The high skills nature of the German economy can be seen in terms of the skills profile of the workforce and other measures of knowledge intensity. Germany's output of higher education graduates relative to population is lower than in the United Kingdom and way below East Asian levels, but the quality is high and has been particularly strong in areas of basic scientists and engineers, although in recent years there has been a drift away from these subjects as in other countries.[12] In 1992, 19 per cent of all degrees awarded in Germany were in Engineering, a lower proportion than in Japan (22 per cent) but higher than in the United States (7 per cent) and the United Kingdom (13 per cent). Degrees in all scientific subjects represented 33 per cent of all degrees, compared with 29 per cent in the United Kingdom and 16 per cent in the United States (see Table 2.2).

Higher education is divided between university courses which graduate students at the *Magister* level (equivalent to a United Kingdom

---

[12] Interviewees at Siemens noted that the number of engineering graduates is in decline, so that by the year 2002 Siemens would need to recruit 3,000 out of a total of 6,000 engineering graduates.

Table 2.2. Science degrees as a proportion of all degrees by country

	Biological science	Physical science	Math-ematics & computing	Engin-eering	All scientific subjects	Science graduates per 100,000 persons aged 25–34[a]
UK	4	6	6	13	29	989
Germany	3	6	4	19	33	650
Japan	—	4	—	22	25	974
USA	3	2	4	7	16	688
TOTAL OECD	3	3	4	13	23	666

[a] Numbers of graduates of any age relative to the young workforce (25–34).

Source: Great Britain 1996.

master's degree) and vocational courses, taken in the *Fachhochschule* and elsewhere. Qualifications at a level equivalent to the United Kingdom level 4 and above would include the *Meister* and *Techniker* qualifications, as well as first and higher university degrees. Qualifications at these levels were held by 19.1 per cent of the total population aged 16–64 in 1997. Although not high by comparison with countries like Japan, the United Kingdom, and the United States, the stocks of adults with higher qualifications are comparable with many other leading countries in Europe. Given that a high proportion of those graduating from university have obtained a master's or higher level awards, German stocks of higher qualified people look impressive. The high concentration of these higher degree holders in various parts of the economy has been noted. Boards of Directors in Germany frequently include persons with Ph.D.s in engineering or other technical areas (Hutton 1995). Recent comparative research on R & D in the electronics industry (Mason and Wagner 1998*a*) indicates that postgraduate scientists and engineers are more prevalent in R & D departments than they are in the United Kingdom.

At the intermediate level of skills, the qualification profile of the working age population in Germany is even more impressive and indeed it is the concentration of skills at this level which most marks Germany out from other advanced countries. Earlier studies (summarized in Green and Steedman 1997) have benchmarked qualifications resulting from three or more years of apprenticeship in Germany as equivalent in standard to the United Kingdom level 3

Table 2.3. Total population by highest qualification attained, by country 1997/8 (per cent)

	Level 3	Level 4 Sub-degree	Degree	Level 5 Higher degree	Level 4 and above	Level 3 and above
UK (1998) (aged 16–64)	18.0	9.0	10.0	4.0	23.0	41.0
Germany(1997) (aged 16–64)	50.6	7.8	—	11.3	19.1	69.7
Singapore (1998) (aged 15 and over)	9.2	7.2	10.2	—	17.4	26.6
S. Korea (1998) (aged 15 and over)	40.9	4.7	13.2	—	17.9	58.8
Japan (1997) (aged 15 and over)	41.8	11.1	13.1	—	24.2	66.0

UK: Working age is defined as males aged 16–64 and females aged 16–59. Level 3 refers to vocational qualifications including those with RSA Advanced Diplomas, BTEC Nationals, ONC/ONDs, City and Guilds Advanced Craft or trade apprenticeships and other professional or vocational qualifications at level 3. Academic qualifications include those with Advanced GNVQs, more than one GCE A level or SCE Highers/Scottish Certificates of Sixth Year Studies (CSYS) at level 3. A certain small degree of upward bias in the figures should be noted. The figures, for example, include trade apprenticeship, which some critics (i.e. Hilary Steedman) consider should not be included. The figures for level 3 also include all those with one or more SCE Higher. Level 4 includes first degree, other degree and sub-degree higher education qual-ifications such as teaching and nursing certificates, HNC/HNDs, other HE diplomas and other qualifications at level 4. Level 5 refers to higher degrees and other qualifications at level 5.

Germany: Working age is defined as males aged 16–64 and females aged 16–59. Level 3 includes *Abitur*, *Fachhochschulreife*, or apprenticeship. Figures for apprenticeship exclude those passing the apprenticeship who already have an *Abitur* or *Fachhochschulreife*. It also excludes those passing whose previous qualification was below the *Hauptschulabschluss*; and apprentices on programmes lasting less than three years (10% of the total). Level 4 includes those with *Meister* and *Techniker, Fachschulabschuluss* (sub-degree), or *Fachhochschulabschluss* or *Universitat* (master's degree).

Singapore: Level 3 refers to post-secondary qualifications. It includes those who have obtained the GCE A level or equivalent as well as those who obtained NTC Grade 2, the Industrial Technician Certificate, Certificate in Business Studies, Teachers Training Certificate, Nursing Certificate, Certificate in Office Skills, Advance Builder Certificate or its equivalent. Level 4 refers to those who have obtained a diploma from polytechnics or institutes of higher education, or those with degree qualification.

Korea: Level 3 refers to those with high school graduate qualifications. Level 4 refers to those with a sub-degree from junior college, or those with a degree from college or university.

Japan: Level 3 refers to those with upper high school graduate qualifications. Level 4 refers to those who obtained a diploma from junior college or College of Technology, or those who obtained a university degree or higher degrees. Data do not include 8.86% of the population (9,449,000) who were attending school and thus had not yet reached their highest educational attainment. The data do not include also 1.01% of the population (1,081,000) whose qualifica-tion level is unknown.

Sources: same as in Table 2.8, below.

National Vocational Qualifications (NVQ). Other level 3 equivalent qualifications[13] in Germany include the *Abitur* and its vocational equivalent, the *Fachhochschulreife*, which give access, respectively, to university and the *Fachhochschule*. Over half the working age population in Germany in 1997 (estimated at 50.6 per cent) had a level 3 qualification as their highest qualification, compared with 41.8 per cent in Japan, 40.9 per cent in Korea, 9.2 per cent in Singapore, and 18 per cent in the United Kingdom. This proportion has remained relatively stable over the past ten years (see Green and Steedman 1997), and appears to have been unaffected by the inclusion of the east German workforce into the count since unification. Based on the Microcensus, calculations for west Germany for 1995 (Green and Steedman 1997) and for all Germany for 1997 yield similar results.

Aggregating the figures for those whose highest qualification is at level 3 with those for people qualified at higher levels, we can see the relative proportion of the working age population in different countries who have qualifications demonstrating their possession of intermediate or higher level skills. On this measure Germany clearly stands above the other countries in this study in the high skills distribution of its workforce. By the same token it has a relatively small stock of working age people who have less than a skilled worker qualification (10 per cent or so). Other indicators further demonstrate the exceptionally skilled nature of the German economy.

Gross expenditure on R & D (GERD) in Germany is below Japanese and US levels but above the UK and the OECD average (see Table 2.4). Similarly the proportion of research scientists and engineers per 10,000 of the labour force (see Table 2.5) is also comparatively high, below Japan and the United States again but well above the UK and the OECD average. Germany is a favourite location for foreign multinationals siting R & D labs (Pearce 1997). As one would expect with such high investment in R & D and with a high tally of researchers and scientists, Germany achieves one of the highest rates of patenting in the world (after the United States) (see Table 2.6), although there has been a decline in patenting in electronics in recent years (Mason and Wagner 1998*a*).

[13] Using here as the benchmark the definition of the National Advisory Council for Education and Training Targets (NACETT) in the UK, which includes level 3 NVQ, 2 or more A levels, or an advanced General National Vocational Qualification (GNVQ) now called a vocational A level.

Table 2.4. Gross domestic expenditure on R & D (GERD) as percentage of GDP, by country, 1997

	GERD/GDP
UK	1.9
Germany	2.3
S. Korea	2.9
Singapore	1.5
Japan	2.9
USA	2.7
OECD TOTAL	2.2

Source: OECD 1999; National Science and Technology Board
<www.psb.gov.sg/statistics_fag/statistics/md.html>

Table 2.5. Researchers per 10,000 labour force by country, 1995

UK	51
Germany	59
S. Korea	48
Singapore[a]	56
Japan	83
USA[b]	74
OECD TOTAL	55

[a] 1996 instead of 1995; refers to both research scientists and engineers.
[b] 1993 instead of 1995.

Source: OECD 1999 National Science and Technology Board, *Singapore (2000)*.

Table 2.6. Annual patents by country

	1990	1994	Total (1990–4)
UK	2,788	2,234	12,539
Germany	7,610	6,731	36,223
S. Korea	225	943	2,889
Singapore	12	51	148
Japan	19,524	22,384	107,152
USA	47,393	56,066	260,130

Source: Toh Mun Heng and Tan Kong Yam 1998: 65–6.

Summary of Skills Profile

The skills profile of the German workforce manifests a pattern of high skills and wide skills distribution underpinned by a strong base of social capital, i.e. the capacity for trust and cooperation. There is an abundance of skilled elites, particularly in the dominant manufacturing areas of chemicals and engineering, which form the core of the export economy where highly qualified scientists and engineers abound. Finance, marketing, and advertising are less developed in the German economy than in countries like the United Kingdom, and we would expect to find a lower concentration of professional elites in these areas. Germany has also been behind the leaders in areas such as software, multimedia, and biotechnology and there is evidence that it has so far failed to fully nurture its elites in these areas. David Soskice, for instance, argues that the highly structured career routes of the scientific professions in Germany encourage a research traditionalism that militates against researchers moving into high-risk areas like biotechnology.[14] However, this may be beginning to change. Certainly these are the areas which have been targeted for new apprenticeships, and the BIBB has recently drawn up new apprentice profiles in these areas.

At the intermediate level skills are widely distributed in Germany. This not only means an abundant pool of technical skills but also a wide distribution of general learning abilities, professional habits and disciplines, and a social valuing of occupational skills in their own right. According to Streeck, in Germany the concept of 'occupation', or *Beruf,* signifies 'a body of systematically related theoretical knowledge [*Wissen*] and a set of practical skills [*Können*], as well as the social identity of the person who has acquired these. Achievement of such an identity is certified by a diploma upon passing an examination and is on this basis recognized without question by all employers' (1996: 145). Similar in meaning to the term 'profession' in Anglo-American culture, but used more widely to refer to all skilled occupations, the *Beruf* belongs to society rather than the employer, having been legally defined in the qualification profile (*Berufsbild*) agreed by the social partners. It implies a breadth of skill and knowledge which can be transferred between contexts—and through the portable qualification between different jobs—and, crucially, an expectation of competence in applying independent judgement.

[14] Comments from interview with David Soskice at Wissencraftzentrum.

The benefits to employers of the surplus of skills are readily apparent. Technically qualified elites are available in the key areas where they are most needed. The abundance of people qualified at craft and technician levels makes it rarely necessary for management and professional level employees to 'work down' to compensate for skills lacking in lower level positions, as has been reportedly the case in the United Kingdom (see Steedman and Wagner 1987). There is no shortage of well-qualified personnel for supervisory and management level positions, not least because direct entry recruits to these positions can be supplemented by the promotion of skilled workers who frequently take higher level (*Meister* and *Techniker*) qualifications (thus also creating higher levels of blue-collar mobility than seen, for instance, in the United Kingdom (see Marsden and Ryan 1995).[15] The traditionally high levels of management and supervisory staffing in German companies may be partly attributable to this and have positive effects in work organization (see Prais, Jarvis, and Wagner 1989, on hotels), although the pressures to introduce lean production methods may alter this picture.

Lastly, but not least in significance, the wide diffusion of broad occupational skills in manufacturing makes possible the flat hierarchies and distinctive forms of multi-skilled teamworking associated with the most advanced production systems in Germany. Professionalization of skilled work in Germany, argues Streeck (1996), leads not only to the wide distribution of responsibilities but also to forms of interaction between seniors and juniors based on mutual professional respect, where exchanges of specialized technical knowledge frame the discourse without reference to formal authority. Workers are given considerable discretion over their own work performance. Likewise cooperation in German-style teamwork (*Qualifizierte Gruppenarbeit*) takes the form of negotiated exchanges between experts with specialist skills, rather than as in the typical Japanese teams of skilled generalists where independent judgement is emphasized less than collectively embodied experience. The German system has been seen as particularly appropriate for the high precision specialized manufacture of the sort in which Germany excels.

Current Problems and Reforms in Skills Formation

The German economy has been under considerable strain throughout the 1990s, partly due to the general competitive pressures of

---

[15] However, mobility of this sort is in decline according to A. Brown (1997).

globalization, and partly because of the huge costs of unification which the government elected to spread throughout the new unified state. This has affected the skills formation system and, particularly, the Dual System, which is at the heart of it. However, the Dual System has shown itself to be remarkably resilient and adaptable so far and it is not generally believed to be in crisis now.[16] Whether it will survive in its current form in the longer term is another matter.

A perennial concern about the Dual System is that it is not producing the right number of places to meet demand. During the 1980s there was a surplus of places and concern that young people were not choosing to take them up. Since 1991 there has been a steady decline in the places available, although academic drift and the shrinking of the youth cohort ensured that there was no overall deficit of places until recently (first reported in November 1999). Companies are not generally exiting the system but many of the larger ones are taking fewer young people on.[17]

The reasons for the decline in the supply of places are various. Companies are complaining that it is becoming too expensive to train apprentices. This is partly due to the increases in apprentice wages agreed in the early 1990s. It is also due to reforms which have reduced the time on the job for apprentices, whilst simultaneously increasing the costs of instruction. Enhanced theoretical requirements in the training mean that *Berufsschule* attendance often absents apprentices from work for two full days per week, since by the time they have completed their extended school hours they often do not have time to return to work. Employers consequently lose their production time for two days. In addition to this, more demanding training objectives mean that employers have to invest more in the actual training process.[18] The new *Länder* also pose a particular problem in terms of apprentice places. There are relatively few small firms which can take on apprentices and the larger firms are still under enormous competitive pressures due to their still substantially lower levels of productivity. Consequently only some 30 per cent of east German youth get a proper apprenticeship with an employer.[19] More generally, there is a concern that hi-tech

---

[16] This is the view of experts such as David Soskice and Karen Wagner at the Wissencraftzentrum, as well as many of the senior HRD staff interviewed in the MNCs. However, opinions on the long-term prospects at the BIBB seem to be more mixed. Some take a fairly optimistic view, but others expressed the view that the Dual System might experience a significant decline in numbers, perhaps recruiting only around 35% of the cohort in coming decades.

[17] Interview with Jochen Reuling.

[18] Interview with Karen Wagner.

[19] In Brandenburg only 30% of youth have proper apprenticeships and only 28% of firms are recruiting apprentices.

companies are avoiding taking on apprentices and that larger companies are increasingly looking to recruit graduates. These trends, taken together with the continuing academic drift of young people towards higher education, could mean a long-term decline both in the supply and demand for places.

The Dual System is clearly adjusting to these trends, however. The deficit in apprentice places in east Germany is made up by additional federal funding. Vocational education is provided by the vocational schools (called OSZ in Brandenburg) and for those with no apprenticeship skills training is provided by state-funded private skills centres. This is generally considered to be second best to proper dual training and only a temporary expediency until the economy is strong enough to provide more company places. Measures are also being taken to introduce apprentice training into sectors where it has not been strongly implanted, in particular in certain service sectors and in small hi-tech firms. BIBB officers are in continual dialogue with firms about providing new places and new training occupations are being established.[20] Plans by the incoming SPD government to introduce a levy to fund increased apprentice places were dropped; however, other measures can no doubt be taken if demand continues to outstrip the supply of places. One view is that apprentice wages in the lower pay sectors will have to come down to achieve this.[21]

The issue of declining demand for apprentice places is also being addressed. In order to make the apprenticeship more attractive, and to meet employer demands for higher skills, a number of new 'dual qualification' initiatives have been introduced. *Berufsakadamien* in Berlin, Thuringen, and Baden-Württemberg provide dual training to higher levels (equivalent to level 4) whilst allowing enhanced progression prospects for their graduates. Trainees undergo three and a half years of apprentice training at the same time as educational studies leading to the *Fachhochschulreife* (i.e. at the level of the full-time courses at the *Fachoberschulen* which give access to the *Fachhochschule*).[22] A similar model has been developed in Brandenburg, after an experimental scheme developed at the Schwarze Pumpe Company. The latter has been notable for the high levels of cooperation between the teachers in the schools and the instructors in the companies and has to date shown good results in terms of student progression (Birke et al. 1998).[23]

---

[20] There have been eleven new training occupations established over the past two years according to Richard Koch.

[21] Interview with David Soskice.

[22] Interviews with Jochen Reuling and Karen Wagner.

[23] Interview with Bodo Richard.

This enhanced apprenticeship model may or may not be generalizable to other areas in Germany.[24] However, there is already in practice a demand-led trend towards this kind of dual qualification. More students are attaining an *Abitur* before entering Dual System training (currently over 20 per cent of *Abiturien* go into the Dual System) and some students train in the Dual System and then go on to university. Attaining good academic and vocational qualifications is seen as a way of hedging bets in an increasingly uncertain job market. If these trends continue, as seems likely, it suggests that the apprenticeship will continue to be a popular option but used in a different way. Young people may well enter it later, or, if they enter early, seek to use it to progress on to higher levels of training.[25] In either case, it suggests a continuing central role for the apprenticeship, providing it can be flexible enough to evolve.

Another challenge for the Dual System arises out of the changing nature of skills demanded by the economy. This not only refers to the need for new training occupations for jobs in areas like multimedia and biotechnology; it also reflects the need for training in generic skills. More jobs are requiring a broad range of skills which cross traditional boundaries. More fluid job roles and rapidly changing job skills profiles also require breadth in skills training and the ability to adapt skills to new contexts and learn completely new skills (Green, Wolf, and Leney 1999). This arguably creates a major challenge for the Dual System which has historically been based on a very strong sense of occupational identity.[26]

Civic and professional socialization has always been an important part of German vocational education, not least for its early philosopher, Kirchensteiner, who saw vocational education as a process of spiritual formation for German youth. German skills formation has traditionally combined this inculcation of professional knowledge and culture with a strong emphasis on precise technical skills and occupational competences. This process is still apparent, despite the increasing fluidity of professional identities in the modern German economy. However, changes in work organization and occupational roles have engendered here, as elsewhere, an increasing emphasis on more generic training in key skills. Employers place increasing stress on IT, teamworking, communicating, and leadership skills. The ability to handle uncertainty and

---

[24] Hamburg, for instance, also experimented with *Berufsakadamien*, but with rather less success. Interview at the Ministry for Education, Youth, and Training.

[25] This is the view of David Soskice.

[26] Interview with Jochen Reuling.

change, to take initiatives, and to learn independently is thought important for all employees. Process thinking, using the media, and people development are amongst the skills frequently considered important for managers.[27] These key skills are generally believed to be increasingly important (though not to be emphasized at the expense of specialist and technical skills, as has arguably occurred in the United Kingdom).

The Dual System has adapted to this pressure in a number of ways. In the first place, new systems have been put in place to speed up the process of developing new training profiles. This has traditionally been quite slow and cumbersome due to the need to reach social partner agreement before issuing ordinances on new training occupations. However, the process has now been improved so that a new occupation may reach the stage of ordinances being issued in only two years.[28] In the second place, a number of new training occupations have been developed in areas such as multimedia, biotechnology, mechatronics. In all, eleven new *Berufsbilden* have been developed over the past two years.[29] Thirdly, existing occupational training profiles have been revised to allow for a broader training in a smaller number occupations. The number of training occupations has fallen from around 900 after 1945 to 627 in 1970 and 370 now (and moreover, 80 per cent of apprentices have contracts in just 30 of these) (Green, Wolf, and Leney 1999). In mechanical engineering the twenty different training occupations have been reduced to four main apprenticeships which share two years of common basic training.[30]

Another important area of change has been in the upgrading of the content of many apprenticeships. Requirements in general education have been raised, involving, for instance, more demanding standards in terms of foreign language competence. More emphasis has been placed on certain key skills, and on general knowledge about issues of current significance, such as the environment. There have also been increases in the demands made on apprentices with regard to specialist technical skills (Wagner 1999).

The 1997 ordinances for the new *Berufsbild* (occupational training profile) for mechatronic fitters well illustrates the balance of specialist technical and generic key skills required in modern apprentice training. According to the general description of their job, mechatronic fitters are 'qualified to work autonomously on the basis of technical documents

---

[27] Interview at BMW.
[28] Interview with Jochen Reuling.
[29] Interview with Jochen Reuling.
[30] Interview at BMW.

and instructions and carry out their work in compliance with the relevant provisions and safety regulations . . . to work in teams . . . and to coordinate activities with upstream and downstream operations'. The technical aspects of the training include the various aspects of programming, operation, maintenance, testing, and quality control which come within the field of multi-skilled fitters working on mechatronic systems. However, the training framework plan, which applies to the training company and in the *Berufsschule*, includes other components such as: 'vocational training, labour and negotiating law'; 'development of company taking on trainees'; 'health and safety protection at work'; 'environmental protection'; 'inter-company and technical communication'; and 'planning and management of work routine'. Planning and management skills (Learning Field 6), which typically receive heavy emphasis in German training (Wagner 1999), include: 'dividing up work stages according to functional, technical and economic criteria'; 'setting work routine according to organizational and informational criteria'; 'planning team work and distributing tasks'; 'planning and organizing the workplace'; 'ordering, supplying and preparing material, tools and accessories'; and 'preparing machines for work routines'. Inter-company and technical communication (Learning Field 5) includes: 'collecting and assessing information'; 'having talks with superiors, colleagues and co-workers . . . using appropriate forms and German and English technical terms'; 'applying ways of settling a conflict'; 'handling computers'; 'data protection and security'; and 'writing protocols and reports'.

The *Berufsschule* has a broad mission in Dual System training including general education and occupational theory, and its terms of reference are drawn up by both the *Länder* ministries and the BIBB. According to the general 1991 framework agreement for vocational schools, the *Berufsschulen* have amongst their objectives:

- 'to impart professional competence, specialized competence in conjunction with human and social capabilities';
- 'to develop occupational flexibility in order to cope with the changing demands of the working world and of society, as well as having regard to the growing together of Europe';
- 'to encourage preparedness for continuing and further professional training';
- 'to provide the ability and willingness to act responsibly in terms of the individual shaping of one's own life and in the public sphere'.[31]

---

[31] Translation by Jana Haeberlein with assistance from Caroline Steenman-Clark.

Effects of Economic Adjustment on German Skills Formation

As suggested above, the German Dual System seems capable of adapting to the specific demands arising out of changes in demands for skills and qualifications from employers and young people. However, the bigger test for the system, and for skills formation in general, is how it will respond to the broader changes in the German economy which are occurring as a response to unification, European integration, and globalization in general. The major issue is how far the German national economy can survive in its current form and whether it can maintain its distinctive characteristics as a social market economy based on social partnership.

The German economy is currently under intense pressure. Following unification, a major recession ensued in 1991, out of which recovery was only partial from the mid-decade. By 1998 forecasts were more optimistic with a growth rate back to respectable levels at 2.8 per cent and a new government in prospect. However, since the election of Gerhard Schröder's government coalition of Social Democrats and Greens in September 1998, the picture has deteriorated. Unemployment in March 2001 was 9.3 per cent and GDP growth in 2000 was only 1.9 per cent, well below the 3 per cent average for the Euro area (The Economist, 2001: 136).

There have been three underlying problems. First, unification has placed severe burdens on public finances and made it necessary to retain high levels of taxation. Government has maintained its policy of bringing east German benefits and wages rapidly into line with the west. Since productivity in the east was still barely over one-third of west German levels at the time of unification (Albert 1993), with wages swiftly reaching 80 per cent of western levels, this has meant enormous transfers from the west to the east. The original DM 115 billion German Unity Fund, set up to meet the costs of unification, was the equivalent of nearly half of all household savings, and more has been spent since then (Albert 1993). Secondly, labour costs in Germany are the highest in Europe. Hourly labour costs in 1999 averaged £16.40 in western Germany, 55 per cent of which are wages and the rest additional employment costs, compared with just £9.80 in Britain (Conradi and Smith 1999). Thirdly, increased global competition in consumer electronics (where Germany no longer really competes with Japan) and, more importantly, in high value markets in autos and machine tools has hit German manufacturing hard. Daimler-Benz (now Daimler-Chrysler) is still coming to terms with the shock of the Japanese launch of the Lexus, a landmark in price-competitive quality car manufacture.

Germany's traditional high value export markets are becoming increasingly price sensitive, and German firms are finding it hard to compete. For unified Germany to maintain its traditional high value economy, new markets have to be found to absorb the additional export potential of east German production, and there are some doubts as to whether quality world markets could sustain a unified German economy primarily producing high price goods (Streeck 1997). Certainly this requires German manufacturing to remain at the leading edge of technology in a broad range of sectors, and this it may not be able to do. It has not made notable advances in the hi-tech fields of software, biotechnology, and multimedia to date, and competed rather poorly in electronic consumer goods, where it used to be strong.[32] Innovation in Germany may not be up to keeping the economy ahead in a sufficiently wide range of sectors to maintain the high wage, high price production regime.

German enterprises are already responding in quite radical ways to the new global competitive pressures. Many companies are increasingly siting their operations abroad, with companies like Siemens, Volkswagen, and Daimler-Benz (even before the merger with Chrysler) having the majority of their workforce abroad.[33] A 1999 survey showed that 2,500 German firms planned to create 230,000 jobs outside Germany by the end of the year (Conradi and Smith 1999). Mergers with foreign companies are on the increase and German firms are generally seeking more foreign capitalization (Albert 1993). German foreign direct investment abroad has traditionally been relatively low but is now growing rapidly (Economic Intelligence Unit 1998).[34] Increasingly, large companies are turning to 'lean production' techniques to reduce costs (Streeck 1996), at the same time as bargaining for reduced wage costs. Some companies (particularly in the east) are even pulling out of the sectoral agreements with unions which have been the basis of labour market coordination in Germany.[35] All of these trends threaten to undermine the traditional social partnership basis of the German national economy.

---

[32] It is estimated that in the early 1990s about 20% of German industrial workers were employed in hi-tech sectors such as pharmaceutical, computers, aerospace, and IT, compared with 21% in the USA and 22% in Japan (Max Planck Institut 1998).

[33] Together they had 60% abroad in 1998 (Max Planck Institut 1998).

[34] The proportion of foreign investment in capital spending was around 6% in 1998, which is still comparatively low (Max Planck Institut 1998).

[35] Interview with David Soskice.

The growing emphasis on international finance in Germany throws into question the durability of the so-called 'Rhinemodel' of producer capitalism (Albert 1993) with its emphases on 'patient capital' and social partnership. The reduced role for domestic banks and increases in foreign capitalization and private equity ownership are likely to give shareholders more power than they have been allowed to date, and thus to shift priorities towards short-term profit-making. This might not only reduce long-term investment in R & D but could also reduce company commitment to training. Were many companies to pull out of the sectoral agreements which reduce problems of poaching in German industry, then incentives to invest in training would be further reduced.[36] Foreign direct investment abroad may threaten jobs at home, keeping the burden of social insurance high.

Having substantial numbers working abroad causes problems for co-determination arrangements in German companies which have not yet been tackled, since employees abroad are not currently represented. Joint ventures and mergers with foreign companies which do not practice workplace democracy in the German fashion will likewise tend to undermine co-determination arrangements. In 1996, 728 companies were co-determined under the terms of the 1976 Law (with only 75 companies with more than 2,000 employees excluded); and 98 per cent of plants with over 250 workers had works councils. However, the 'co-determination free zone' has increased by about one-fifth since the mid-1980s. Government policy is still to maintain co-determination as a central foundation of the German economy, but it is recognized that, if companies are to remain competitive, it will have to adjust, so that there is greater flexibility and more emphasis on local bargaining and local solutions (Max Planck Institut 1998). Any substantial weakening of co-determination arrangements might encourage more firms to abandon the high skills, high wage system and to adopt strategies for competition based on price. This would undermine the basis for high skills training as well as weaken the institutional basis for implementing the Dual System.

The skills formation system in Germany has been notable for its adaptability and it continues to adapt to the needs of the changing economy. How far it can continue to do this will depend in the short term on the general health of the economy—and the willingness of employers to provide places. In the long term it will depend on how far the institutional basis of the German high skills/high wage economy

---

[36] Interview with David Soskice.

survives in the face of global pressures. The best guess is that it will remain distinctive but have to adapt substantially.

SINGAPORE—THE DEVELOPMENTAL HIGH SKILLS MODEL

Singapore, a small island state with scarcely four million inhabitants, is by size one of the wealthiest countries in the world. After three decades of growth averaging 9 per cent per annum (Ashton and Sung 1994)—above the average even for the tiger economies—it is now the richest country in Asia (after Japan) and the third richest in the world, passing Switzerland in GNP per capita (PPP) in 1996 (Lee Tsau Yuan 1998). Of all the East Asian economies, it has weathered the financial crisis best, with currency and stock market devaluations at a fraction of its neighbours' level, and unemployment still moderate by OECD standards (4.5 per cent in September 1998) (Lee Tsau Yuan 1998: 1). Singapore's manufacturing and regional 'hub' services faced a tough ride during the regional crisis, and growth is unlikely to be maintained at its former levels (it was at 4.6 per cent per annum in January 2001 (The Economist, 2001; 135)). But the fundamentals of the economy are still sound.

Singapore has a transparent and trusted financial sector and government reserves are amongst the highest in the world (at $80 billion in 2001) (Committee on Singapore's Competitiveness 1998; The Economist, 2001; 138). Unlike many of its East Asian neighbours, Singapore has not based its expansion on public or private debt and was consequently not so badly hit by the crisis in foreign investor confidence. Tough government measures to reduce business costs were implemented to maintain competitiveness during the crisis and to maintain the high levels of foreign direct investment on which the economy relies, and now it is beginning to ride the wave of regional recovery as planned. By all accounts Singapore's competitiveness strategy through its years of independence has been remarkably successful and sustained as attested by its first place ranking in the WEF Global Competitiveness Report in 1997. However, Singapore is not yet, and does not yet regard itself as, a high skills economy.

Skills formation has undoubtedly been important to Singapore's development. As a small island, with no natural resources or advantages other than its strategic location, it had to create its comparative advantages where it could, including through its human resources, and governments have been proactive and strategic in raising skills supply to meet future economic demands (Ashton, Green, et al. 1999). In the early years after self-government in 1959, economic development did not make large demands on skills. Employment growth was mostly in semi- and unskilled work and experienced engineers, managers, and technicians could be imported from abroad as and when required (Wong 1992). Educational expansion, first at primary and later at secondary levels, was promoted to spread basic English language literacy throughout the population and to nurture national identity and social cohesion. For a new, multi-racial state, with no history of nationhood and fragile inter-ethnic relations, nation-building was a high priority, and education, alongside compulsory national service and integrationalist housing policies, was a primary instrument for this, focusing as much on values formation as knowledge and skills acquisition (Castells 1992; Green 1999a). The shift towards export-oriented industry after 1965 made more demands on domestic skills prompting the government to set up a Technical Education Department at the Ministry of Education (MOE) and to instigate numerous joint training schemes with foreign MNCs to meet skills demands.

From the mid-1970s onwards, there was a concerted drive by government to develop more technology and skills-intensive industry which was accompanied by rapid skills upgrading of the existing workforce and massive expansion of post-secondary vocational training and polytechnic education. It was apparent to government policy-makers by this time that Singapore would face increasing competition within the region as a low wage, low cost manufacturing base, not only from South Korea and Taiwan, which were already rapidly industrializing, but also from up and coming states such as Malaysia, Thailand, and Indonesia. The key to continuing growth appeared to lie in reconfiguring Singapore's comparative advantages as a regional base for foreign direct investment, so that MNCs would continue to operate there but for reasons other than the availability of low cost labour for routine assembly work. In other words, the Singapore government wanted to upgrade its manufacturing and service industries into higher value added sectors which would allow the rising standard of living upon which its own political legitimacy rested.

In 1978 it launched its 'Second Industrial Revolution' strategy designed to accelerate the country to a higher technological plane, thereby removing it from competition with the low wage countries in the region (Rodan 1989). Generous tax incentives were given to MNCs for hi-tech investment, dramatic improvements were planned for the social and physical infrastructure, and a 'corrective wage policy' was introduced to raise the price of labour and encourage capital intensification.

The new wages policy introduced in 1979 had three strands. The National Wages Council recommended substantial increases in minimum wages; employers were required to pay an additional 4 per cent in national insurance contributions on top of their already substantial contributions to the Central Providential Fund; and a Skills Development Fund (SDF) was introduced, funded by a levy on employers of 2 per cent of wage costs for each worker receiving S$750 or less per month. Taken together these measures increased total wage costs in the economy between 1979 and 1981 by over 41 per cent (Rodan 1989).

In addition to deliberate wage-enhancing measures, designed to encourage capital intensification and upskilling, other measures were taken to drive the economy technologically upmarket. Various industries were earmarked for development—including automotive components, machine tools, medical instruments, computer peripherals, optical instruments, software, and wafer fabrication—and generous incentives were offered for investment in R & D and new plant and machinery in targeted areas. Government funding for public R & D institutions rose from S$10 million in 1981 to S$50 million in 1982. With massive expansion of science parks, industrial districts (in Jurong), and land reclamation, amongst other projects, total development spending as a proportion of government budget spending was projected to rise from 31.6 per cent in 1979 to 55.3 per cent in 1982 (Rodan 1993: 155).

At the same time heavy investment was undertaken in upgrading skills to meet the new demand. Enrolments in universities and polytechnics increased by 49.4 per cent between 1979 and 1983; Institute of Technical Education (ITE) skills centres took on an additional 7.5 per cent; and new institutes of technology were set up in collaborating with major investor governments—i.e. the German–Singapore Institute of Production Technology; the Japan–Singapore Institute of Software Technology, and the French–Singapore Institute of Electro-Technology. A National Computer Board was founded with plans to spend over S$170 million on computer education for Singaporeans between 1982 and 1986.

The initiative overall did achieve some upgrading within the economy but not to the extent planned. Foreign investment continued to flow in, with an annual rate rising from S$6,349 million in 1979 to S$12,717 million in 1985; at the same time value added per worker rose from S$23,992 to S$42,377 (Rodan 1993: 174). Investment in low value added areas like textiles declined, whilst increasing in capita-intensive areas like chemicals, electrical and electronic machinery, and computer component and peripherals manufacture. Manufacturing grew but considerably behind the rate for the economy overall, with a share of

GDP dropping from 23.7 to 20.6 per cent between 1980 and 1984. The shift to highly value added was restricted mainly to more automated and higher value added product assembly, rather than to R & D and design. Whilst US manufacturing companies were relatively amenable to capital upgrading of their operations, Japanese companies were less so, and in fact in due course many of the major Japanese manufacturing operations (Aiwa, Sony, Toshiba) were to move out to countries with lower wage costs.

In 1985 Singapore experienced a major recession. This was partly precipitated by the recession in the world economy; but it also underlined emerging weaknesses in the competitiveness strategy based on upgrading manufacturing. Growing trade protectionism in the United States and Europe revealed constraints to policies for growth based on exporting high value manufactured products, and increasing robotization of production in countries like Japan reduced the comparative advantage in offshore manufacture and stalled foreign direct investment expansion. This was the cue for a new course in development strategy which was less reliant on manufacture and more oriented towards services and particularly business and financial services.

The New Economic Policy launched in 1986 placed more emphasis on services and regional economic integration. The government relaxed its attitude to foreign investment in low skill manufacture, freezing wages and reducing business costs to maintain Singapore's competitiveness in the region, whilst at the same time seeking to develop its manufacturing-related service industries and its role as a leading broker in regional development. Comparative advantage was now seen to lie less in exporting goods than in providing and exporting services, where Singapore could leverage on its advantages as an English-speaking nation, with excellent transport and communications infrastructures and a good business environment. In 1991 the government launched its new vision for the next three decades in a document entitled *The Next Lap*, which foresaw Singapore surpassing Switzerland in technological sophistication and wealth in the coming decades. The key to continued growth was to turn Singapore into the 'business hub of the Asia Pacific', where it would play a key role in regional development, particularly in relation to the Singapore–Malaysia–Indonesia 'growth triangle'. Central to this vision was further improving the transport and telecommunication infrastructures and the skills base to make Singapore an attractive centre for the regional headquarters of the MNCs, providing not only manufacturing facilities but also upstream R & D capability and downstream capacity in advertising, marketing, distribution, and logistics.

The recent crisis has not fundamentally altered this new trajectory except in emphasizing the importance of Singapore reducing its vulnerability to external shocks by diversifying its international linkages, strengthening its external economy, and developing its own world-class companies. According to the October 1998 report of the Committee on Singapore's Competitiveness (1998), manufacturing and service industries will remain the twin engines of growth, but Singapore must move rapidly towards a 'knowledge-driven economy' which aims for world-class excellence in a range of service industries. Manufacturing must shift towards higher value added activities upstream and downstream, developing competitive clusters and emphasizing the niche areas, like computer components and peripherals, where Singapore has already established a strong presence. High technology growth areas are identified as wafer fabrication, biotechnology, software development, and data storage. In the service sectors the emphasis is still on financial services, international trading, transport and logistics, exhibition management and tourism, with growth potential identified in regional health care, cultural and education services, multimedia, international publishing, direct marketing, IT and communications, and e-commerce. The desire to turn Singapore into the premier services hub of the region is accompanied by an acknowledgement that this will require an enormous further upgrading in human resources.

Singapore's competitiveness strategy has indeed relentlessly moved the economy up the value added chain over the last three decades, and this has necessarily involved a substantial increase in workforce skills and capabilities. This is clear from the changing occupational profile of the workforce, with professionals increasing their share of total employment from 12.2 to 19.7 per cent, and technicians and associate professionals from 9.6 to 17.6 per cent between 1984 and 1996 (Ashton, Green, et al. 1999). However, this does not yet mean that Singapore's competitiveness relies chiefly on its workforce skills. This is the future vision but, as the Committee on Singapore's Competitiveness acknowledges, 'to realize this vision, we require a quantum jump in capabilities' (1998: 6). The World Economic Forum placed Singapore first in its 1997 Global Competitiveness report and Moody's Investment Service rated its banks the strongest in Asia and seventh in the world (Committee on Singapore's Competitiveness 1998); however, its skills ranking was much lower. The competitiveness of the Singaporean economy is currently primarily based on factors other than workforce skills.

Rapid economic growth in Singapore has, from the outset, depended heavily on inward foreign direct investment and exports. As its leaders recognized from the beginning, there was no real alternative to this strategy for development. Domestic markets were too small to build up a domestically-oriented economy, and there was little in the way of indigenous capital and local entrepreneurialism to develop growth internally (Rodan 1989). Investment from US and European MNCs could both provide investment for jobs and reduce Singapore's vulnerability as a small island with fragile relations with its major Chinese and Malaysian neighbours. MNC investment was systematically courted by government—and particularly by the Economic Development Board (EDB) (see Schein 1996)—to provide jobs and growth by making the country attractive for business.

Initially, Singapore was attractive to foreign investors because of its strategic location; its low cost, disciplined, and predominantly English-speaking workforce; its honest and competent bureaucracy; and because of the transport and logistics infrastructures inherited from its entrepôt trading history. The government created additional comparative advantages for investment by ensuring political stability and social order, a compliant trade union movement, world-class IT and telecommunications infrastructures, and an attractive physical environment. It also adopted consistently pro-business attitudes, providing generous subsidies for investment and training and doing everything possible to ease the entry of foreign firms (Castells 1998). The EDB provided comprehensive 'one-stop shop' services for new MNCs, and the government generally has provided transparent procedures and consistent and predictable regulation of the business environment (Schein 1996). These factors have been at the heart of economic competitiveness.

Singapore's Skills Profile

Singapore's skills profile has improved radically over the last three decades, but it is still weak by the standards of the advanced nations. The proportion of the active population with higher education (level 4 and 5) qualifications in 1998 was 17.4 per cent compared with 24.2 per cent in Japan, 23 per cent in the United Kingdom, 19.1 per cent in Germany, and 17.9 per cent in South Korea (see Table 2.3). Deficits in intermediate skills are equally marked. The proportion of the workforce whose highest qualification is at a level 3 equivalent in 1998 was 9.2 per cent, compared with 50.6 per cent in Germany, 41.8 per cent in Japan, 40.9 per cent in South Korea, and 18 per cent in the United Kingdom.

The younger age groups are much better qualified than the adult population as a whole. Thirty-eight per cent of the active 25- to 29-year-old population have higher education degrees (level 4 or above), compared with 46.5 in Japan, 34.8 in South Korea, 28 per cent in the United Kingdom and 14.9 per cent in Germany (see Table 2.7). Intermediate qualification levels still lag behind with only 12.2 per cent having level 3 as their highest qualification compared with 65.8 per cent in Germany, 59.5 per cent in Korea, 44.6 per cent in Japan, and 17 per cent in the United Kingdom. However, the proportion with at least level 3 (i.e. qualified at least to higher craft and technician levels or their academic equivalents) is now ahead of the United Kingdom (49.8 per cent compared with 45 per cent), although still way behind Korea (94.3), Germany (80.7), and Japan (91.1 per cent). Calculations on qualifications flows in 1994 (Steedman and Green 1996) showed the number of Singaporeans achieving at least a level 3 qualification to be equal to 50 per cent of the 17–19 cohort, compared with an estimated 39 per cent

Table 2.7. Population aged 25–29 by highest qualification attained by country, 1997/8 (per cent)

	Level 3	Level 4 Sub-degree	Degree	Level 5 Higher degree	Level 4 and above	Level 3 and above
UK (1998)	17.0	9.0	15.0	4.0	28.0	45.0
Germany (1997)[a] (aged 25–28)	65.8	5.3	—	9.6	14.9	80.7
Singapore (1998)	12.2	15.5	22.1	—	37.6	49.8
S. Korea (1998)	59.5	34.8	—	—	34.8	94.3
Japan (1997)[b]	44.6	23.2	23.3	—	46.5	91.1

[a] Level 3 includes *Abitur, Fachhochschulreife,* or Apprenticeship. Figures for Apprenticeship exclude those passing the apprenticeship who already have an *Abitur* or *Fachhochschulreife.* It also excludes those passing whose previous qualification was below the *Hauptschulabschluss*; and apprentices on programmes lasting less than three years (6% of the total).

[b] Data do not include persons whose qualification levels are unknown as well as those who were attending school and thus had not yet reached their highest educational attainment. The proportion of the former group is 0.28% (22,000) in 1987 and 0.8% (76,000) in 1997. The proportion of the later group is 1.05% (82,000) in 1987 and 1.66% (157,000) in 1997.

Sources: UK: *Labour Force Survey,* Autumn, 1998, provided by DfEE; Germany: own calculations based on German Mikrozensus provided by Federal Statistics Office, Germany; Singapore: Ministry of Manpower, *Report on the Labour Force Survey of Singapore,* 1998; S. Korea: *Labour Force Survey,* 1998, provided by National Statistical Office in Korea; Japan: Management and Coordination Agency, Statistics Bureau, Japan, *Employment Status Survey,* 1997.

for that year in England and Wales. The equivalent figure for 1998 was 64.3 per cent, compared with 52.1 per cent in England (Green 2000b). It will take some years before Singapore's qualification levels reach the standards of the most advanced countries. Nevertheless, the speed of advancement has been dramatic.

Singapore's major skills problem is that over 60 per cent of employees over 40 lack full secondary education with a similar proportion lacking full English language competence, since their education was in non-English primary schools. Because of their lack of basic skills, training participation amongst this age group is low, with a mere 10 per cent of those on SDF-funded courses being over 40. This poorly educated group is having difficulties keeping up with the skills demands of constantly upgraded jobs. They present an increasing problem for skills upgrading, since they represent a growing segment of the workforce until the year 2010, although, of course, new entrants to this age band will be better educated.[37]

Comparatively low levels of workforce skills in Singapore are mirrored in the levels of R & D. In its brief developmental period Singapore has experienced rapid technological upgrading and, like other Asian NICs, has shown itself highly adept at technology transfer. However, it has not yet reached the standards of advanced nations in terms of leading-edge technological innovation and R & D intensive manufacture. Gross Expenditure on Research and Development (GERD) as a proportion of GDP was 1.5 per cent in 1997, considerably behind Japan (2.9 per cent), Germany (2.3 per cent), South Korea (2.9 per cent), and the United Kingdom (1.9 per cent) (see Table 2.4 and Loh 1998: 62). Research scientists are proportionally less numerous than in comparator countries, even on a generous measure which includes research engineers for Singapore but not the other countries. In 1995 there were 56 per 10,000 in the labour force in Singapore compared with 83 in Japan, 74 in the United States, 48 in South Korea, and 51 in the United Kingdom (see Table 2.5 and Loh 1998: 62).

It is certainly true that the Singapore economy has become more research-intensive over recent years. GERD rose by a factor of 22 from S$81 million in 1981 to S$1,792 million in 1996, and research scientists per 10,000 of the labour force from 10.6 to 56.3 over the same period (Loh 1998: 52). However, R & D is still mainly concentrated in public sector institutions (rather disproportionately) and in foreign MNCs (which employed 61 per cent of the research scientists and engineers in 1996).

---

[37] Interview with the Productivity and Standards Board.

The latter tend to retain their fundamental research and design activities at home, using their Singapore R & D centres mainly for adapting products for local needs. Local companies have tended to rely more on licensing and joint venture agreements for technology development, although there is a trend for more researchers to be based in this sector in recent years.

In terms of patents registered, Singapore has lagged behind world leaders and other Asian tiger economies even in relation to its population size. In the period 1990–4, it had 148 patents compared with 260,130 in the United States, 107,152 in Japan, 36,223 in Germany, 12,539 in the United Kingdom, 5,268 in Taiwan, 2,889 in South Korea, and 279 in Hong Kong (although there was an upward trend from 12 to 51 over the period) (Loh 1998: 66). Despite the improvement over time, Singapore is still not in the front rank of technology. As Lawrence Loh comments in a recent comparative survey of the indicators: 'Singapore has attained remarkable GDP growth despite its lower levels of technology inputs' (1998: 61).[38]

Despite its fast rising educational attainment, the Singapore economy has a number of critical deficits in terms of its human capital. In the manufacturing sector (which employs 23 per cent of the workforce), there would appear to be an ample supply of new recruits with adequate education and good labour discipline for jobs at operator levels, and a rapidly expanding supply of technicians (although this never seems to be enough despite the 32 per cent—16 per cent in engineering—of young people now attaining higher technician level diplomas) (Green 2000b). However, there is a shortage of local research scientists and engineers and of senior managers, particularly for the local firms, and there is a considerable problem in the upgrading of older blue-collar workers.[39] According to Lim Swee Say (1998), then Vice President of the NTUC, Singaporean engineers are known to be disciplined but not very creative.

The service sector faces even greater deficits in terms of local skills. For the lower and intermediate level jobs, there is an abundance of potential new recruits amongst the younger generation who have excellent basic educational skills and, arguably, a high level of certain

---

[38] The assessment is endorsed by Tan Kong Yam and Toh Mun Heng who write that 'the key existing weakness in the Singapore economy is the lack of availability of skilled manpower such as qualified engineers, competent senior managers and, consequently, their relatively high renumeration. . . . The other key weakness is in the area of science and technology, with low rates of expenditure on R and D as a share of GDP, low number of patents granted and low domestically established brand names' (1998: 23).

[39] Observation from interview with Council for Professional and Technical Education (CPTE).

important social and 'emotional skills' (Goleman 1996). However, there are significant shortages of capable and experienced professionals in key areas where creativity and innovation is required. The advertising industry is dominated by foreigners, with few Singaporeans recruited to creative and design positions.[40] The media, an area earmarked for development by the government, also lacks talent in key capabilities such as multimedia and broadcasting technology development.[41] Financial services and banking have grown fast in recent years and are seen as key areas of expansion in the future. The strategy is 'to position Singapore to be Asia's management and distribution point for financial services in the region' (Committee on Singapore's Competitiveness 1998: 55). However, some foreign banks say they tend not to employ Singaporeans because they lack the necessary experience, drive, and aggressiveness. In particular, a shortage has been identified in high calibre skilled personnel to support growth in key areas such as fund management, debt markets, and risk management (Committee on Singapore's Competitiveness 1998: 154).

Perhaps the key gap in local human capital for future development in Singapore, however, is the lack of innovators, risk-takers, and entrepreneurs (Lim Swee Say 1998). The qualities necessary to perform these roles are not naturally generated in schools in Singapore which have generally stressed social conformism more than individual creativity. 'To promote entrepreneurship in our society, a complete mindset change amongst Singaporean is required', according to the Committee on Singapore's Competitiveness (1998: 92). Some have doubts whether this is achievable. 'Another uncertainty', writes Lee Tsau Yuan in his review of Singapore's future prospects, 'is whether Singapore can indeed succeed in developing a culture of innovation and risk-taking and entrepreneurship. In tightly-run Singapore, how much loosening, if at all, is needed to encourage creativity remains an open question.... What is not certain is whether a political loosening up is necessary to create the buzz, and if so, how to do it without embarking on the slippery slope into Chaos' (Lee Tsau Yuan 1998: 16).

---

[40] 'Asia, in general, has long suffered from a shortage of genuinely creative individuals—for one thing, this is surely the reason that the advertising industry in this part of the world has long been dominated by westerners' ('Seeking Creative Solutions', *Straits Times*, 17 Oct. 1997).

[41] 'At the moment, Singapore's capabilities in media and communications are not as strong as those of New York, London, and Hong Kong, which are the focal points of the world's major mass media and informative resource companies. We trail in key capabilities such as multimedia and broadcasting technology development' (Committee on Singapore's Competitiveness 1998: 154).

Despite very rapid advancement in skills formation, Singapore is thus clearly not yet a high skills economy in the same sense as Germany or Japan. Its dramatic economic growth over the past thirty years could not have been achieved without this rapid advancement in skills, to be sure, and the government has placed great emphasis on achieving skills upgrading. But Singapore's high level of competitiveness compared with our other countries cannot be attributed in the main to skills in the narrow sense of the term. However, in some respects, other than gross levels of qualifications, Singapore does share some important skills advantages with Japan and Korea (Green 1999a).

The education system is highly efficient in imparting foundation skills and knowledge in mathematics and science. Singaporean 13 year olds came top out of 41 countries in the Third International Maths and Science Study (TIMSS) and almost 20 per cent of 18 year olds gain an A level in Maths (Green 2000b). This provides an excellent platform for the later acquisition of applied and technical skills, not least in engineering, which accounts for almost half of all graduates (see Green 1999b). The education system has also been a very effective instrument of socialization, not only in helping to nurture that strong sense of national identity and confidence which was so important in the development process, but also more generally in imparting social attitudes deemed necessary to create a cohesive society with hard-working and disciplined labour. Many of the ingredients for the development of a high skills society are in fact present in Singapore, not least with a strong societal basis of trust and cooperation—although arguably this is still much weaker than in Japan.

This takes its own form and has been achieved in a different way from Japan. Capacity for trust and cooperation in the public sphere—as opposed to within the family—does not have deep cultural roots in Singapore as in Japan. Confucianism is relatively weakly implanted and there is a stronger and growing element of Western-style individualism (Chua 1995). Japanese models of company-loyalty and teamworking were heavily promoted by government in the 1980s, but this was not considered a success (Rodan 1989), since Western-style labour markets encouraged high levels of job-hopping and since workers were inclined to hoard information, skills, and power.[42] Income distribution is also relatively unequal compared with countries like Japan and Germany (wage spread being similar to that in the United States—see Table 2.8), and social cohesion in Singapore can hardly be attributed to

---

[42] Interview with the Productivity and Standards Board.

Table 2.8. Household income: ratio of top 20% to bottom 20% of households

Singapore	13.7	:	1
USA	13.2	:	1
UK	8.3	:	1
Taiwan	5.3	:	1
Japan	2.7	:	1

Source: From tables 11.2 and 11.3 in Lowe and Ngiam Tee Liang 1999: 238–9.

egalitarianism, as it sometimes is in Germany and Japan. Social solidarity in Singapore has in fact been engineered from the top down through a relentless and concerted ideological process of nation-building. Integrationalist housing policy, education, and a generally rising tide of incomes through rapid growth have helped to shore it up, and it remains a young and fragile phenomenon. Nevertheless, Singapore has achieved a high level of social order and work discipline with all the attendant social skills in abundance throughout the workforce. This has undoubtedly been a major economic advantage. Whilst not having achieved large high skilled elites, nor wide skills distribution, Singapore most certainly has a basis of social capital on which to build these.

Current Initiatives to Achieve High Skills

The Singapore government clearly recognizes the size of the task facing the country to attain the skill levels needed to support the realization of its vision of a high value added economy: 'In order to achieve this vision,' argues the Competitiveness Committee, 'our strategies towards human and intellectual capital development must be holistic: from nurturing skills, creativity and talent at all levels in the workforce to the development of entrepreneurship training' (1998: 85). Current plans certainly reflect this holistic approach, characterized as they typically are by an uncompromisingly system-wide approach. Government agencies responsible for education and training, from the Ministry of Education (MOE) and the EDB to the recently formed Ministry of Manpower (MOM), have a fully integrated plan for skills upgrading, spanning reforms in schooling and higher education, new initiatives in enterprise-based training, and policies for attracting foreign talent. Targets and public expenditure commitments are ambitious and implementation is characterized above all by thoroughness and concerted action.

Plans for the higher education sector involve a substantial shift towards higher level qualifications and skills. A previous target to put 40 per cent of young people through polytechnic courses leading to (level 4) diplomas has been achieved, and now the goal is to expand university first degree and postgraduate education. A third new university for business studies, as well as four new branches of top foreign universities, are being set up (Brown and Lauder 2000*b*; Green 2000*b*) and overall intake onto first degree courses is to increase substantially, through additional home student registrations and through attracting more foreign students (through substantially reduced overseas student fees). This reverses an earlier policy designed to cap numbers going to university to prevent any socially destabilizing effects from the over-production of graduates. Postgraduate and research programmes are also due for expansion and the universities are currently working hard to recruit more prestigious foreign professors, although this is proving difficult in the humanities and social sciences where suspicion still lingers about limitations on academic freedom in Singapore. Talk of turning Singapore into the 'Boston' of Asia may be somewhat optimistic, but there is clearly scope for Singapore to become a centre of regional excellence in higher education provision in certain fields. Singapore is clearly too small to be a world leader in research, but the government hopes that it may attain world-class standards in certain niche fields, such as biotechnology.[43] The infrastructure for applied research and technology transfer is already good, with fourteen publicly funded research institutes and centres. The latest (1996) National Science and Technology plan sought to promote more basic research and to persuade more of the MNCs of the adequacy of Singapore's research base for conducting fundamental R & D.

A similarly ambitious programme for upgrading workforce skills has been set in train. Singapore-based companies already have a quite respectable record in training, with an average spend in 1997 of 3.1 per cent of payroll, a great deal of which was heavily subsidized by the government. The Skills Development Fund is currently funding one in three employees annually in some kind of training activity (Committee on Singapore's Competitiveness 1998: 18), and the Productivity and Standards Board is involved in promoting or delivering a wide range of Human Resources Development (HRD) programmes and activities including on-the-job training (OJT) courses, instructor and supervisor training courses, mentoring schemes, job redesign schemes, and the

---

[43] Observations from interview at CPTE.

new company standards award known as People Developer. Its latest major programme, known as CREST, is designed to put 50 per cent of the workforce by 2002 through programmes to enhance 'critical enabling skills'. This huge initiative, budgeted at S$2 billion, is aimed at all employee levels, from operators up to top senior managers, and will be delivered, for the first time in Singapore, by a variety of private providers, including the British Council. The seven 'CREST Skills', derived largely from Marzano's work in the United States, are: 'learning to learn' (developing effective learning strategies); 'literacy' (interpreting, analysing, and using information); 'communications' (more effective listening and communicating); 'problem-solving and creativity' (identifying potential problems and generating innovative solutions); 'personal effectiveness' (self-esteem, goal-setting, planning careers); and 'group effectiveness' (teamwork, negotiating, conflict resolution, etc.).

The programme is very ambitious but may face some problems. Like many schemes for promoting generic skills, CREST fails to specify the level and nature of targeted competencies with much precision, and it will consequently be hard to evaluate the effectiveness of the programme. There is also a danger that the scheme will simply duplicate much of the training that is already done in the larger firms, with companies re-branding existing provision to gain the 80 per cent subsidy. However, it may have a positive impact on smaller firms, which do not currently do enough of this type of training or who only do it with selective groups of employees.[44] The Productivity and Standards Board's aim is clearly saturation in what it considers to be key skills.

The school system is undergoing comprehensive reform aimed chiefly at promoting IT skills acquisition, increased creativity, and independent learning capability amongst students. Three major programmes, as well as allied in-service teacher training, are currently being implemented throughout the school system to achieve this.

IT Masterplan is a S$2 billion initiative which aims to provide the equipment and skills throughout the school system to make up to 30 per cent of curriculum delivery IT-based by the year 2002. All teachers and students are to have their own e-mail accounts, and there will be a desk-top or laptop computer for every two students and every two teachers. Many schools are already have a number of LCD projectors,

---

[44] Information from interviews at the Productivity and Standards Board and the British Council.

which allow teachers to deliver lessons from the computer in the classroom using programmes like Power Point. In due course most classrooms will be equipped with these. Most schools also have their own Local Area Networks, and these are being wired up to a Wide Area Network, which will link schools with the MOE and libraries. In time the system will be incorporated into the broad-band multimedia network—termed Singapore ONE—which will link up all homes and offices in Singapore. As well as providing the hardware, the MOE aims to make all teachers competent with IT-based teaching so that the new technologies can stimulate a revolution in pedagogy and learning methods. Teachers are being systematically trained in IT and IT-based teaching and customized learning software is being developed by private companies, working with the MOE, which is being made available to schools.

Despite being very resource-hungry, this initiative is not seen primarily as a means for efficiency saving. There is no complementary plan, for instance, to reduce student contact time with teachers, although the content base of the curriculum is being slimmed down. The initiative is about promoting IT skills and new forms of learning. It is hoped that enhanced access to information sources will encourage student initiative in sourcing and handling information and lead to creative learning through new forms of project work. Whether the new tools can stimulate more creative thinking remains to be seen, but Singapore children at the end of this will certainly be amongst the most IT literate in the world.

In many ways more ambitious still is the programme to develop creative thinking, currently aimed at the non-technical streams in secondary schools. Characteristically labelled 'Thinking Schools— Learning Nation' (TSLN),[45] this is tasked with transforming the whole way students think and learn. Eight core thinking skills have been identified—analysing, organizing, remembering, information gathering, focusing, evaluating, generating, and integrating—and these are taught both through a dedicated thinking skills lesson each week, and through infusion into the main curriculum subjects. Teachers are being trained in using these techniques, as well as IT, through a programme which involves everyone in 100 hours of in-service training each year, much of which is conducted on Saturdays.

---

[45] It is characteristic of Singapore that the term 'learning nation' is used in preference to 'learning society'. National identity remains a key issue.

Whether the MOE's systematic—and somewhat programmatic—approach to changing the way students think and learn will work remains to be seen. There are considerable barriers to the adoption of new methods, not least from conservative teachers and parents who value the traditional methods of drilling and rote learning, and from students whose instrumental attitudes towards learning puts a premium on the acquisition of diplomas rather than learning for its own sake.[46] There is also the problem of how creative thinking sits alongside the traditional emphasis on conformism in schools.

There is a view, particularly within Western cultural analysis, that the nature and meaning of creativity differs substantially between Western and 'oriental' cultures. Levi-Strauss, for instance, maintained that individual creativity in non-Western societies was anathema to systems of shared values and shared themes in art, whilst Gardner has argued that Chinese culture emphasizes 'basic skills before creativity' (quoted in Hickman 1991). Whether or not such cultural differences exist in general—and they may be simply a construct of Anglo-centric thinking about the nature of creativity and art—it is certainly the case that children in Singaporean schools have traditionally been taught to put social values and the social good above personal interests and self-expression and that this inevitably inflects the ways in which they can be creative. Indeed, alongside the TSLN programme is another major initiative, known as National Education, whose express purpose is to teach children respect for shared national values. Arguably, the dual emphasis in Singaporean schools on value consensus, on the one hand, and on thinking skills and innovation, on the other, is likely to develop its own singular notion on creativity in the learning process which may differ from the kind of creative individualism that is venerated in Western learning.

Singaporean teachers talk about 'managed creativity' or 'bounded creativity' signifying that although students are being taught to think flexibly and to find new solutions to problems, they are doing this within the constraints of the existing system of shared values. They are not being asked to challenge fundamental value paradigms. As one teacher put it: 'they are taught to think more, but not to think differently'. The stress within TSLN on thinking processes and techniques, including those assisted by IT, fits in with this approach. Creative thinking in TSLN is less about stimulating imagination and originality, as in the Western ideology of artistic production, and more

---

[46] Interview with Professor Gopinathan.

about advanced problem-solving techniques whose most proximate models probably lie in engineering.[47] The methods are no doubt well suited to achieving incremental gains in the way Singaporean children approach their studies without endorsing an unacceptable level of individualism and socially non-conforming self-expression. How far they can stimulate the mind-set changes needed to nurture a new generation of entrepreneurs, 'blue skies' researchers, and innovators is another question (Brown and Lauder 2001*b*).

JAPAN—THE HIGH SKILLS MANUFACTURING MODEL

Japan achieved an unprecedented economic transformation in the post-war era. Growth rates in the 1960s and early 1970s were twice those of its major competitors—10.2 per cent and 8.7 per cent compared to an average 5 per cent and 4.4 per cent for the other six members of G7 (Perkin 1996). Whilst growth slowed thereafter, in part due to global conditions, comparatively high rates were still achieved through the 1980s, allowing Japan to emerge as an economic superpower. The share of value added in high-technology manufacturing increased from 9.6 per cent in 1980 to 14.5 per cent in 1995 while the share of manufacturing in total output decreased from 29.2 per cent to 25 per cent over the same period (OECD 1997*b*). Growth in the national economy brought a substantial increase in living standards and, moreover, the increased wealth has been fairly evenly distributed (see Table 2.1).

Economic success has been owed in part to cyclical factors, such as the opening of the global markets, to political factors such as *pax-Americana*, and to policy factors, including a prudent industrial strategy (Castells 1998). Success has also been supported, to a significant degree, by a highly educated workforce. Its contribution has involved a combination of widely distributed general education with an emphasis on social skills (i.e. cooperation, loyalty) and other company-specific institutional/tacit skills (Takeuchi and Nonaka 1995). This has resulted in the

---

[47] Students at Nanyang Girls High School, an elite independent secondary school, are encouraged as they go about the school to observe their environment and to think of better ways of organizing things—'like an improved system of guttering'. When they are taught to think of creative solutions to problems, they are reminded of the constraints within which these solutions must operate. National Education is about reminding students of the constraints (and opportunities) that constitute Singapore, as a vulnerable, small island state.

maximum utilization of individual-based skills, and their integration and mobilization to achieve company objectives. Furthermore, the unique institutional mechanisms of Japan's corporate sector have facilitated the development of these skills. These make Japan an example of a high skills manufacturing economy, although in its own distinctive way.

Japan's high economic performance has been based mainly on the success of its large manufacturing companies, notably in the automobile and electronics sectors. These companies excelled most by increasing operational efficiency and perfecting the quality of existing models. As part of the second wave of global industrialization, Japan adopted a 'catch-up' strategy, which allowed it to climb quickly up the technology ladder to reach the standard of the advanced (first wave) industrial countries. Relying on—and learning from—imported technology, its companies have gradually developed their own innovative capacities and have increasingly moved up the value added chain, particularly in medium-high technology areas and high-priced goods sectors.[48] By 1996 Japan had captured the second largest share of world trade in three major manufacturing product areas, namely automotive products, machinery and transport equipment, and office machines and telecommunication equipment (WTO 1997).

The strong economic performance was underpinned by a unique institutional base in the economy, notably with the *keiretsu*, mutual shareholding, and main banks. These three terms refer to the interlocking systems of company ownership and interaction which reinforce mutual reliance and obligation, through good times and bad. These relationships extend to the system of subcontracting, in which large companies work and grow in close association with small and medium-sized enterprises (SMEs) through determined areas of specialization and the clear demarcation of responsibilities. The unique system of interlocked companies and the main bank have provided a stable business environment in which companies could take long-term perspectives on their business investment. As discussed below, this long-termism is a basic condition for Japanese skill formation.

Despite the global presence of its top MNCs, the Japanese economy is, in many ways, distinctively national in character. Even in terms of international trade, the proportion of exports in the total GDP is surprisingly modest at only 10 per cent, as compared to 16 per cent in the United Kingdom and 26 per cent in Germany (Perkin 1996). Japan's

---

[48] The equivalent figure for the medium-high technology sector increased from 31.1% to 32.7% while that for the low technology sector decreased from 27.2% to 25% (OECD 1997*b*: 139).

massive trade surpluses result not only from its good export performance but also from the small size of its imports. The latter can be
attributed to various covert barriers to trade (such as prohibitive standards regulations and impenetrable retailing sectors), supported by the
unique preferences of Japanese consumers who, for both quality and
nationalistic reasons, are willing to pay more for domestically produced
goods (Green 1998). In financial matters, Japanese companies pay out
unusually low dividends to shareholders who are largely Japanese
and who are less demanding of high returns. This allows Japanese
companies to reinvest profits and focus on long-term performance
without meeting demands for short-term returns (Hutton 1995). At the
consumer level, Japanese households accept low rates of interest on
savings which tend to keep corporate borrowing rates low. These characteristics suggest that Japan still has a markedly national economy
both in terms of the cultural predisposition of consumer and producers
and in terms of a range of state policies which are best described as neo-
mercantilist (C. Johnson 1995). Producers tend to be shielded from
foreign competition and investments (and rely heavily on the acceptance of fellow citizens). Mutual shareholding enables Japanese
companies effectively to block a hostile takeover attempt by foreign
companies.[49] While the opening of its economy is often promised, it has
been difficult—or almost impossible—for foreign companies to pene-
trate markets in which strong corporate interconnections predominate.
The main question is whether the protection of domestic firms has
resulted in inefficiencies which are hampering the country's growth
prospects.

The defining characteristic of skill formation in post-war Japan has
been the high degree of coordination and mutual reinforcement
between its management, production, and the formal education
systems. The management system is known for its emphasis on developing long-term relations between employee and employer. Employers
provide job security and internal promotion, while employees, in turn,
provide loyalty and long-term commitment to the company. The social
and emotional elements of in-company skill formation are very high.[50]
As Dore and Sako (1989) suggest: employees are emotionally identified

[49] T. Boone Pickens who held 26% of the equity of Toyota's partner firm (Koito) could not buy
a single further share from members of the group even though Toyota itself had only 15% of
Koito's equity (Green 1999a).

[50] Figure 2.3 shows that Japan's labour productivity is strong on a per worker basis, but is less
strong on a per hour basis. This suggests that its high labour productivity has been achieved by
long working hours, indicating the strong presence of social skills, manifested in a dedication
to hard work and loyalty.

with their companies, and workers do not have to be convinced to get involved or to upgrade their skills with concrete prospects.

Japanese companies are acclaimed for their commitment to training, although this does not necessarily show up in typically inadequate comparative figures on training investment by employers. This is largely attributed to the predominance of on-the-job training. Learning on the job is expected and senior workers are often assessed in part on the basis of their contribution to training. Such training is broad and highly company-specific. In production, employees gain an overall picture of the production process and locate their specific role in the entire productive process. This assists the coordination tasks, spotting of problems, and devising of collective solutions (Sakamoto et al. 1998). Continuous improvement owes much to the suggestions from these skilled and experienced production workers. Job rotation also cultivates broad knowledge, although it also delays specialization (normally until after eight to ten years of service). The strong emphasis on company-specific skills focuses attention in skills formation onto post-employment training, leaving the school system free to develop general education rather than occupational skills. Recruitment to firms is thus based on the general aptitude of applicants and their general education credentials—as, for instance, in the ranking of an applicant's university—thus increasing the exam pressure to gain admittance to the most prestigious universities.

The school system, based on the uniform curriculum and teaching style, has been highly successful in raising the standard of education with relatively low inequality in student achievement outcomes. The principle of equal opportunities for every student is reflected in the comprehensive and mixed-ability forms of public primary and lower secondary schooling. This, and the typical belief that all children, regardless of their innate abilities, can achieve if they try hard enough, encourages widespread attainment (Green 2000a). Social skills or specific personal aptitudes, much appreciated by employers, are also taught as an important part of education. There is substantial emphasis on group activities in schooling and the importance of 'cooperation', 'hard work', and 'co-existence' are promoted not only in the designated class but also through the whole school ethos and many aspects of school life.

Despite Japan's competitive position not all sectors have performed equally well. Indeed, large companies have tended to perform better than companies in general. For example, while the banking sector grew rapidly in the 1980s, it suffered severely from the recession of the 1990s.

A cross-industry examination of productivity reveals the relative weakness in the SME and non-manufacturing sectors. Average productivity of SMEs in the machinery, retail, and textile sectors is 60–70 per cent of that of large companies and the figure in other services—transport, communication, and food—is reportedly 30–40 per cent (Chusho Kigyo Cho 1997). The lower productivity in these sectors has been overlooked until the economic downturn in the early 1990s. It is now being debated whether their inefficiency is holding up Japan's economic recovery.

Japan's Skills Profile

A wide distribution of general skills and a developed social-institutional capacity for skill utilization places Japan in an internationally competitive position as a high skills manufacturing economy. This characterization is demonstrated in the skills profile of the workforce as well as other related indicators.

The wide distribution of skills is evident from the fact that 66 per cent of those aged 15 years and over possess qualifications which are at or above the equivalent of NVQ level 3 in the United Kingdom. This figure is considerably higher than that of the United Kingdom (41 per cent) and Singapore (26.6 per cent), while Germany (69.7), and to lesser extent Korea (58.8), project comparable figures. Among the younger population, aged 25–29, the equivalent figure exceeds 90 per cent in Japan. Furthermore, a high general standard of skills is clearly reflected in the qualification level of the manufacturing workforce. In 1997 the proportion of workers with more than level 3 was 95 per cent for professional and technical workers, 69.9 per cent for crafts, mining, manufacturing, and construction workers, and 50.2 per cent for (lower level) plant and machine operators (Management and Coordination Agency 1998).

The proportion of the working population with higher degrees and above is also high. The proportion of the population with at least a degree is 13.1 per cent, which is below the level for the United Kingdom (14 per cent), but similar to Korea (13.2 per cent) and better than Germany (11.3 per cent) and Singapore (10.2 per cent). If we include the figure for the population with sub-degree qualifications, the figure increases to 24.2 per cent in Japan, and this is the highest among the comparator countries, with the next two highest being the United Kingdom with 23 per cent and Germany with 19.1 per cent. For the population aged 25–29 in Japan, the proportion with at least sub-degree qualifications is robust at 46.5 per cent. The country possesses a large supply of engineering graduates as well. The share of engineering degrees amongst first degrees generally is 22 per cent, which is the highest among the comparator countries. However, the number of students choosing liberal arts and humanities has increased gradually in recent years, resulting in a relative decline in science and engineering majors.

Based on the ranking of universities from which employees graduate, the highest concentration of high skills is observed in large companies in Japan (Dore and Sako 1998).[51] The concentration of engineering graduates from prestigious universities (namely Tokyo University and Tokyo Kogyo University) in large companies is extremely high. Some 53 per cent of their engineering graduates are in companies with 10,000 or more employees, and 20 per cent of them are in companies with 3,000 to 9,999 employees (MOL 1999a: 343).

The strong profile in higher education, however, is not normally interpreted as an indicator of a large stock of high skill elites as discussed in the case of Germany. This is largely due to a strong emphasis on general skills and broad knowledge in the curriculum, which, until 1991, accounted for nearly one-third of the degree curriculum.[52] Thus, apart from some science degrees such as medicine, higher education qualifications are generally seen to impart general skills and knowledge and/or a greater capacity for learning, rather than specialized skills and knowledge. The participation in postgraduate studies has been modest, although the proportion of graduates advancing to postgraduate studies has increased rapidly from 6.8 per cent in 1990 to 9.4 per cent in 1996 (MOESSC 1997).

Japan presents a solid profile of intermediate skills as well. If we take graduation rates from high school (upper secondary) as a benchmark for the equivalent of the NVQ level 3 in the United Kingdom, 41.8 per cent of the Japanese population is qualified at this level.[53] The figure

---

[51] According to one study, 70% of graduates of universities with a standard deviation score entry rating of over 70, found jobs in companies with more than 5,000 employees, while only 7% of graduates of universities rated 45 or less did so (Takeuchi quoted in Dore and Sako 1998: 93).

[52] The stipulation of the curriculum hours for general education has been removed since reforms in higher education in 1991.

[53] It should be noted, however, that there is a certain degree of upward bias in the level 3 figures. The graduate certificates of high school are not graded and there is no national examination taken at the end of high school as in the English system. Another point which should be mentioned is that the overall profile of the level 3 qualification is considerably 'general' in nature. While 95.9% of the students who completed compulsory education progressed on to high school in 1996, enrolment in vocational high schools accounted for only 26.1% of total secondary school enrolment (MOESSC 1997). The tendency of academic drift is apparent, as over

compares unfavourably with 50.6 per cent in Germany due to a higher progression rate to higher education. However, it compares favourably with 40.9 per cent in Korea, 18 per cent in the United Kingdom and 9.2 per cent in Singapore.

Japan's strength in basic skills, such as numeracy and literacy, has been demonstrated in various international surveys. In the Third International Maths and Science Study Japanese students came third in the maths test after Singapore and Korea, and fourth in science following Singapore, Korea, and the Czech Republic. Previous International Evaluation of Educational Achievement (IEA) studies have also shown that these skills are relatively evenly dispersed (Green 2000).

Although it would be hard to demonstrate quantitatively, it would seem that Japan's continuous improvement and cumulative innovations owe much to a broad dispersal of social skills as well as to company-specific institutional skills. Social skills include teamwork and communication skills as well as 'emotional intelligence' (Goleman 1996), and are closely tied to personal aptitudes such as discipline, cooperation, and work effort. The strong emphasis which the school system places on these skills results in them being highly dispersed in the Japanese workforce. The presence of other, related, types of skills should also be noted. These include the 'institutional knowledge' which come from in-company experience and involve understanding work norms, the corporate culture, and various assumptions and expectations of the work environment (Takeuchi and Nonaka 1995). Such skills are tacit and informal in nature but equally important in a knowledge-driven economy (DTI 1998*a*). Koike (1997) highlights the ability of Japanese workers to deal with unexpected situations ('intellectual skills'), although the technical difficulty of quantification makes international comparisons impossible.

The high skills nature of the Japanese economy has also been demonstrated in the strong innovative capacity of Japanese companies. As shown in Table 2.6, the number of patents obtained by Japanese companies in 1994 was the second highest in the world (22,384), following only the United States (56,066). Moreover, 88.6 per cent of total patents obtained by Japan in 1995 were in high and medium-high technology, which indicates a significant effort in keeping a leading

40% of high school graduates progress on to higher education. Even in terms of its curriculum, general subjects sometimes account for up to 60%. It is an accepted view that, in most cases, real technical training and specialization occur in-company after employment. Thus, although school-based vocational training is still important for SMEs, it plays a rather minor role in skills formation in Japan.

edge in a knowledge-driven world (OECD 1997*b*: 134). While Japanese companies imported innovations from other countries (50.6 per cent from the United States in 1993), they also exported their own innovations abroad (31 per cent to the United States). The largest proportion of imported technology in the United States in 1993 came from Japan, which was followed by Germany with 8.2 per cent (ibid.).

This strong innovative capacity has been supported by a relatively high level of investment in R & D. Investment as a proportion of GDP in 1997 was 2.9 per cent (the same as Korea), 2.7 per cent in the United States, and 2.3 per cent in Germany (see Table 2.4). Furthermore, 70.3 per cent of total R & D investment is accounted for by the private sector (ibid.), indicating that the drive to sustain a knowledge-based economy is largely led by private corporate initiative. The number of researchers per 10,000 workers was 83 in 1995, which is the highest number in the six-country comparison in Table 2.5. However, much of the effort is dedicated to adapting existing products and inventions.

The skills effect of the Japanese workforce has been articulated in four basic ways: highly adaptable and flexible working practices, efficient OJT, concerted and coordinated work practices, and a maximum utilization and mobilization of skills. A high level and broad distribution of general skills supports the country's capacity to adapt to the changing needs of business through flexible and multi-task/skills work practices. Sound basic skills, in particular in mathematics, have given Japanese workers an advantage in coping with the rapid advancement of technology (i.e. the introduction of computer-aided and numerical control systems). A wide distribution of skills provides a strong basis for effective OJT in which workers absorb new skills and knowledge on the job. It has allowed employers not only to focus on providing a relatively high level of technical/professional training, but also to provide such training in a fairly uniform manner (including understanding highly technical manuals).

A wide distribution of skills (and the relative weakness in specialized skills) has also meant that the inequality in general skills and knowledge among workers is relatively small. This has allowed a type of teamwork in which practically everyone can understand and contribute to *kaizen* (continuous improvement), or in which engineers and production workers engage in problem-solving literally at the same table (MOL 1999*b*: Aug. 6–15). This has, no doubt, facilitated well coordinated production efforts. Strong social skills, which range from work attitudes such as loyalty, commitment to company-specific shared knowledge, and tacit skills, have contributed to maximizing the utilization of skills to achieve common objectives. This tendency has been multiplied by a high level of workers' emotional association or even self-identification with their peers and company. Notwithstanding the long working hours which have resulted, workers' emotional commitments have also allowed Japanese companies to achieve continuous high performance which perhaps would not be possible with simply a collection of individuals with a high level of skills.

Current Economic Challenges

Since the early 1990s, the Japanese economy has faced serious economic challenges which now represent the biggest economic crisis in the post-war period. It began with the tightening of monetary policy to halt the speculative bubble in asset values which produced an economic boom in the second half of the 1980s. The bursting of the bubble economy after 1990 resulted in the decline of public and business confidence and a sharp decline in investment and domestic consumption. The GDP growth rate dropped from 6.2 per cent in 1988 to 4 per cent in 1991 and a mere 0.1 per cent in 1993.

The problem was compounded by a surging yen and intensified competition in the global market on efficiency, quality, and value added productions in the high-priced market. These conditions in the international market made the situation particularly difficult for the locomotive of the Japanese economy: export manufacturing. Many manufacturing companies responded by further enhancing value added production and new product development, and by moving production to low-cost bases in neighbouring Asian countries. While financial companies had performed strongly during the bubble economy, the recession left them with declining asset values and a heavy burden of bad loans, which prompted many to resort to high-risk, high-return investments in other Asian markets (Wade 1998).

The Asian financial crisis could not have hit Japan at a worse time: it was finally seeing signs of recovery from the earlier recession, with a growth rate of 3.6 per cent in 1996 (Dore 1998: 774). Japan's trade with the Asian region accounted for almost 40 per cent of its total trade, while heavy investment in the region exacerbated the situation. The succession of sharp falls in Asian currencies and share prices in 1997 was too great for some Japanese financial companies to cope with.

During the long recession, many Japanese companies have made considerable efforts to avoid laying off employees. Despite the financial burdens created by the long-term employment and seniority systems, companies were generally more concerned with the decline of worker morale which would result from redundancies. However, the country once acclaimed for its low unemployment rate suffered from a record high unemployment rate of 4.8 per cent in March 1998, which almost exceeds the figure in the United States. This manifests the scale of the strain which the recession imposed on the corporate sector. As the recession has continued, many of the pre-recession practices (from competent bureaucracy, to the business and management system, to the education and training system), which were formerly considered to be determinants of economic success, are now being questioned.

Various causes and diagnoses of the crisis have been put forward by the experts on Japan. The problem is partly seen as exogenous, whereby external forces are perceived as the main sources of the crisis; and partly as cyclical, whereby a combination of 'ill-judged and ill-timed policy measures, or unlucky' circumstances have been to blame (Whittaker and Kurosawa 1998; Johnson 1998; Dore 1998). However, the slump has also been seen as a sign of more deep-rooted structural or systemic defects. The structural problems revolve around the heavy reliance on export demand, mass-production manufacturing, and a gradual shift from manufacturing into services. Systemic defects include the mutual reliance and obligations exemplified by *keiretsu*, main banks, cross-shareholding, and other interlocking relations, which, as a side-effect, have led Japan to cronyism and prevented the operation of effective checks and balances (Johnson 1998).

Responses to the Current Economic Crisis

The economic crisis has prompted Japan to reconsider the basis of its competitive strategy. This reflects the realization that efficiency improvement in large-scale manufacturing may reach its limit and not be able to provide the basis for future growth. As a result, there is much debate regarding the need for a paradigm shift from its traditional 'catch-up' strategy to a new 'innovation' strategy based on Japan's own inventions or discoveries. It must shift its competitive base from 'how to make' to 'what to make' (Nakayama 1999). This would allow it, so it is argued, to capture new—and highly lucrative—market niches.

Arguably, such innovations will be based on basic science and research (or unexploited discoveries made elsewhere), as well as new creative product developments. It reflects a belief that innovation is seen as the only way to survive in the already crowded global market. Increased attention has also been placed on venture business (VB) as a potential source of Japan's next sunrise industries and new source of employment.[54] At the same time, a need is felt for Japan to strengthen other longer term weaknesses in its economy, notably the lack of efficiency of its white-collar workers and the lack of competitiveness of its SME and service sectors, which are largely confined to the protected domestic market. In terms of sectors, the business community expects growth in the next five years to be highest in information technology, medical and social work, education and leisure, and business-support (MOL 1999*a*: 362). However, their interests in expanding or moving into knowledge-intensive hi-tech industries such as biotechnology and new chemicals and synthetic fibres show a slight decline compared to the last five years (ibid.).

In the search for solutions to the recession, efforts have also focused on the institutional structure. The reform effort has included a financial sector package called 'Big Bang' designed to loosen monetary policy and financial regulations, stimulate domestic demand, and increase transparency. Reform has also attempted to promote a more open-market economy with fewer interlocking relationships, more similar to the Anglo-American model. These reforms are gradually changing the nature of the economy. For instance, banks are selling the shares of close customers, while trading companies are selling shares of companies which do less and less business through them (Whittaker and Kurosawa 1998; EPA 1999: 125). The first clear sign of a breaking up of *keiretsu* came about in May 1999, when the Mazda group announced the sale of all of the mutually held shares of one of its old partners (Nikkan Kogyo Shinbun Sha 1999). In addition, an increase in direct financing (as opposed to indirect financing through main banks) has been reported, and this is making companies more sensitive to movements in the stock market and the short-term interests of shareholders. Although the full extent of the changes and their impact remain to be seen, there is a concern that such short-termism may further erode the basis for the internal labour market and make employers think twice about investing in training.

---

[54] The Advisory Committee for Industrial Structure (MITI) announced a series of support schemes, ranging from special taxation to VB, to the establishment of VB ranking institutions (Nikkan Kogyo Shinbun Sha 1999).

Do these broader changes in the Japanese economy suggest that Japan is adjusting itself to the Anglo-American model which is largely driven by short-termism? And how far can the skill formation system in Japan survive in the light of broader institutional changes? It requires more time to provide definite answers. Changes have been slow so far, and there is also considerable counter evidence to a shift towards the Anglo-American model. Recent studies on changing attitudes towards 'corporate governance' and 'employment practices and employee–employer relations' among Japanese managers reveal unchanged support for the existing practices (Inagami 1999).[55] While companies attempt to be more responsive to the needs of shareholders, a substantial part of their efforts is devoted towards increasing investors' understanding of and support for the company's long-term strategies (Miyauchi and Tahara 1999). This is, they seem to believe, the best and perhaps only way to be truly responsive to shareholders.

Soon after the Asian crisis, the majority of the Japanese managers thought that the convergence of its economy was inevitable (Dore 1998). However, two years on, the downside of the Anglo-American model is also highlighted, and some critics claim that Japan will be different (MOL 1999*b*; Terashima 2000). Although future discussion will inevitably be affected by the economic situation, many protagonists are currently re-stressing the benefits of long-term employment for both employers and employees and arguing that it should continue to be a basic principle and practice of Japanese employment (MOL 1999*a*: 160–5; MOL 1999*b*: July). OJT is also emphasized in this context as the most efficient and effective form of training (ibid.).[56]

There is one more issue which needs to be considered for the analysis. Despite the increased signals of a decline of traditional Japanese systems, some companies are instead enhancing their existing *keiretsu* relations, although only in the strategically important areas (Nikkan Kogyo Shinbun Sha 1999 and MOL 1999*b*). It should be noted that a handful of large Japanese companies (mostly MNCs) have been able to generate a continuous surplus despite the overall downturn in the national economy. The monolithic picture of Japanese companies

[55] According to studies on attitudes towards (personnel) restructuring, approximately 60% of the respondents across industry claim that they would maintain long-term employment as much as possible (MOL 1999*a*: 246; EPA 1999). While there exist many ways to cope with business shortfalls, 44% of SMEs and 49% of large companies said that they find the layoffs the most difficult to practise (EPA 1999: 161).

[56] A study shows that 66.2% of companies who responded claimed that they would enhance OJT as their priority HRD effort, although 62.1% of them also said that they wanted to enhance skill development which is also useful outside the firm (MOL 1999*a*: 417).

is gradually eroding, as companies, depending on the type of business and industry increasingly take different approaches to the challenging economic environment.

The economic downturns that began in the early 1990s have drastically changed the context in which the existing skill formation used to operate. As in the past, there is a high expectation that human resources in Japan will contribute to overcoming the crisis. However, as Japan attempts to reinvent its competitiveness, it is imposing considerable challenges to the existing skill formation system.

The severe economic pressures have affected the existing system of skill formation in two general areas. First, efforts to develop a new economic strategy based on the innovatory high value added products and sunrise industries places a high premium on a new set of non-traditional skills. These include creativity, autonomy, risk-taking as well as certain specialized professional skills. This presents a marked shift in emphasis from the general and teamworking skills which were traditionally appreciated and which provided the basis for Japan's past success. Secondly, the economic pressures have highlighted weaknesses of the skill formation system, which existed prior to the recession but were less noticeable when the economy was generally performing well. These problems fall into two general areas: the inadequate skills of white-collar workers and the growing shortage of technical workers felt especially by SMEs. The new skill requirements and the longer term skills deficiencies are considered in more detail in the subsections below.

Changing Skills Requirements

A more intense focus on high value added production, new product development, and non-traditional business activities requires companies to develop their innovative capacity. This, in turn, requires them to employ or train creative workers. While Japanese companies— and notably those in manufacturing—have demonstrated strong innovative capacity in applied science, employers and policy-makers are increasingly concerned with the weakness of, and lack of innovation in, basic science. This has resulted in repeated calls for more creative talent, including scientists and basic researchers.

One effort to help tackle this problem was the reform of the Standard Law (in labour) in September 1998, which provided an official endorsement for flexible working hours for those who are responsible for jobs which require creativity, or already possess specialized skills (MOL 1999b).[57] Although the ministry continues to provide strong support for long-term employment, it has recognized the necessity for increasing labour mobility/fluidity given the limited supply of specialized talents. Its White Paper (MOL 1999a) also places greater emphasis on the respect for individuality and individual choice in achieving potential in one's working life (even though it may involve changing employers rather than staying with the same employer for a long time). However, there is a danger that the promotion of creative talent may undermine the development of cooperative workers who are vital for the integrative system (Sakamoto et al. 1998).

The new business environment also requires more autonomous and innovative workers as well as the generation of more risk-taking entrepreneurs. Many employers find that their workers are very proficient at following blueprints or other instructions but that without such guides they have difficulty knowing how to proceed (NIRA 1994). This problem has its roots in the education system where students are trained to give maximum effort under pre-set conditions.[58] That attitude has traditionally met the requirements of employers. The lack of risk-taking entrepreneurs is another area of concern. The differences in attitudes between young Japanese and American students[59] were revealed in a study in 1993 which compared their career paths and perceptions towards occupation. Only 11 per cent of the Japanese students expressed an interest in setting up their own businesses, while the figure for American students was 26 per cent. Furthermore, while some 40 per cent of Japanese students expressed a desire to be promoted in already established companies, only 22 per cent of American students had such a career path in mind (EPA 1999: 344).

Another area of concern is the shortage of professional workers such as lawyers, accountants, and financial experts. This shortage has become important with the increase in business transactions taking place in the public sphere, as opposed to more traditional private or bilateral transactions. For example, the increased propensity of large companies to solicit direct-financing—rather than indirect financing through major banks—has resulted in increased demands for highly qualified accountants and financiers who can meet public reporting requirements and

---

[57] The reform also permits a maximum three-year (formally one-year) employment contract for specialized people, allowing both employers and employees to make flexible employment arrangements if they wish.

[58] Interview with Yoshiyuki Kudomi, 1999.

[59] Engineering students of Tokyo University, Tokyo Kogyo University, and MIT.

negotiate complex deals. Furthermore, as knowledge and information have become crucial competitive assets, lawyers and other legal specialists who can protect and negotiate the trade of such intellectual property rights are becoming increasingly important (Inoki 2000).

Skills for White-Collar Workers

With the decline of manufacturing employment and the growth of the service sector, the proportion of white-collar workers has increased steadily from 50.8 per cent of the workforce in 1985 to 54.5 per cent in 1998 (MOL 1999*a*: 368). For their part, firms are finding that the ability to increase productive efficiency is now reaching its limits and increasing the efficiency among white-collar workers (in advertising, planning, marketing, information technology) is necessary to increase the profitability and the overall productivity of the company. The emerging new market for highly skilled white-collar workers exists alongside a traditional emphasis on manufacturing skills and a traditional de-emphasis of white-collar skills. Thus, the development of an adequate skill formation system for white-collar workers is seen as an urgent requirement (MOL 1999*a*).[60]

Shortage of Technical Workers

An increased number of science and engineering graduates are finding employment in the banking and financial sectors.[61] While large companies are well equipped to attract the declining number of engineers and technicians, or are better able to overcome the shortage through mechanization, the capacity of SMEs is limited in this regard.

[60] One of the reasons for the de-emphasis of white-collar skills can be attributed to the technical difficulty of defining and assessing their skills. In response, the government has developed the 'Business-Career System'. The attempt, begun in 1993, provides matrices in which general responsibilities for each white-collar job at different grades are benchmarked and the level of skill and qualifications required to fulfil the responsibilities is suggested. It also lists the names of approved training institutions for obtaining qualifications. However, the extent of use of this system, as well as the impact of the system on the productivity of white-collar workers, remains to be seen.

[61] It is said that in an affluent Japan, technical jobs, which are often characterized as: dirty (*kitanai*), dangerous (*kiken*), and demanding (*kitsui*) (called 3K jobs in Japanese), are no longer attractive occupations for young Japanese.

A shortage of technical workers, especially in SMEs, is therefore a major concern for the future viability of manufacturing in Japan.

Along with the issues directly linked to (or revealed by) the current economic problems, underlying demographic and social changes are adding to the strain on the existing pattern of skills formation. Ageing is a general concern affecting most parts of the Japanese economy. Some 22 per cent of the total workforce is above the age of 55. This problem is particularly acute among skilled craft workers, where the average age of casting and gilding workers is now over 50 years (Seki and Ukai 1992). Furthermore, the average age of skilled workers is significantly higher in SMEs, where 40.6 per cent are 50 years and over while the equivalent figure for large companies is 14.1 per cent (CKC 1997). With fewer young people entering technical occupations, this is seriously hampering the transfer of skills to new generations.

There are also changes in the progression of youth and declining standards in education. The high school drop-out rate has increased,[62] and absenteeism in compulsory education has almost doubled over the last seven years from 66,817 students in 1991 to 130,208 in 1999 (MOESSC 2000). A growing body of evidence depicts an alarming picture of demoralized youth. This includes those who are tired of studying hard to win intense educational competitions, those who have lost the desire to learn and the aspiration to progress in school, and those who have lost interest in participating in competitions altogether (Amano 1997; Kudomi 1999).[63] As a wide distribution of skills and relative equality in student attainments has been the fundamental basis for the Japanese skill formation, the impact of the changing profile of the young may be far-reaching.

Reforms in the Formal Education System

The policy discourse for the reform of the formal education system is largely in line with the new skills requirements. In addressing the

[62] From 1.9% in 1992 to 2.6% in 1998 (MOESSC 1999).

[63] Aggravated by the current severe employment situation, those who are neither in education nor work (including temporary work) has increased from 6.2% in 1989 to 15.5% in 1998 among graduates, and 5.6% to 7.9% among high school graduates (MOL 1999a: 324). It is also reported that 50% of the graduates in one high school in Tokyo neither progressed on to higher education nor entered full-time jobs. They claim that they prefer taking part-time casual jobs until they find 'what they really want to do'—the so-called self-discovery syndrome. This may be interpreted as evidence that young people are becoming autonomous and choosing their way by rejecting the existing pattern of school–work transition. However, this also indicates that their skills level (even basic skills) is not high enough to secure jobs with prospects (Terashima 2000). One thing that is clear is that they are out of the existing skill formation system altogether.

generalist inclination in higher education, there has been a major reform of higher education to create more 'specialized' talents (MOESSC 1998*b*, 1999). The reforms in school have emphasized the importance of cultivating 'creativity', and granting greater respect for 'individuality' as it is assumed to foster the creative capacity of individuals (CCE 1996, 1997). However, the reform efforts in formal schooling should be understood in the context of growing social problems at Japanese schools as discussed above. Reports on disrupted classes, school violence, and bullying are numerous and these problems taken together are by far the predominant educational issue in contemporary Japan. The rigid and highly competitive nature of schooling is largely to blame, it is argued, so that the reforms place substantial importance on loosening up the system and providing students with more 'room to grow' (*yutori*) (ibid.; Green, Ouston, and Sakamoto 1999). In practical terms, a reduction in school days has been proposed and the content of curriculum is being reduced to focus on 'essential elements'.

The promotion of *yutori*, reduced curriculum hours and content, the increased respect for individuality and choice may be necessary for the promotion of creative talent and the improvement of the general welfare of students. However, there is a risk of widening the inequality of student attainment and lowering the general standard of education, as mentioned (Green 2000*a*). This has serious implications for the existing high skill model based on a high diffusion of skills and the efficiency of widely practised OJT in the workplace. A widening skill and knowledge gap among workers may not allow the kind of cooperation in which technicians and engineers work together literally at the same table (MOL 1999b: Aug. 6–15). This skills gap may differentiate workers to the extent that the existing 'single-status' management practice is difficult to continue.

Changing Notions of Competence and the Japanese Management System

Reforms in human resource management have been taking place gradually since the 1970s. However, the financial burdens triggered by the recession have accelerated the process and brought more defining changes to the system. The nature of the changes is notable in two ways. One is a growing tendency in adapting the performance-based payment system, shifting away from the traditional seniority-based system.

'Performance' was not necessarily neglected even in the past system (Kumazawa 1997). However, there has been a growing shift in emphasis to 'performance' elements (as opposed to seniority) in determining the level of payment and the prospects for promotion. Secondly, an increasing number of companies are adopting two-tier systems of human resources which distinguish between those employees who have long-term prospects of becoming 'core personnel' and those who are employed with short-term prospects to meet immediate needs.[64] The use of part-time and contract workers has been increasing, and their proportion is now near 20 per cent of total employees (MOL 1999*a*: 301).[65] There are concerns about whether these short-term employees possess a long-term commitment to the company and whether they are motivated to participate in cooperative and coordinated work practices.

Japan's past success has been built on a competitive strategy characterized by increasing efficiency and quality in large-scale goods production. It has been supported by a skills formation system involving a broad diffusion of general skills, extensive on-the-job training, supportive in-company institutions, and cooperative work practices. The severe recession has called into question the country's competitive strategy and prompted debate about the need for a paradigm shift. Such a shift might involve a more creative, innovation-based approach, focusing on different markets and requiring different work practices. Such a change would have far-reaching implications for the existing skills formation system. It would require the promotion of much greater individuality, risk-taking, and creativity in both the education system and the workplace and it might require a more differentiated and less egalitarian approach to personnel. It is not yet known whether such a highly creative and specialized sector of the economy would function as the backbone of the Japanese economy as manufacturing has done. The main concern with shifting the competitive basis is whether Japan has the inherent strengths and characteristics to make such a new strategy successful, or whether the shift will undermine the strengths of the existing system.

In this regard, the calls for a more free-market, Anglo-American approach to the economy must be viewed with extra caution. On the one hand, many of the reforms regarding transparency and corporate responsibility, as well as efforts to open the domestic market to greater outside competition, may be beneficial in reducing domestic inefficiencies. However, tampering with the institutional structures of

---

[64] Interview, director of personnel, major electronics company, May 1997.
[65] In the fourth quarter of 1998, the proportion of part-time workers was 4.45% in construction, 12.21% in manufacturing, 36.81% in retails and restaurants, and 19.01% in service.

corporate governance and inter- and intra-company relationships while promoting the inequalities that characterize innovative sectors may undermine Japan's traditional strengths.

THE UNITED KINGDOM—HIGH SKILLS/LOW SKILLS MODEL

The United Kingdom stands out from the other countries in this study in that its model of economic competitiveness has not been associated with wide skills distribution, as in Germany and Japan, nor even a rapid movement towards this, as in Singapore. The model can be characterized, rather, as one of skills polarization, where competitiveness in some sectors is based on high labour productivity derived from skilled elites, but where in many other sectors such competitiveness as there is derives primarily from other sources, such as capital productivity and flexible labour. A limited distribution of skills throughout the workforce has been linked with high and rising rates of income inequality and relatively high ranking on many of those social indicators, which are often taken as evidence of a lack of social capital—i.e. divorce, crime, incarceration, and so on (Brown and Lauder 2001a). Although patchy, and despite improvements, the overall picture is still one of rather indifferent levels of competitiveness in the national economy, combined with considerable social problems, although the latter are not the specific subject of this chapter.

Despite improving rates of growth in recent years, the United Kingdom economy still achieves rather average levels of productivity. This, as was argued earlier, appears to derive largely from continuing deficits in labour productivity, which are only partially disguised by rather high levels of capital productivity. Figures for the market sector during 1994–6 show United Kingdom labour productivity per hour worked as lagging well behind other competitor countries, with the United Kingdom benchmarked at 100 against France (126), west Germany (126), and the United States (137) (McKinsey Global Institute 1998: exhibit 2). IMD figures for 1998 show comparative productivity gains against Germany, but the gap with leading economies remains substantial, particularly in manufacturing.[66] This is not to deny that in many sectors—such as banking and financial services, aerospace,

---

[66] On DTI figures for 1996 (DTI 1998b), the UK was not far behind Japan on total labour productivity (100 against 103), but well behind in manufacturing.

pharmaceuticals, telecommunications, media and entertainment (Finegold 1999)—there is strong evidence of skills-based competitiveness. Nor does it overlook Britain's relative strength in many leading edge industries such as biotechnology, multimedia, and—more tendentiously—e-commerce, although productivity in hi-tech industries as a whole is still thought to be behind Germany, France, Italy, and Japan (DTI 1998*b*). It is also compatible with many firms operating on a low skills, low productivity basis remaining profitable, particularly where they are able to compete on low labour costs.

However, it does mean that the overall competitiveness of the economy remains indifferent. In 1997 the United Kingdom ranked nineteenth in the world in GDP per capita (at PPP), behind Finland, Ireland, and Italy (DTI 1998*b*, chart 3.10). By 1998 it had overtaken Finland and Italy, but remained behind Austria (106), Belgium (110), Canada (110), Denmark (116), France (103), Germany (101), Ireland (106), Japan (107), the Netherlands (109), Norway (128), Switzerland (121), and the United States (149) amongst other countries (see Scarpetta et al. 2000). GNP per capita (at PPP) in 1998 was $20,314, ahead of Korea (at $13,286), but behind the United States (at $29,240), Singapore (at $25,295), Japan (at $23,592), and Germany (at $22,026) (IBRD/WB 2000).

Economists have been unable to demonstrate conclusively that skills are the major determinants of productivity, not least because they are notoriously difficult to measure directly (Ashton and Green 1996). Other factors may clearly be involved such as capital investment in R & D, plant, and machinery. The United Kingdom ranked fifth amongst the G7 nations for business investment in R & D in 1995 (down from third in 1987) (DTI 1998*b*) and capital investment per worker has undoubtedly been low relative to a number of comparator countries. Between 1983 and 1993, for instance, for every £100 invested per worker in the United Kingdom, Germany and the United States invested nearly £140, France almost £150, and Japan over £160. Current estimates for the late 1990s (O'Mahoney 1999) suggest that capital intensity is still higher by 30 per cent in the US economy, by 40 per cent in France, by 50 per cent in Japan, and by 65 per cent in Germany. McKinsey Global Institute estimates that only 5 per cent of the lower labour productivity in the United Kingdom can be explained by lower capital investment, but whatever the precise figure it is clearly significant.

However, there are clearly good reasons to think that inadequate supplies of skills and poor utilization of skills have been part of the reason for low productivity in many sectors of the United Kingdom economy. Evidence for this comes from a number of sources. Perhaps most convincing are the National Institute of Economic and Social Research (NIESR) comparative studies which look at skills and productivity in matched plants and establishments in Britain, France, Germany, and the Netherlands. These have covered sectors as diverse as engineering, furniture production, clothing and biscuit manufacture, food processing, and hotels,[67] and all have tended to show lower productivity in the United Kingdom cases compared with other countries even where market niches and machinery vintages were similar. Higher productivity in the continental plants and establishments was related to the greater ability of shop-floor workers to perform a wide range of tasks leading to higher quality products and services; a reduction in downtime from machinery breakdown; and the earlier introduction of new technologies. In clothing manufacture around 40 per cent of machinists had a relevant vocational qualification in Germany and none in the United Kingdom. In the study of hotels, three-quarters of the hotel housekeepers were found to have served an apprenticeship in Germany—none had in the United Kingdom. In each case lower levels of skills in the United Kingdom plants were shown to be inhibiting productivity.

A number of related explanations have been put forward for this apparent linkage between low skills and low productivity in many sectors of the United Kingdom economy. Finegold and Soskice argued in 1988 that the United Kingdom was caught in a 'low skills equilibrium' in which the majority of enterprises staffed by poorly trained managers and workers produce low quality goods and services (1988: 22). The cause of this long-standing phenomenon was seen to be 'a self-reinforcing network of societal and state institutions' which served to stifle demand for improvement in skills levels. The institutional pathology was seen to be evident in: the education and training system; industrial relations; the financial markets; the organization of industry, firms, and the work process; and ultimately in the structure of the state itself. The analysis is often now seen as too 'static', not least by one of its own authors (Finegold 1999), but it undoubtedly had the merit of pointing to a range of factors which appear to interact with each other.

The low demand for skills has also been seen as the key issue in the work of others such as Keep and Mayhew (1998), Albert (1993), and Hutton (1995). Keep and Mayhew (1998) argue that skills demand has remained low because firms in the United Kingdom have access to a

---

[67] Daly, Hitchens, and Wagner 1985 and Mason and van Ark 1996—for engineering; Steedman and Wagner 1987—for furniture; Steedman and Wagner 1989—for clothing manufacture; Mason, van Ark, and Wagner 1996—for food processing; and Prais, Jarvis, and Wagner 1989—for hotels.

variety of competitive strategies other than those based on high skills. These include seeking protected markets, growth through takeover, shifting investment abroad, seeking monopoly power, and cost-cutting and resort to new variants of Fordism. Most notably many firms have remained profitable by concentrating on low-cost and low-quality product and market strategies, where competitiveness relies on flexible and low wage labour. Examples range from the avowedly cheap group of retail discounters (including Aldi, Netto, and Kwik Save amongst food retailers) to economy air services (such as Ryanair and Easyjet) to fast food outlets and low-cost domestic retail banking. The strategy can work, particularly in the United Kingdom where there is a substantial constituency of consumers with low disposable income. Likewise Albert (1993) and Hutton (1995) have argued that shareholder or consumer capitalism in the United Kingdom and the United States makes lower demands on skills than the 'producer' or 'stakeholder' capitalism more typical in continental Europe and Japan, because of the uniquely dominant position of the financial sector. Where large profits can be made from mergers and acquisitions and from asset-stripping, not to mention from the booming trade in financial instruments such as options, futures, and other derivatives, productivity through high skills may not seem so essential (Soros 1998).

Parallel arguments can be made about the supply of skills, both from historical and contemporary points of view. Historians have long been aware of the relatively late development of mass public education in England by comparison with most of northern continental Europe, and of the origins of this in voluntarist policies favoured by the dominant nineteenth-century traditions of Political Economy and Liberalism. Britain's early consolidation as a nation-state, based on insular territorial integrity, a dominant language, and the ancient institutions of Crown, Church, and Parliament, led to a relatively weak impulse towards state formation in the early nineteenth century and the consequent absence of a major spur towards educational development (Green 1990). The early and successful industrial revolution, combined with the overwhelming strength of the City, arguably led to further complacency about the importance of promoting mass education through state action (Hobsbawn 1977). Victorian educational voluntarism cast a long shadow across twentieth-century school reform which has been evident in the continuing priority given to elite over mass education, the relatively weak institutionalization of first secondary then post-secondary schooling, and the continuing low status accorded to technical and vocational education. By the 1980s the United Kingdom, and particularly England, still had amongst the lowest rates of participation in post-compulsory education and no high-status vocation tracks (Green 1997*a*). The system lacked coherence and transparency, reform was often ad hoc and poorly planned and there was an unusually sharp divide between academic and vocational education, with vocational students typically undertaking no general education (Green 1998).

Workplace training has suffered from similar institutional inertia. Voluntarism still dominates policy which only rarely takes recourse to the interventionist strategies which have been used to institutionalize employer supply of training in the other countries in this study. Training levies (currently used extensively in—amongst other countries—Austria, Denmark, France, Ireland, Korea, the Netherlands, and Sweden) were tried following the 1964 Industrial Training Act but were progressively phased out after 1973, never to return. Employers are under no statutory compulsion to provide training for young employees in skilled occupations (as in Germany) and adult workers have no statutory right to training leave (as they do, for instance, in France and Italy). There are no obligations for firms to join Chambers of Commerce (as in for instance Austria, France, and Germany) or other organizations which may exert institutional pressure towards greater investment in training, nor are firms bound by many sectoral agreements linking jobs and pay with qualifications (as in for instance France, Germany, Italy, and the Netherlands). Licence to practise laws and regulations are relatively minimal in the United Kingdom, compared with many other countries, such as Austria and Germany, which limits the incentives of employers and individuals to invest in skills. Statutory minimum wages are set very low in the United Kingdom, meaning that they neither have the effect that the higher minima in France have in discouraging youth employment and early exit from education, nor the more radical effects of the tax on low wages in Singapore which forces employers to raise skills and pay levels or alternatively to pay into the general SDF fund for training. Actions to strengthen product and process standards are one of the few interventions to raise the workplace supply of skills, but Investors in People remains voluntary.

Slack statutory obligations and weak social partner institutions reduce employer incentives to invest in training; in fact they may provide positive disincentives as unregulated labour markets encourage 'poaching' and make employers fearful to invest in the training of employees they may later lose to rival employers (Greenhalgh 1999). The finance-driven nature of 'shareholder' capitalism may also reduce the supply of workplace training. As Hutton (1995) and others have argued, shareholder power in UK companies is such as to encourage short-termism in investment generally and particularly in training and R & D, which can be the first casualties of cost reduction policies. Employers and the UK government resisted signing up to the Maastricht 'Social Chapter' agreements on employee representation on company boards, although this applies nevertheless for MNCs which trade extensively in Europe. Works councils and supervisory boards, where employee representatives can exert pressure for increased training, are much rarer in the United Kingdom than in continental Europe (Woolcock 1996). Likewise there is no widespread tradition of the main bank system as in Germany and Japan, whereby banks provide long-term 'patient' capital to firms in exchange for an active role in company decision-making through strong board representation. Shareholder power on company boards, combined with the liberal laws on mergers and takeovers, put UK company directors under unique short-term pressures to focus on short-term quarterly financial statements which in turn may discourage long-term investment in skills (Albert 1993; Hutton 1995; Woolcock 1996).

The above presents something of a pathology of skills formation in the United Kingdom, where institutional structures and incentives in every sphere serve to reduce the supply of and demand for skills. In fact, as we shall see, the picture now is somewhat more complicated than this. On the one hand, the supply of skills, particularly at the graduate level, has increased dramatically over the last decade, although there are still substantial deficits in intermediate skills, and although there is a continuing problem of low demand for and utilization of skills in many sectors. On the other hand, productivity and competitiveness in many areas, including in important new fields such as biotechnology and multimedia, is apparently very good in the United Kingdom and may be supported in this case by just the kind of flexible and voluntarist system of skills formation which is described above as the problem (Mason and Wagner 1998a). This dualism suggests the need for a more complex theorization of skills formation and skills utilization which is more sensitive to sector specificities, than the traditional models which are very much based on experience in manufacturing.

The Skill Profile in the United Kingdom

The description of the British skill/competitiveness strategy as one based on high skills elites and skills polarization is borne out by analysis of the current stocks and flows of qualifications and by other more direct measures of skills.

At the higher education level Britain's output of qualifications has been impressive for some years. Data from labour force surveys (see Table 2.3) shows that 23 per cent of the adult population in 1998 had a degree or higher degree compared with 19.1 per cent in Germany (1997), 17.4 per cent in Singapore (1998), 17.9 per cent in Korea (1998), and 24.2 per cent in Japan (1997). The majority of graduates included in this UK population obtained their degrees when higher education enrolment was much lower than it is now. Between 1989 and 1996 the total supply of first degree graduates in the United Kingdom increased by 89 per cent (Mason 2000), and the current level of participation amongst under 21 year olds is in excess of 30 per cent.[68] Graduate qualification levels have consequently risen considerably amongst the younger adult age cohorts. Rates of participation in other countries have, of course, also risen, although more notably in East Asia than in comparator European countries like Germany. The result is that the United Kingdom has strengthened its position in relation to Germany (and probably other continental states) in terms of graduate qualifications in the workforce, but has slipped behind the very high rates in East Asia. Amongst the 25 to 29 year olds in the adult population 28 per cent now have degrees (see Table 2.7) compared with 14.9 per cent in Germany, 37.6 per cent in Singapore, 34.8 per cent in Korea, and 46.5 per cent in Japan. Increasing participation in higher education since the early 1990s does not yet fully show up in these figures, nor do the 500,000 extra places in higher education announced in 1999. It is likely that when these rises in participation are translated into higher education qualifications, the United Kingdom will still appear to be in a strong position regarding its qualification of elites.

In terms of the distribution of higher education qualifications between subjects (see Table 2.2), the United Kingdom has a lower proportion of degrees in science generally than Germany but a higher proportion than most of our comparator countries and a much higher proportion than for the OECD as a whole. Engineering degrees awarded increased between 1987 and 1997 but more slowly than for degree qualifications as a whole (Mason 1999) and form a much smaller proportion of the total than in Germany, Japan, and Singapore. Given that Britain has a smaller manufacturing base than these countries, this may not

---

[68] According to OECD figures, the UK now has the highest graduation rate in Europe (OECD 2000a).

indicate a problem with higher level engineering skills, despite the reports of some higher level skills shortages in engineering which occur at various points in the economic cycle (Mason 1999). However, there is evidence that the quantity and quality of output of short-cycle sub-degree qualifications in engineering may be inferior to competitor countries and in need of rectification given the continuing decline in entry to Higher National Certificate (HNC) and Higher National Diploma (HND) sub-degree courses engineering (Steedman et al. 2000). In fact there is a case generally that the mix of sub-degrees and degrees needs to be altered in favour of the former which can be obtained more rapidly and more economically by students, which offer better rates of return at least to less academically qualified students (see Deardon et al. 2000), and which often meet the needs of the employment market as well as vocational degrees. However, broadly speaking the output of higher education in the United Kingdom seems to compare well with comparator countries and generally to meet the demands of the high skills elites competitiveness strategy.

The problems lie more at the level of intermediate skills and with those who have no or only very low qualifications. Only 18 per cent of the adult population in the United Kingdom in 1998 had a level 3 qual-ification as their highest compared with 50.6 per cent in Germany, 40.9 per cent in Korea, and 41.8 per cent in Japan. Only Singapore, with 9.2 per cent having this as their highest qualification, had a bigger problem in this respect. Figures for the 25–29 population show that the United Kingdom still has substantial deficits in intermediate level skills, with only 17 per cent having this as their highest qualification, and with other countries showing higher proportions of young people qualified at this level than for their populations as a whole.

The output of qualifications at level 3 in the United Kingdom has of course improved substantially in recent years. The National Advisory Council on Education and Training Targets (NACETT) calculates that around 52 per cent of the relevant age cohort (taken as 19–21 year olds) in 1999 were achieving a level 3 qualification, compared with around 40 per cent in 1994. This improvement shows up in the stock figures in that in 1998 only 55 per cent of 25–29 year olds had no qualification at level 3 or above, as opposed to 59 per cent for the population as a whole. However, whilst the United Kingdom has improved its rates of qualifi-cation amongst young people during the past decade so have other comparator countries. In Germany, Japan, and Korea, less than 20 per cent of 25–29 year olds have not achieved this qualification level. The United Kingdom still has a far higher proportion of young people with low-level qualifications than other comparator countries. According to Labour Market and Skills Trends 1998/9 (DfEE 1999a), 27 per cent of young people reach 19 without a level 2 qualification and 18 per cent with no qualification at all.

Measures of qualifications clearly do not capture all of the skills in a population and Britain, which has been historically rather less credentialist in its approach to skills than its continental neighbours, has skills in the workforce that are not codified in qualifications. More direct measures of skills, however, confirm the comparative prevalence of low skilled individuals in the workforce. The International Adult Literacy Survey (IALS) (OECD/Statistics Canada 1995), for instance, tested for levels of literacy (defined as Prose Literacy, Document Literacy, and Quantitative (arithmetic) Literacy) in representative samples of adults over 16 in eight countries, with results published for Belgium (Flanders), Germany, Ireland, the Netherlands, Sweden, and Great Britain. In the British and US samples around 22 and 21 per cent, respectively had only the lowest level (i.e. one on a five-point scale) of literacy, whereas the proportion in Germany, Sweden, and the Netherlands was in each case only around half of this level (Steedman 1999a, 1999b: 23). Similar results for the United Kingdom were reported from the National Child Development Survey (NCDS) of 37-year-old panel members in 1995. On a four-point scale from very low skills to good skills, 19 per cent of the sample tested demonstrated low or very low levels of literacy. In numeracy, 19 per cent of men and 27 per cent of women tested had very low skills (Bynner and Parsons 1997).

The polarization of skills and qualifications in the high skills/low skills system in the United Kingdom is originally a function of the unequal outcomes of initial education and training. To some extent we may expect these highly differentiated levels of attainment of individuals leaving initial education to be attenuated over time through later acquisition of skills and qualifications from further learning, either in formal education or at the workplace. However, the studies which directly measure the basic skills of adults in the labour force, such as NCDS and IALS, do not give much evidence that this is the case at least as regards literacy and numeracy. Evidence on adult acquisition of qualifications in the United Kingdom is very sketchy, so it is not possible to provide any clear picture of how learning continues through the adult lifecourse. However, the evidence on the incidence of training at the workplace, inadequate also though this may be, does give some indication as to why this may not have much impact on the problem of skills polarization.

International surveys of training at the workplace are not able to provide any very reliable comparisons between countries, even in terms of the more measurable types of formal training. The most extensive international survey to date was the European Commission's 1994 Continuing Training in Enterprises Survey (CVTS) (EC 1999*a*) based on an achieved sample of 45,000 firms of ten or more employees in twelve member states. This found that 82 per cent of employers in the United Kingdom sample had offered training in the previous year as against, at the top, 87 per cent in Denmark, followed by 85 per cent in Germany, 77 per cent in Ireland, 62 per cent in France, and, at the bottom, 13 per cent in Portugal. United Kingdom employers were more likely than employers in most other countries to report giving training but in terms of hours of formal training course attendance per 1,000 hours worked, their performance was average at 8.7 as against Germany (9.9), France (11.1), Netherlands (12.1), and, at the low end, Italy (3.6). Greenhalgh's (1999) comparative analysis of this data for France and the United Kingdom suggests that whilst UK firms tend to offer more incidents of training than French firms, these are typically of rather shorter duration than in France, and amount overall to rather less in terms of quantity.

Several surveys are conducted in the United Kingdom to measure the quantity of employer provided training. They tend to show, like the CVTS, that most employers report providing some training, and also that the amount of training is increasing. The former Department of Employment's Employers' Manpower and Skills Practices Survey (EMPS), for instance, found that 90 per cent of workplaces were reported to have offered training in the previous year, but that 'most were not doing very much' (S. Dench 1993: 2). This is confirmed in evidence from the UK Labour Force Survey (LFS). Results from the Spring 1998 LFS showed that 72 per cent of the sample reported having received no training in the previous thirteen weeks and that 45 per cent of those had never been offered training by their current employer (Keep 2000). What most surveys show is that whilst reported incidents of training are quite numerous, they are often very brief (and may be mainly concerned with initial induction for many employees).

Further, what training is provided is shared very unequally between different types of employee. Generally, the evidence is that most of the training goes to those already well qualified and in more senior full-time positions. Low-level, part-time, and contract workers do particularly badly. The extent of this inequality of distribution was demonstrated in the 1988 DfEE's National Adult Learning Survey (NALS) in which 90 per cent of managerial and professional employees reported having had some structured learning within the past three years as against less than half of the manual workers in the sample (Keep 2000). The 1997 Report of the National Advisory Committee on Continuous Education and Lifelong Learning (Fryer 1997) estimated that 30 per cent of adults had no formal education or training since leaving school.

The evidence above on qualifications stocks and flows, tested skills, and workplace training provides clear evidence of substantial polarization of skills and qualifications within the United Kingdom population. The school system has long been criticized for producing a diversity of attainment outcomes with a 'long tail of underachievement' (Green and Steedman 1997). Despite Britain's deserved reputation for 'second chance' education in its colleges and universities, this is not, apparently, rectified to any significant extent by further learning after school in formal education or in the workplace. In fact, as regards workplace learning at least, it would seem that the opposite is the case. Employment based training would seem to reproduce and increase the gaps in skills and qualifications attainments between individuals and groups. This tends to confirm the analysis that the United Kingdom skills formation system is a high skills/low skills system.

Skill Shortages and Gaps

The evidence on skills shortages and gaps is notoriously tricky to interpret, first because results are very sensitive to the economic cycle and secondly because they normally rely on what employers perceive as a problem. The CBI Quarterly Industrial Trends Survey asks employers if a shortage of skilled labour is 'likely to limit your output over the next three months'. Fifteen per cent said 'yes' to this at the last peak in 1998, compared with 25 per cent at the earlier peak in 1989 (Skills Research Group 2000). The 1998 Skills Needs in Britain Survey (SNIB), based on a sample of 4,000 establishments employing 25 or more staff, found 23 per cent of employers reporting hard to fill vacancies, 19 per cent in manufacturing, and 22–25 per cent in services. The most cited hard to fill vacancies were in catering, sales and service, and health-related occupations and amongst road transport operators, engineers, and technologists (Skills Research Group 2000). SNIB found skills shortages in technical and practical areas, in computer literacy and IT, in general communications and customer handling skills, and in management skills. The most recent survey on 'The Extent, Causes, and Implications of Skills Deficiencies' (Hogarth et al. 2000) found that 15 per cent of establishments surveyed reported hard to fill vacancies in at least one occupational area with 61 per cent of these in associate professional and technical occupations, i.e. those requiring intermediate level skills.

Despite the relative consistency of these findings, however, they give only a poor guide to the true extent of skills deficiencies, since they are based on employers' perceptions of immediate or immediate future needs. They do not tell us whether the skills available are adequate from the point of view of optimum productivity in a given sector or in terms of more general societal needs. For this, more detailed sectoral analyses are needed which look not only at skills supply, but also at skills utilization and productivity. The general findings from the NIESR studies which aim to do this have already been cited. Other recent sectoral studies are also insightful and give a fuller sectoral picture of where the UK skills formation system works adequately and where it does not.

Banking and financial services is one of the more successful sectors in the United Kingdom. Business services as a whole account for 20 per cent of total GDP and employ around 17 per cent of the United Kingdom workforce (Hasluck 1999). Despite a slump in the early 1980s, the financial services sector picked up again and achieved a 64 per cent increase in gross output during 1991–6, including productivity growth. Growth has not been held back apparently by any shortages of skills. Hasluck concludes his survey by remarking that 'there is little evidence of any significant skills shortages at present in financial services, nor is there much evidence of a sector specific skills gap'. This is despite evidence from studies by Steedman (1999a) and Quack, O'Reilly, and Hildebrandt (1995) that skills levels in the sector are weaker than in Germany, France, and the Netherlands, with the United Kingdom having only 60 per cent of its workforce with level 3 or higher qualifications compared with over 80 per cent in Germany and the Netherlands (Steedman 1999a).

Apparently the UK banking and financial services sector is highly competitive despite not having particularly high levels of skills. The reason for this paradox may be simply that the kind of high skills/low skills skill set produced by the UK skills formation system is quite appropriate for this sector. As Hasluck shows, skills have become increasingly polarized within the sector. On the one hand, there has been an increasing demand for highly skilled specialist professionals, most obviously those dealing with new and highly technical financial instruments, but also more generally in customer care and specialist sales areas. On the other hand, there has been a significant deskilling at the middle and lower ends, with declining demand for the skills of the traditional branch manager, and experienced counter staff, and a large increase in routine process operators doing tele and web sales and data entry. This kind of skills polarity seems well served by the current skills formation system.

Another sector which appears to have been well served by the skills system, at least in its developmental phase, has been the new hi-tech sector. As Hendry's recent study of 'The New Technology Industries' (1999) indicates, the United Kingdom is well placed in advanced materials, biotechnology, and opto-electronics. The biotechnology industry in the United Kingdom is the second largest in the world, with an estimated 30 per cent share of the European biotechnology business which is equal to that of France and Germany combined. Opto-electronics, which involves technological development in fibre optics, lasers, and sensors, is also a major growth industry with the United Kingdom ranking fourth in the world after Japan, the United States, and Germany. Each of these areas are heavily dependent on fundamental science in which the United Kingdom excels, and they have benefited, according to Hendry, from the innovation and technology diffusion policies in the United Kingdom. However, as Hendry also points out, there are growing skills shortages in these sectors, particularly in terms of technician skills and project management skills. Liquid Crystal Display (LCD) technology was developed in the United Kingdom but was lost for commercial exploitation to Japan. There must be some danger that the same pattern may be followed in the other technologies. Britain's high skills elites system appears to have served these industries well in their developmental phases, but one wonders how it will serve them as the industries grow from their small-scale scientific development into the phase of large-scale commercial exploitation. The same may be true of e-commerce, which has flourished in the early developmental stage in the United Kingdom, helped by the abundance of young entrepreneurs with computer skills, enterprise, and access to venture capital, but now faces problems in generating sustained profitability.

Engineering is an area that has arguably already suffered from the UK high skill/low skill system. Previous NIESR comparative studies of the United Kingdom, Germany, and the Netherlands—using matched plants based on selected product areas in metal products and mechanical engineering—found that the larger proportion of production workers trained to craft level in the continental countries contributed positively to productivity performance. Continental craft workers had greater ability to reach demanding quality standards under daily pressure of small and medium batch production and to switch flexibly between different products and tasks (Daly, Hitchens, and Wagner 1985; Mason, van Ark, and Wagner 1996). In recent years the numbers employed in craft level jobs in engineering have declined while the proportion holding appropriate craft qualifications has risen (from 43 per cent in 1988 to 53 per cent in 1998) (Mason 1999). However, the 1998 survey of the Engineering and Marine Training Authority (EMTA) found that one-third of engineering employers were reporting a gap between the current skills of their workforce and what was required to meet their business objectives. Despite the enrolment of over 16,000 engineering trainees on modern apprenticeships during 1996–8, Mason argues that the sector is still experiencing structural problems in training, particularly at the level of intermediate skills (Mason 1999).

Hi-tech electronics, however, according to another comparative study of the United Kingdom and Germany by Mason and Wagner (1998a), has fared rather better. The United Kingdom has received substantial foreign investment in this area and has expanded substantially in computer assembly. Its share of OECD exports in computers in 1985 was similar to Germany's (at 10 per cent) but rose in 1994 to 11.1 per cent against a drop in Germany to 7.6 per cent. The United Kingdom has also slightly closed the gap with Germany in the share of OECD exports for telecommunications equipment, rising from 4.2 per cent in 1985 (to Germany's 8.7 per cent) to 7.1 per cent (to Germany's 10.2 per cent) (Mason and Wagner 1998a). Trends in patenting in United Kingdom electronics since the 1980s have also shown a closing gap with Germany. Mason and Wagner's study of electronics components firms in Germany and the United Kingdom (1998b) shows equal levels of employment of engineering graduates in the two countries but with Germany employing more postgraduates who have typically gained substantial practical experience. However, systems of skills transfer in the United Kingdom appeared to lead to greater innovation in products. Germany relies heavily on the intermediate research institutes (like the Fraunhofer institutes) for skills transfer, particularly to the SMEs. Mason and Wagner judge this strongly institutionalized system to be weak at supporting risky innovative areas in high technology, and not so efficient at promoting interchanges along the supply chain. The United Kingdom, on the other hand, relied heavily on job mobility and interactions with customers and suppliers to stimulate skills transfer and this appeared to be more conducive to product innovation.

The evidence above on patterns of skills utilization by sector, although inevitably selective, is nevertheless suggestive of the strengths and weakness of the United Kingdom skills formation system. The high skill/low skill mix it produces would seem conducive to competitiveness in certain areas: in particular in sectors which rely heavily on high-level skills in science and the creative arts or which benefit from labour market flexibility and loose networks (i.e. pharmaceuticals, biotechnology, Formula 1, media and entertainments, advertising); and in sectors like banking which are characterized by skills polarization. On the other hand, in manufacturing and service industries which rely heavily on intermediate skills, it would appear that the system works less well. One of the paradoxes for the United Kingdom system is that whilst aggregate skills levels may appear to be rising (Ashton, Davies, et al. 1999), and whilst there is increasing demand for the high level skills that it produces effectively, it is also the case that currently the majority of employment and output in the United Kingdom, as in other countries, is still in industries and services which depend for their competitiveness on intermediate level skills, and it is these which are in deficit. Furthermore, the increases in demands for skills are most evident at the level of associate professional and technician employment (whose share of employment rose from 7 to 11 per cent between 1981 and 1997) (DfEE 1998). The skills formation system in the United Kingdom is not particularly strong at qualifying people at this level either, at least compared with the East Asian states.

Current Contradictions in Skills Formation and the Potential Impact of Recent Reforms

Skills formation and competition strategy in the United Kingdom are subject to many of the pressure points and trade-offs (see Chapter 5) that are characteristic of advanced capitalism in the current global economy. Specifically, there are four sets of contradictions or tensions which define the boundaries of policy-making in the current United Kingdom context. These can be stated broadly as the tensions between (1) company profitability and national prosperity; (2) flexible labour markets and social partnership; (3) high-technology and intermediate-technology manufacturing and services; and (4) more generally, between economic and social priorities.

The high skills/low skills model of skills formation appears to serve some of the higher technology industries well, as evidenced by the increasing United Kingdom share of world trade in high skills sectors such as chemicals, office machinery, electrical goods, and aerospace between 1976 and 1994 (Crouch, Finegold, and Sako 1999). It also allows many firms to remain profitable on the basis of either high skills inputs or through cost competitiveness based on low wages or efficiency generated through flexible labour markets and employment contracts. This has proved in recent years to be a viable if not spectacular set of competition strategies for many sectors. However, the conditions which allow these outcomes are also conditions which block other outcomes which may be in the interests of long-term growth and social cohesion. Profitability in firms, and more generally, capital productivity, does not necessarily generate the high output per capita on which national prosperity depends. It certainly does not necessarily deliver relative income equality and social cohesion. High-technology production and services may be highly productive, but they do not employ the majority of the workforce and nor do they generate the majority of national income (Crouch, Finegold, and Sako 1999).[69] Labour market flexibility, which underpins profitability in many companies, appears from our comparative studies to be antithetical to the development of high skills diffusion which in turn can promote relative wage equality and higher productivity (see Chapter 3). Yet flexible labour markets remain central to national competition strategies. In fact, on many measures, the United Kingdom appears to be moving increasingly towards the US model of high technology and labour market flexibility (Due, Madsen, and Jensen 1991), with all the polarization of skills and incomes that this implies (Brown and Lauder 2001a) but without the US's advantages in terms of large domestic markets, economies of scale, and dollar domination (Thurow 1996).

Chapter 5 will analyse the current direction of UK skills formation policy in further detail. However, a few points should be made here which derive from the analysis above and which suggest that UK policy is still following a fairly 'path-dependent' trajectory.

First, government policy on economic development, or at least that part which comes under the Department for Trade and Industry (DTI), is largely oriented to the hi-tech sector, with far less emphasis placed on those industries which, although declining, may be a far greater source of current employment and output. The DTI White Paper (1998a), *Our Competitive Future: Building the Knowledge-Driven*

---

[69] Even in the USA, hi-tech industries employ relatively few people. The information technology 'titans' as Edward Luttwack calls them, including Intel, Novell, Oracle, Sun Micro, Amgen, Cirrus, Intuit, MBC Soft, Picturel, Apple, Microsoft, Cisco, Bat Net, Sybase, Peoplesoft, Informix, Am.Online, Autodesk, Cordis, and Adobe, between them only employed 128, 420 staff in 1995, compared with 721,000 employed by General Motors (Luttwack 1999: 79).

Economy, largely concerns itself with developments in biotechnology, e-commerce, telecommunications, and such areas. The analytical paper which supports this (DTI 1998*b*) bases its analysis firmly on the contention that the hi-tech sectors are the future, and that it is the value added from knowledge in these sectors which will determine future competitiveness. The paper quite rightly points out strengths in these areas, noting that the United Kingdom is the third largest earner of royalties and licence fees from abroad and the second largest exporter of computer and information services. It is also one of the major recipients of inward investment after China and the United States, and the only major country where foreign affiliates' share of manufacturing R & D is higher than their share of production. This last point may partly reflect the fact that manufacturing R & D spending is comparatively low and somewhat obscures the extent to which foreign direct investment is financing low skills assembly work in many areas. Nevertheless, it is a justifiable tribute to the strength of the UK's high skills science base. The main point is how to exploit this commercially more effectively, and DTI strategies include a variety of supply-side measures for promoting entrepreneurship, SMEs, and university spin-off companies.

Apart from the partnership with Wellcome Trust to modernize the British Science and Engineering base, new public investments are modest in size and act primarily as pump-priming devices. The overall policy emphasis is more on building networks and clusters and on deregulating the business environment. The analytical report calls for a 'new approach' to industrial policy which avoids 'old-fashioned state interventionism' and a 'naive reliance on markets'. The new role involves 'acting as a catalyst, investor and regulator to strengthen the supply-side of the economy' (DTI 1998*b*: 5). For the most part this entails addressing market failures through improving access to finance, removing impediments to investment in R & D, strengthening inter-firm collaborations and purchaser–supplier partnerships, and encouraging entrepreneurship and improving workforce skills. In contrast with our comparator countries, and particularly the East Asian states, this is a 'light touch' approach to industrial policy.

The third point which arises from our comparisons is that UK policy on skills formation remains highly supply-side focused. There has been a wide array of new initiatives to increase the production of skills, notably with the New Deal programmes for the young unemployed, the Modern Apprenticeship and the University for Industry. However, few measures, with the exception of the Investors in People standards, actively intervene to raise employer demands for skills. Licence to practise laws remain comparatively minimal, sectoral agreements on jobs and qualifications are limited, and the Cruikshank Commission has not recommended any major changes to company governance that might encourage more long-term approaches to investing in R & D and skills. Indeed the determination to maintain flexible labour markets may be seen as a positive disincentive for firms to adopt new product market strategies that involve transforming their work organization and human resources policy in the direction of high skills.

Lastly, despite a substantive shift away from dysfunctional competition in education and training provision (manifested in the creation of a new and powerful Learning and Skills Council to plan and fund all post-16 provision: DfEE 1999*b*), and despite a new emphasis on 'partnership', there are no plans to break with the predominantly voluntarist paradigm that has dominated UK training. Compulsions on employers (i.e. levies, employee rights to paid training leave, compulsory membership of employers' organizations, etc.) remain against government policy, and do not feature amongst the many proposals of the National Skills Task Force (1999, 2000). Partnership is encouraged through such measures as the Union Learning Fund and Lifelong Learning Partnerships, but it remains on a voluntary and largely non-statutory basis. This distinguishes it clearly from the model of social partnership still dominant in continental states which is entrenched in statutes and regulations and long-term institutional structures (Green, Wolf, and Leney 1999). Partnerships as loose and ad hoc networks may have advantages in the kind of high skills eco-systems described by Finegold (1999), where individual incentives for collaboration are high. It is less clear that they can be used to enlist and bind unwilling partners to the provision of collective goods, where their interests do not motivate them in that direction.

Despite the plethora of new initiatives in skills supply, therefore, it would seem that the institutional infrastructure and regulatory framework for increasing the demand for high skills in the United Kingdom is still relatively weak. It might be said that this does not matter so long as the individual incentives are in place. Certainly the government can point to the rapid increase in higher education participation—facilitated by supply-side reform but mainly driven by market demand—as evidence that a market-led partnership approach can work. Indeed the proposals of the National Skills Task Force, like those in the Government White Paper *The Learning Age* (DfEE 1998), are largely premised on the notion that with adequate information, available loans, and accessible and appropriate provision, individuals and employers will make rational choices to invest in more education and training.

However, the evidence that 'rational choice' works in skills formation is not overwhelming. Certainly, it has not been the underlying premiss in the comparator countries in this study, where institutional structures, regulatory frameworks, and normative regimes all play a major part in incentivizing investment. Even in the United Kingdom, there are plentiful examples where initiatives based on rational choice assumptions combined with small incentives have not been as successful as hoped. Career Development Loans, for instance, have had low take-up and only 0.03 per cent of eligible firms have taken out Small Enterprise Training Loans. Full evaluation of the Individual Learning Account pilots has yet to be undertaken, but it seems unlikely that their take-up will meet expectations. The £150 deposit from public funds may not prove sufficient incentive to many individuals for them to invest more in training and many employers may not wish to match the investment for non-specific training (Keep 2000). Significantly, it may be that the scheme succeeds fully only where trade union–management agreements are involved, that is to say where there is an institutionalized social partnership underpinning individual decisions.

Even where a supply-side approach may raise participation in life-long learning, it may not be mostly amongst those who most need it or who have been most excluded hitherto. In fact the evidence of the past ten years is that increases in participation often fail to reach those most excluded and more often reproduce rather than redress inequalities of skills attainment. Furthermore, where participation in skills acquisition does increase, it may not be in areas in most demand in the labour market; nor will these increased skills necessarily be utilized by employers. Government proposals for new foundation vocational sub-degree courses will in this sense be an interesting test case. Labour market analysis suggests that this is a level at which skills shortages exist. But will individuals sign up and will employers then make use of them when they graduate (Mason 2000)? On past experience, 'rational' or other choice has led declining numbers into sub-degree courses, whilst enrolment has increased in vocational degree courses, particularly for qualifications such as media studies and journalism for which employers show little interest.

Britain's flexible skills formation system clearly continues to offer significant promise in key respects. It is good at furnishing creative talents and proves more responsive than many systems to the immediate demands of employers. However, expectations that it will lead to high skills diffusion seem based more on hope than evidence or past experience. This may be the system best matched overall to current competitiveness strategies, but it may be those strategies which are most in need of reform.

SKILL FORMATION SYSTEMS AND THE GLOBAL ECONOMY

The analysis presented above clearly shows that there are markedly different dominant competitiveness strategies in our comparator countries, each one served by different systems of skill formation. There are also variations within countries, according to sector, in the dominant strategies and these are served more or less well by the dominant national skills formation system, sometimes with sector-specific compensation mechanisms. Broadly speaking, we have identified four singular national paths to a high skills economy which are characterized by distinctive and complex articulations of competition strategies and skills formation systems.

The first model, characterized by Germany, comes closest to our definition of a 'high skills society'. The German economy bases national competitiveness primarily on high productivity manufacturing in a range of quality goods sectors relying predominantly on scientific elites and on high-quality intermediate skills. The skills system that serves this generates wide skills distribution and high levels of social trust, and promotes high average incomes and wage equality.

The second model—the 'high skills manufacturing model'—exemplified by Japan, is in some ways a variation of the first, although it has different historical origins, owing more to the shaping influence of the developmental state than to European-style social partnership regulation. Like the German model, it bases national competitiveness primarily on efficient quality production in manufacturing sectors, relying predominantly on intermediate skills, but in this case with markedly poor competitiveness in both service and some small firm sectors, and with a mediocre record in pure science which has impeded rapid advance in high-technology sectors such as biotechnology (Castells 1998). Japanese skills formation has been built around high levels of general education widely distributed throughout the population. This has been achieved through a highly controlled and standardized school system, which successfully cultivates the attitudes of cooperation, group solidarity, and teamwork necessary for the distinctive management systems that have powered manufacturing efficiency in large firms. Like Germany, Japan also relies heavily on the training provided by employers, although in this case less through apprentice-style occupational training than through the continuous training which large firms can deliver on the basis of highly structured internal labour markets (Ashton and Green 1996; see Chapter 3). The Japanese system, like the German system, has been instrumental in generating wide skills diffusion, high levels of trust and labour cooperation, and relative wage equality (although with marked horizontal differences between large and small firm sectors and between men and women: see Chapter 3).

The third model—the 'developmental high skills model'—exemplified by Singapore is arguably not yet a high skills model at all, although it is moving rapidly in that direction. Here human capital is becoming increasingly important, but growth and competitiveness have relied more to date on other factors such as wage competitiveness, infrastructure, and maximization of geo-political advantages by a strongly developmental state (Castells 1998). Insofar as domestically generated skills have played a major role in Singaporean competitiveness, it has been through the creation of a highly competent elite of bureaucrats and engineers, rather than the creative, scientific, and entrepreneurial elites who have played the leading role in Germany, the United Kingdom and the United States. In addition to this, Singaporean education and initial training has improved itself rapidly to the point where it is now turning out new cohorts onto the labour market where the vast majority have acquired good basic skills and social competences, and solid technician level vocational training. Singapore is also heavily reliant on the import of specialist skills.

The fourth model—the 'high skills/low skills model'—exemplified by the United Kingdom (and the United States) bases competitiveness on high levels of innovation and productivity in some hi-tech and innovation-led manufacturing and service sectors as well as on flexible labour markets and capital productivity. The skills formation system which articulates with this generates a polarized combination of low skills and high skills elites, typically mirrored by high levels of income inequality.

In each of these cases there is a striking (though not surprising) symmetry between national skills profiles (and the outputs of the skills formation systems which generate them), dominant competition strategies (and the skills demands they generate), and patterns of sectoral competitiveness (analysed in terms of contributions played by skills to competitiveness). Put simply, and focusing on the primary contrast in skills regimes, the distinction is between countries which have highly polarized skills profiles (the United Kingdom and the United States) and competition strategies requiring—or capable of accommodating— bi-polar skills sets, and countries with wide skills distribution (Germany and Japan) whose competition strategies leverage on the advantages that these create. Taking two exemplary cases the pattern has been as follows.

The United Kingdom skills formation system generates a bi-polar profile of skills with large numbers qualified at high levels, large numbers with only low-level skills and few or no qualifications, and a small proportion of the labour force with intermediate level skills and qualifications. This distribution of skills more or less matches the imme- diate needs of the different sectors according to their dominant competition strategies. The abundant skilled elites with their scientific, creative, and entrepreneurial talents meet the primary demands of the high skills and knowledge-based industries like pharmaceuticals, advertising, and the media and support their high value added, innovation-based competition strategies. Sectors like financial services that utilize both skilled elites and massed ranks of low skill workers are also apparently passably served by the polarized skills profiles of the labour force, at least for the moment. At the other end of the scale in terms of competition strategies are those industries which compete to a large extent on price and flexibility, benefiting from low levels of labour market regulation and an abundance of relatively cheap, flexible labour. A skills formation system which produces a large number of less qualified people with little labour market bargaining power serves these industries according to their chosen competition strategies.

The German skills formation system, on the other hand, has a far flatter distribution of skills and qualifications, turning out new cohorts of labour market entrants where the overwhelming majority are quali- fied at intermediate levels, but with an adequate concentration of skilled elites. German national economic competitiveness depends to a large extent on its high-quality, medium-tech, manufacturing industries and these rely for their competitiveness on the specialized professional competencies of the elites and on the pervasiveness of intermediate skills in the workforce. A widespread ethic of professional competence, encouraged by the careful cultivation of *beruf* identity through the Dual System, also makes an important contribution to high trust, high- performance, multi-skilled workplaces.

Recent evidence on the relative trading success of different high, medium, and low skills sectors in the different countries demonstrates how these skills/competition strategies translate into national competitiveness on the world markets. Crouch, Finegold, and Sako, in their recent study (1999), analyse the changes in export shares of a range of countries' high, medium, and low skilled sectors. High skilled sectors are taken to include: petrol, gas, chemicals, dyes, paints, pharmaceutical, and office equipment; intermediate sectors to include: engines, machine tools, metal machine tools, and non-electric machines; and low skilled sectors to include: meat, rubber, leather goods, rubber goods, and textiles.[70] Figures for 1994 show Germany and Japan to have much larger shares of world trade in intermediate sector products by comparison with their shares for high and low skills sector products. The United Kingdom has a low share for intermediate skills sector products compared with its share for high and low sector products. The rough ratios from high to medium to low sectors are 10:26:5 for Germany; 12:16:3 for Japan; and 8:6:2 for the United Kingdom. The bell-shaped pattern of the relative shares for Japan and Germany matches the similarly shaped distribution of qualifications levels of the workforce, where intermediate skills predominate. Likewise the sharp declining line of the United Kingdom ratios reflects a skills distribution where intermediate qualifications are poorly represented and high qualifications well represented.

On various criteria each of our countries (including Singapore) have claims to be highly competitive economies. In terms of per capita income Germany, Japan, and the United States have been in the top

Table 2.9. Country sector exports as a percentage of total world exports in 1994

Country	High skills sectors	Intermediate skills sectors	Low skills sectors
Germany	1.067	2.608	0.524
Japan	1.253	1.698	0.306
UK	0.886	0.646	0.238
USA	1.679	1.699	0.479

Source: Adapted from Crouch, Finegold, and Sako 1999: 103–5.

[70] The classification of industries into high, medium, and low tech categories is, of course, a very approximate business and the classifications used in this case could no doubt be challenged on a number of fronts. For our purposes here the results are suggestive, but we would not wish to place too much weight on them.

rank for decades and have now been joined by Singapore. In terms of growth Germany, Japan, and Singapore all performed well up to 1990, although Germany and Japan not since. The United States has been a moderate growth country until the last decade but now has faster growth than many other large advanced countries. The United Kingdom has been neither high growth nor high income relative to these countries for most of the last thirty years but has been catching up in the last decade. All of these countries, except perhaps Singapore, could claim—in different ways—to be high skills economies.

However, only Germany (and to a lesser extent Japan) meet the more exacting social and economic criteria of the 'high skills society'—that is to say only these countries both base aggregate competitiveness primarily on high skills and achieve relative skills and income equality through a policy of wide skills distribution. Germany has used its skills formation system to transform most jobs into skilled jobs; Japan has done the same in the large firm manufacturing sector, although not in other sectors of the economy (where the majority of women employees work under poorer conditions: see Chapter 3).

Until quite recently, advocates of the high skills society could claim with some confidence that the form of high skills formation found in Germany and Japan—variously known as the 'Rhine model' or 'associational' capitalism in Germany and 'relational' or corporate capitalism in Japan, achieved markedly better social outcomes than the Anglo-Saxon model of 'stockholder' capitalism. Japan and Germany both had comparatively good records on employment until relatively recently and still retain amongst the lowest levels of income inequality in the developed world. However, post-1993 recession in Japan and post-unification slow growth in Germany have increased unemployment markedly in both countries, calling into question the former claims to being socially inclusive societies. Neither were ever quite so in fact, given that in Japan women were largely excluded from the high skill high wage jobs, and given the marginalization of immigrant workers in Germany (see Chapter 3). But they were certainly more so than the Anglo-Saxon countries. Now, with rising unemployment in both countries, there is a growing group of adults who are excluded from the high wage, high skills economy.

Claims typically made that deregulationist economies like the United Kingdom and United States are better at job creation and limiting unemployment need to be heavily qualified, however. The United States has indeed created more jobs per adult of working age during the Clinton years than most other advanced countries, and the United

Kingdom also has a good record (Thurow 1996). However, despite higher rates of employment growth in high skilled jobs, the absolute majority of new jobs in the United States have been in low-paid service sector occupations. The unemployment rate advantage in the United States is largely wiped out if one includes the 1.8 million behind bars as part of the unemployed (Luttwak 1999). In fact in 1990, the United States had a lower proportion of 15–80 year olds in full-time employment than Austria, Denmark, Finland, Italy, Greece, Japan, Portugal, and Sweden, amongst other countries (Crouch, Finegold, and Sako 1999).

The social achievement of the Anglo-Saxon model in the past ten years has been its ability to reduce unemployment levels, albeit largely through the creation of large numbers of low-paid and insecure jobs in the service sector and with rapidly increasing inequalities of income (Thurow 1996). The social achievements of the high skills society model in Germany (and other northern continental European countries such as Denmark) have been on a much broader range of fronts.

Germany has been relatively successful in creating well-paid skilled jobs in the manufacturing sector, and has maintained relative income equality across the employed population. Living standards, especially in the west, have been considerably higher than in the United Kingdom and much more equal than in both the United Kingdom and the United States, with average incomes for the employed some 30 per cent higher than in the United Kingdom and costs of living considerably lower. For those not in paid work, living standards have been maintained at relatively high levels through generous social benefits, with pensions worth almost double their value in the United Kingdom and initial redundancy pay at almost full-wage levels (Streeck 1997).

Germany (like Denmark and until recently Sweden) has an expansive welfare state, whose social outcomes would appear beneficial on most indicators of social health. Rates of crime, suicide, incarceration, and divorce are far lower in Germany (and particularly Japan) than in the Anglo-Saxon countries (Perkin 1996; Thurow 1996), and Germany ranks highly on the measures of social capital and trust that are typically used in the comparative surveys, such as the World Values Survey. High levels of social capital in communities and society generally are thought to have numerous potential benefits in terms of effective public administration (Putnam 1993) and civic participation (Foley and Edwards 1999). There is also evidence that they are beneficial to economic growth (Knack 2000; Knack and Keefer 1997). Recent cross-national analysis of data on welfare states and economic competitiveness by Gough (1999) shows mixed results as to whether welfare spending associates positively with competitiveness across a range of states. However, there are strong positive correlations between the *outcomes* of welfare spending and economic competitiveness.

The main conclusions of the analysis presented here, therefore, are threefold. First, that there are different routes to national economic competitiveness which make quite different demands on skills, even amongst those countries in which high-level skills may be seen to play an important role in competitiveness strategies. Secondly, that in terms of their social outcomes there are few countries (and in our sample only Germany and to a degree Japan) where high levels of skills diffusion have led to what might be called a 'high skills society', i.e. where skills play a key role in both economic competitiveness and social cohesion. Lastly, each of the high skills models dominant in the different countries are currently under severe strain due to the pressures of the global economy. The remainder of this chapter looks at the likely future prospects of the competition strategies and skills formation systems in four of the comparator states: Germany, Japan, Singapore, and the United Kingdom. One question asked is how far these systems are likely to converge under the common pressures of globalization.

Germany—The High Skills Society at Risk

The German high skills model has come under increasing pressure during the past ten years, raising questions within Germany about how far the society can sustain its generous welfare system and high social costs (Albert 1993; Castells 1998; Streeck 1997). The immediate pressures have come from the process of unification. This has incurred the German state and taxpayers enormous costs. It also raises the fundamental question as to how far the west German high skills system can be transferred into the new eastern *Länder* where productivity is substantially lower and where businesses are generally less competitive. Even were skills and productivity levels in the east raised to west German levels, the fundamental question raised by Streeck remains: how far can the world market absorb the increased output of German high value goods upon which generalization of the model across Germany would rest? Global competition has increased competitive pressures in high-priced markets and there is considerable doubt as to whether an enlarged German high skills society could remain at the leading edge in a sufficiently wide range of quality trade goods sectors to sustain the model (Streeck 1997).

The most obvious signs that the German model cannot sustain itself in its current form lie in the increasing tendency of the German MNCs to abandon the traditionally national economy in favour of a fuller, and more purely profit-driven, integration into the global economy. Increasingly German firms are siting substantial proportions of their operation abroad or acceding to merger deals with foreign MNCs—both of which result in a haemorrhaging of skilled jobs from Germany (Martin and Schumann 1997). Global pressures on profits, the need for increased foreign capitalization, and the opening up of eastern European labour markets for profitable investment have all fuelled this tendency.

Martin and Schumann calculated that in 1996 a Volkswagen worker in Nuremberg costs some thirty times more than his/her counterpart in Lithuania and similar labour cost advantages now apply in a host of countries which might be suitable for German MNC investment. The consequence of this is that many of the major German manufacturing firms are now basing most of their production abroad. Siemens, Volkswagen, and Daimler-Benz (even before its merger with Chrysler) had a majority of their employees abroad. Only one-third of IG Farben staff work in Germany (Martin and Schumann 1997). It is not only foreign-basing which is causing job losses in Germany. The increased productivity of German operations threatens the loss of domestic jobs where commensurate trade increases do not follow. Altogether between 1991 and 1995 more than 300,000 jobs were lost from the German auto sector with annual output remaining the same (Martin and Schumann 1997).

The most visible threat arising from this increased internationalization of German firms is rising unemployment at home. Increased productivity with static market share in key manufacturing industries, combined with increases in foreign-basing of operations, inevitably leads to job losses in manufacturing which are not easily balanced by job creation in the service industries. Germany's tradition of high wages and labour protection makes it difficult to reduce the resulting unemployment through the creation of low-paid and flexible jobs in the service sector as the United Kingdom and the United States have done (Crouch, Finegold, and Sako 1999).

Large German companies are beginning to adapt to global pressures by adopting the profit-maximizing strategies of their US rivals. Evidence that this trend is beginning to affect a range of traditional practices is provided in a detailed recent study of institutional change in the German economy by Ronald Dore (2000).

Mergers, acquisitions, foreign capitalization, and foreign-basing are part of the macro picture of corporate change in the increasingly globalized German economy. Where once both outward and inward investment in the German national economy were quite low by the standards of advanced economies, now this is beginning to change. According to Dore (2000), inward investment rose only modestly between 1990 and 1997 from $111 billion per annum to $138 billion, but the rash of recent corporate mergers since suggest that this is now increasing fast. Meanwhile, the stock of German investment abroad grew from $152 billion to $326 billion (Dore 2000: 196). Increasingly, the large companies are reducing their reliance on German banks and raising more investment from abroad. More and more German companies in general are now quoted on the stock exchanges, and individual Germans are investing more in equity (Dore 2000).

The gradual shift towards a 'shareholder' model of the firm is also evident in the erosion of certain institutional practices which have been key to the German model of co-determination. The IAD research institute found that coverage by collective agreements fell between 1995 and 1997 in west Germany from 53 per cent to 49 per cent of firms and in east Germany in 1997 only 26 per cent of firms were covered (quoted in Dore 2000). Even where agreements are in place, they are increasingly sidelined by local arrangements. One recent survey found that local deals were undercutting national deals in 11 per cent of cases in west Germany and in 30 per cent of cases in east Germany (see Dore 2000). As Martin and Schumann put it: 'The old concept of Deutchland LTD is . . . breaking down, and a new quite different corporate culture is taking over. In many big German companies, "shareholder value" is now the magic formula of the hour—which, in the end, simply means the old idea of profit maximization to the benefit of the shareholders' (1997: 128).

The erosion of the traditional model of co-determination and national capital in Germany, along with the increasing international-ization of firms, inevitably puts the German high skills model under pressure. As profit and shareholder value increasingly dominate cor-porate culture, so the long-termist and corporatist/stakeholder values which underpin high skills investment are weakened. Pressures to raise efficiency through the adoption of 'lean production' methods also chal-lenge the high skills system with its model of banking skills surpluses (Streeck 1997). There are, of course, strong forces which are resisting corporate pressure to erode skills and wages, but with a weakening system of co-determination it is far from clear that such changes can be resisted in some sectors at least.

The effects of all these changes on the competition and skills formation systems may not be dramatic or sudden, but they are likely to be felt over the coming years. There is evidence of a drift away from the Dual System of apprentice training on the part of some larger companies (although we also found evidence of strong support for the Dual System, see Chapter 3). A number of large firms are increasingly employing graduates and developing internal, customized systems of lifelong training, rather than the front-loaded and occupationally-based forms of generic skills training represented by the apprenticeship system. Firms complain that the latter is too expensive and that the standards of apprentices are dropping. Firm-specific training may increasingly be seen as preferable in a global economy where large firms are in head to head competition and where workforce-specific skills may form an embedded part of the exclusive technological advantage of a particular firm (Crouch, Finegold, and Sako 1999). The secular decline of apprenticeship systems across Europe (excepting in the case of the Dutch and Danish hybrid apprenticeship systems) tends to support the argument that there is a widespread shift towards the internal labour market, firm-based model of training (Green, Wolf, and Leney 1999). In Germany, young people for their part are increasingly opting for higher education, with some of them also doing apprentice training as a hedge to improve their labour market security.

With pressures from German employers for the creation of more lower paid and lower skilled jobs at the periphery, the likely prospect would seem to be that Germany's hitherto flat skills distribution will begin to polarize. There are rapid increases of graduates at one end. At the other, more people are excluded from the high skills labour market, either because they have failed to gain an apprenticeship or because the apprenticeship they have gained is in one of the low status occupations where training, skills, and pay are eroding.

Given the long time lags involved in changing the skill stock profile of a workforce, it would be decades before Germany reached the bi-polar profile of skills of the United States and the United Kingdom. However, without major and concerted resistance from unions and other constituencies in Germany, each new cohort of entrants to the labour market may come to resemble this pattern of skills distribution more as time goes on.

The German 'high skills society' model is certainly not terminally sick and there seems little prospect of a rapid convergence with the polarized shareholder model of the United Kingdom and the United States. However, major adjustments are undoubtedly underway which may well erode the distinctiveness of the system.

Continuity and Change in Japan

Japan, still in prolonged recession, faces even greater challenges than Germany. Japanese manufacturing, though still strong in parts, is being squeezed by global competition from countries with lower costs and which vie with Japan on efficiency, as comparative advantages accruing to Japan from its legendary management systems seem to be diminishing. At the same time the economy suffers from marked inefficiencies and low productivity in its small firm and service sectors—the latter is particularly problematic as service sector employment inevitably grows—and from sluggish advance in leading edge sectors such as biotechnology. Japan maintains an impressive output of engineers, but is failing to produce the creative talents in key areas of science and ICT, and this is retarding science-led innovation in the growth industries. The prolonged crisis has led to widespread talk amongst policy-makers and business leaders about abandoning the Japanese economic model which served growth so well for thirty years but which now appears to be failing the 'knowledge-based economy'. The rhetoric of change is widespread, with powerful demands for the dismantling of characteristic industrial policy measures, for large doses of privatization and deregulation, and for a general shift towards the market-based, shareholder model of the Anglo-Saxon economies (Dore 2000). How far these changes will go, and how far the distinctive Japanese model of skills and competitiveness will erode, is open to debate.

At one level it seems clear that the Japanese developmental model has run its historical course. The very success of Japanese development has so globalized the major firms and so exposed the economy to international finance markets, that there is now less scope for the state 'administrative guidance' which, to Chalmers Johnson (1982) and Castells (1998), played such an instrumental role in the years of rapid growth. Full integration into the global economy has made it increasingly difficult for the bureaucracy to control financial flows, trade, and therefore industrial policy. Financial globalization has deprived the Ministry of Finance of much of its power to determine interest rates, while MITI is increasingly sidelined through the sheer global power of the MNCs. Many sectors have been substantially deregulated in recent years (including petrol retailing, domestic airlines, and telecoms), and the bureaucracy has less control than in times past over investment planning. Not only has the developmental state less leverage than hitherto: it may also involve a degree of rigidity and standardization that, as Castells (1998) argues, is incompatible with advanced knowledge productive in an 'information age' and out of touch with the social demands of a maturing democracy. It is not necessary to agree with Castells that the developmental state per se is finished—it still thrives in Malaysia, Singapore, and China, in a different form. However, in Japan, it may well have served its historical purpose. As Castells writes: in contemporary Japan there is an 'incompatibility between the developmental state—the actor of Japanese development and the guarantor of Japanese identity—and the information society that this state decisively helped bring to life' (1998: 241).

However, this by no means indicates that Japan is adopting an Anglo-Saxon model of shareholder capitalism or that its economy will increasingly converge with American norms. Institutional structures in the labour market and in corporate organization, and by extension in the skills formation system, remain distinctive and changes to them have been modest.

Dore's analysis of institutional change in key areas of Japanese exceptionalism show clearly how limited have been the changes so far in the institutional base of the economy. The main targets for reform to date have been to the systems of cross-shareholding, 'relational trading', and lifetime employment, all held by advocates of shareholder capitalism to be serious barriers to efficiency. However, despite changes on the margins, these practices seem quite strongly in place across large sectors of the economy.

Cross-shareholding between member firms within *Keiretsu* has been supported in Japan as a means to protect firms from cyclical crises and hostile takeovers, and as a way to encourage cooperation and diffusion of good practice between firms. Some firms are now beginning to depart from this as part of the drive to weed out inefficiency and to promote greater shareholder power and there has been a significant decline in the volume of shares owned in this way—from 21 per cent of all shares in 1987/92 to 16 per cent in 1999. However, much of this divesting of cross-held shares may be a cyclical phenomena resulting from recessionary conditions which are forcing firms to raise cash. Japanese managers have apparently not defected en masse from their former belief in the system. According to a recent survey of 100 firms (quoted in Dore 2000), only one respondent thought that the demerits of the system outweighed the benefits. Some of the largest *Keiretsu*, including Mitsubishi, Sumitomo, and Mitsui, actually hold more cross-shares than formerly, and still 95 per cent of firms sampled do hold them (Dore 2000). So whilst it may be that governments and firms are anxious to convince investors (and particularly foreign investors) that cross-shareholders will have less influence and traditional shareholders more influence on corporate policy, group solidarity inside the *Keiretsu* still prevails.

Lifetime employment and seniority wages have also been the target for reform by governments and some business leaders. New legislation in 1998 allowed more scope for short-term contracts within professional and semi-professional occupations and there has been a growing tendency for younger corporate employees to change jobs during the early years of their careers. Whilst seniority pay systems used to dominate in large firms for the first ten years of employment, some firms have now reduced the norm to five years. Some firms are also reducing the 'core' of workers who are deemed to be covered by lifetime employment practices. However, Dore's surveys do not suggest that practices have changed that radically in either case. Personnel managers generally favour retaining existing levels of pay differentials and do not want revolutionary change in payment systems (although many of the younger employees might). The trend figures on job tenure do not show any radical change. The percentage of the workforce classified as temporary was 10.6 in 1990 and 11 per cent in 1996. Voluntary quit rates were lower at 13 per cent in 1993 than in 1975, although they have increased somewhat since. Despite stories of ruthless downsizing in a few high-profile cases, a 1998 survey of firms by the Ministry of Labour found that only 3 per cent of them were contemplating dismissals (Dore 2000).

Another pillar of the Japanese system has been the so-called 'relational trading' between companies whereby firms and their subsidiaries and suppliers maintain a high level of cooperation and trust in order to maximize skills and technology transfer and to maintain quality. Again, Dore finds 'no evidence of substantial change in sub-contracting patterns' (Dore 2000: 140). A 1998 study of Toyota, Honda, and Nissan showed strengthening commitment to long-term relations with core supplier firms but weakening commitment to peripheral ones (Dore 2000).

Japanese skills formation policy is undoubtedly changing. This is partly on account of economic pressures from business leaders to generate more creative talents and specialist skills to keep Japan up with the leaders of the 'knowledge economy'. However, equally, and perhaps more, the changes to the education system are coming from social pressures and from the demands of the population at large. Parents have been concerned for years about over-competition and consequent bullying and stress amongst schoolchildren and this is encouraging policy-makers to reform the school system. Japanese society is also becoming more stratified and more individualistic in its expectations which is eroding the former commitments to standardized and egalitarian school structures and processes. Taken together these forces are encouraging policies to 'liberalize' and diversify the school system (Green 2000a). These will no doubt have the effect of creating greater differentiation in outcomes amongst school students leading to some increases in skills polarization.

However, it seems unlikely that Japan will move towards the kind of bi-polar high skills model seen in the Anglo-Saxon countries. One reason for asserting this is that the societal commitment to achieving universally high levels of general education and basic skills remains strong, which makes unlikely a reversion towards the kind of United Kingdom system which produces a long tail of underachieving and unqualified school leavers. This is in part a cultural issue. Societies with strongly embedded beliefs in the value of education do not easily shed these beliefs, even where economic realities might work against them for some sectors of the population.

There is also another sense in which Japanese skills formation is likely to remain distinctive. Its emphasis on moral and social education has long marked it out and this has been sustained in different ways through many different political and economic climates. Despite, and perhaps in reaction to, policies to liberalize and diversify schooling, the government retains a strong—and perhaps recently reinforced—commitment to the development of national values (albeit alongside the somewhat instrumental preference for internationalizing the curriculum). The ways in which national and international perspectives are reconciled in education in the future will no doubt change. What may well persist, however, despite global pressures, is the strong commitment to education for social as well as economic purposes.

Japan is certainly changing significantly. The classic 'Johnsonian' era of the 'developmental state' has probably run its course, and with it the developmental skills formation system (Ashton, Green, et al. 1999). What is now emerging is a new hybrid model. More competition-driven structures of schooling co-exist with distinctive relational labour market structures and skills transfer systems and still powerful government controls over the process of values socialization. As Castells acknowledges, Monbusho doggedly retains its fundamental mission in terms of 'the preservation of Japanese identity, the transmission of traditional values, and the reproduction of meritocratic stratification' (Castells

1998: 245). Convergence with the dominant Anglo-Saxon models of economic competition and skills formation thus seems even less likely here than in Germany. However, much will depend on whether Japan retains its position in medium-high technology production, since that is the core around which skills formation policy has been shaped.

The Puzzling Survival of Developmentalism in Singapore

Singapore remains in many ways unique, not least in its size and forms of government (Castells 1998). Compared with Japan, it is still a very young country and has neither fully passed through its early phase of nation-building nor relinquished its embattled survival mentality. In fact, in most respects, it is still a vigorous and successful developmental state. Its competition strategies and skills formation system are still consonant with the developmental state model and, despite strains and tensions, still seem to work.

The stresses and tensions have already been discussed and two in particular highlighted. Singapore's continued march towards a high skills, high wage economy requires a quantum leap in the domestic output of creative and entrepreneurial skills, as well as the continuing import of foreign talent. Policies to achieve this are being implemented rapidly, but they face some major contradictions. Measures to generate more individual creativity and entrepreneurialism are likely to challenge the conformity-enhancing aspects of schooling. Yet these have played a vital role in developing the social discipline and order which has been crucial to Singapore's economic success. At the same time, the continuing import of foreign elites, combined with the growing international mobility of new globalized Singaporean elites, undermines the characteristic national loyalty of key sections of society which has been another important condition of growth in the developmental state. The trade-offs involved in high skills competition strategies thus involve considerable dangers for a society that cannot yet afford to lose the competitive advantages that accrued through high levels of social order and discipline.

In the longer term, there are also major political contradictions between democratization and state developmentalism. Planning and concerted policy implementation have proved to be relatively effective in a highly managed society. However, increasing demands for individual choice and democratic participation will, over time, make centralized management of these processes much more difficult. There are already signs that middle sectors of Singaporean society are increasingly impatient with their paternalistic system (Ooi et al. 1998). With social inequalities likely to increase over time, this may well extend to larger sections of the population.

How long Singapore maintains its current system will probably depend, to a large extent, on the durability of current growth rates. Economic pragmatism has encouraged potentially restive groups to acquiesce in the current system, and they may continue to do so for some time so long as Singapore continues its spectacular rise and so long as most are seen to benefit. In the immediate future, therefore, the developmental model of skills formation may well survive, albeit with increasing stresses and strains. In the longer term Singapore will no doubt have to face the implications of the waning of its developmental phase, just as Japan is having to do now. But by that time the regional strength of 'Chinese capitalism' may offer quite different dominant models of skills formation and quite different opportunities for convergence.

The United Kingdom and the Hollowing Out of the Economy and Skills

The United Kingdom is subject to the same global pressures as Germany, Japan, and Singapore but has responded in quite distinctive ways. It now faces a somewhat different set of problems from those countries. Whilst Germany, Japan, and Singapore have maintained the strong manufacturing sectors based on intermediate skills—which continue to provide the social ballast of numerous skilled craft jobs— the United Kingdom has allowed its traditional manufacturing base to decline in many sectors. This has created a distinctive hollowing out of the economy, and a substantial erosion of craft level skilled employment.

Insofar as traditional manufacturing is replaced by new areas of hi-tech manufacturing and high value services this need not be a problem. Britain has grown faster than the other countries in hi-tech and high skill manufacturing (as Crouch, Finegold, and Sako's 1999 analysis of trends in world trade clearly shows). It also has a world competitive position in advanced services such as advertising, media and financial services, and the pioneer e-industries. This provides great comfort to supporters of the so-called 'weightless economy' vision of the future. However, 'living on thin air', as Leadbeater has dubbed the condition of the 'new economy' (Leadbeater 1999), is only an attractive proposition to those who are actually included in this economy. The majority, of course, will not be.

The major problem for the 'hi-tech' version of the high skills economy is that there are rather few high skills jobs in the hi-tech sectors. This is most obviously true in the heartlands of the new hi-tech industries, including biotechnology and software production, where even in the United States—which leads the world—few people are employed. Microsoft's output may rival that of some medium-sized states, but in 1995 it only employed 15,500 people. Indeed, as noted above, the whole of the IT industry in the United States, according to Edward Luttwak's estimates, only employed 128,420 staff in 1995, compared with 721,000 employed by General Motors (Luttwack 1999: 79).

This is also true more generally of the so-called knowledge-based industries. Banking and financial services, like medical care services, certainly employ large numbers of highly skilled and highly paid professionals. But they also rely on rather larger armies of generally low-paid staff who may be very skilled but whose skills are not fully rewarded in the knowledge-based economy. Where large-scale job creation does occur in the new hi-tech manufacturing industries, it is likely to be through the mass production of products which are currently only being developed by the knowledge professionals. These may involve high precision skilled work, as in the production of computer chips, but it is not work that will necessarily be reserved for the countries which have developed the technology. Britain may have provided the science that created Liquid Crystal Display technology, but it is not the major producer of the flat screens which arise from it.

The dilemma facing the proponents of the 'hi-tech' or 'knowledge economy' route in Britain is not thus primarily how to develop the high skilled elites—this is already quite successfully accomplished. The dilemma is how to employ the remainder who are not knowledge professionals and for whom there are fewer opportunities for high skilled and highly paid work. No country has achieved a majority of employment in the knowledge jobs of Reich's symbolic analysts. Countries which allow a substantial hollowing out of their manufacturing may find it particularly difficult to sustain even majoritarian high skills employment and may be headed for the 20:80 society predicted by Martin and Schumann (1997) for the globalized advanced states.

The British 'knowledge-driven economy' version of high skills economy also faces particularly acutely the problems of social exclusion which accompany uneven distributions of skills and opportunities. These arise in part from the polarization of incomes and work quality that are the inevitable concomitant of the other face of the dominant competition strategy—competitiveness through flexible labour markets. For all the emphasis of current New Labour policies on reducing social exclusion through enhancing skills and employability, there are few signs to date that this is reducing social exclusion in a society of polarized jobs and incomes. Active employment policies may be successful in increasing the circulation of marginalized groups. Certainly, there is some evidence that long-term unemployment can be alleviated in this way (Crouch, Finegold, and Sako 1999). However, the basic divisions between the work poor and the work rich are not changed fundamentally.

United Kingdom education and training policies have concentrated on raising the aggregate level of skills and qualifications and to a degree they have been successful in this, although other countries have been raising theirs with equal vigour. What has changed very little is the uneven distribution of skills and qualifications. In fact arguably, the traditional bi-polar pattern of skills production has been exacerbated by recent policies. Policies to expand higher education have successfully increased graduation rates. On the other hand, policies to address the problem of the under-qualified—that is the marginalized fifth who leave school without useful qualifications and the seven million adults who have problems with literacy and numeracy (Moser 1999)—have so far largely failed. School inequalities remain at the root of this problem. However, they are reinforced by adult continuing education and training policies which fail to encourage those most in need to pursue the lifelong learning which is currently espoused as the solution to all problems.

As we argue throughout this book, the major problem for the United Kingdom version of the high skills economy remains that it is unable to increase substantially the demand for high skills employees. Improving the mechanisms to increase the supply of skills has not proved enough, even when backed by improved information and a saturation campaign for lifelong learning. Fundamentally there remains a problem with the economic and social incentives. Where most employers are still not demanding high skills, many people will not be persuaded to acquire them, particularly in a culture where the rationale for learning has become so instrumentally tied to economic advancement.

It would be comforting to suggest that there could be a cultural revolution which would raise aspirations for learning and skills as a social and spiritual benefit. It is certainly time that more were invested in creating such a climate. However, what might be achieved is likely to be limited in the absence of policies to raise demand for, and the utilization of, skills *across* the economy. Greater wage equality and social inclusion is only won through a broader diffusion of skills, and only by widening the reach of high skills employment will the incentives be created for the wider acquisition of those skills.

3

Innovation, Skill Diffusion, and Social Exclusion

HUGH LAUDER

It appears that innovation is relatively easy, as far as the production of new ideas is concerned. The initial idea itself is rarely the crucial part of any invention. . . . It is the social conditions for their sustained development that is more central.

(R. Collins 1986: 115)

INTRODUCTION

This chapter is concerned with three issues: those of innovation, skill diffusion, and exclusion in relation to education and training systems and the labour market. In the past labour markets have been analysed in terms of their ability to generate economically efficient outcomes and the degree to which they provide equitable and meritocratic access (see Chapter 1). In these analyses consideration of a nation's stock of skills has been prominent. However, in an economic context in which knowledge and skill change rapidly the question of skill diffusion assumes greater significance. Neither human capital theory nor the more sophisticated models of economic growth have been able to capture its dynamics since theoretically they are only able to focus on the stock of skills.[1] Nor, indeed, have policy makers given skill diffusion

---

[1] Human capital theory assumes that the postulate of rational egoism coupled to rational judgements about the future of the labour market will ensure that individuals will gain economic advantage by upskilling. In other words, skill diffusion must be on this theory merely

much consideration. While raising the stock of skills is clearly a necessary condition for a high skills society, it is not sufficient. Given the rate of innovation, a central concern must be how the development of the stock of skills is adapted *and* transferred through the relevant sectors of the economy in order to capitalize on innovations. National competitiveness depends in significant part on the nature and speed of the processes by which skills are diffused. If they cannot be diffused rapidly and effectively, the opportunities for innovation, development, and production will be lost.

Skill diffusion is one aspect of skill formation that we define as the societal capacity for high skills. It focuses on two questions. The first concerns the way education and training systems can be kept abreast of the skill requirements necessary for leading-edge technology. The second relates to the transfer of such skills to small and medium-sized companies (SMEs). One of the fundamental problems in relation to high skill formation is how small and medium-sized companies can sustain industrial intelligence, R & D, training budgets, and learning for continuous improvement to keep up with best practice. This is especially significant when the SME sector is being drawn increasingly into the global economy through exports. For example, approximately 70 per cent of the SME sectors in Austria, Belgium, and Italy are involved in exports (DTI 1997).[2]

Education and training (ET) systems and labour market structures act as conduits for skill diffusion: the way ET and labour markets are integrated and structured will more or less efficiently diffuse knowledge. In effect ET and labour market structures generate national systems of skill diffusion, just as it is now recognized that there are national systems of innovation (Nelson 1993; Lundvall 1992). The key question, then, is: what are the advantages and disadvantages of different ET and labour market structures in diffusing skills?

However, in asking these questions we need to be aware of the wider issues relating to ET and labour market structures and, in particular, questions of exclusion. There is little point in considering the effectiveness of skill diffusion systems if a large proportion of the workforce is excluded from acquiring, and changing their skill sets in response to innovation. The major concerns about exclusion relate to gender and poverty. For example, women have often been seen as 'shock absorbers'

a matter of the pursuit of individual self-interest based on a collection of individual judgements. Growth theories be they of the neo-classical or endogenous kind build stocks of skills into their models but that is as far as they can go. See also n. 6.

 [2] The figure for the UK is just over 40%.

within capitalist economies, being hired in times of boom and fired during slumps. The very nature of this function, it has been argued, has excluded them from the training needed to acquire the skills at the cutting edge of innovation. The issue here is whether women perform the same function in all ET and labour market systems or whether various types of labour market allow for different opportunities for women.

Similar points can be made in relation to poverty. People in poverty are more likely to underperform in education (P. Brown and Lauder 2001a) and are more likely than others to be unemployed or in low skill work as adults. The question, then, is whether some types of labour market are more likely than others to generate low skilled, insecure, and poorly paid work, thereby creating the structural conditions for inter-generational cycles of poverty.

THE NATURE OF INNOVATION AND SKILL DIFFUSION

The pivotal issue relating to skill diffusion concerns the processes of skill transmission in relation to innovation. Innovation should not be understood merely in technological terms (R. Collins 1986; Cooke and Morgan 1998), nor solely in relation to scientific research and development, although technological change brought about by R & D is an important factor in the demand for new skills. Changes in the social relations of production also generate the demand for different types of skills and indeed changes in how we understand innovation. The clearest example of our changing understanding of innovation lies in the importation of elements of Japanese production techniques in most advanced economies. This has brought with it the notion of innovation through continuous improvement on the production line (Elger and Smith 1994).

It should be stressed that different economic sectors will transfer skills in different ways. For example, in the automotive industry skills are usually developed by a combination of theory, practice, and work socialization, which usually begins with an apprenticeship at the shop-floor level which is then developed into specialisms through further training. Even within manufacturing there appear to be different optimal routes for knowledge transfer which in turn have implications for the kinds of institutions and networks necessary for carrying skill diffusion. Mason and Wagner (1998a) note that while Germany is superior to the United Kingdom in intermediate technology manufactured goods, this is not the case in hi-tech electronics. They found that the relative success of the two countries in these two areas is in significant part due to levels of skill and knowledge transfer. The ease with which individuals in Britain could job hop from company to company taking their expertise with them was likely to generate advantages in innovation that could not accrue in Germany because of its more stable employment structure and attendant laws.[3] Rasher and Brown (1997) have also found job hopping and poaching to be the primary means for skills transfer in logic production in Silicon Valley. Strictly speaking we should refer to multiple systems of skill diffusion. However, in each of our comparator countries there are distinct labour market structures and systems of skill diffusion in relation to the ET sector and its links into SMEs.[4] These have been created by their respective national frameworks and it is with them that we are fundamentally concerned.

EDUCATION TRAINING AND LABOUR MARKET REGIMES

In this chapter four regimes of ET and labour market structures in relation to innovation, skill diffusion, and exclusion are examined. These are associated with five of the comparator countries in the High Skills project: Germany, Japan and Korea, Singapore, and Britain. These regimes are labelled, respectively: *occupational, internal, state guided,* and *flexible* and refer to the dominant form of ET and labour market organization in each of these countries. These labour markets are differentiated in terms of occupations, institutions, or networks, which to a greater or lesser extent, privilege or exclude specific kinds of knowledge and workers. Each of these labour market regimes structure the flow of knowledge, skill, and innovation in different ways opening up different kinds of opportunity for knowledge and its transfer. Consequently,

[3] In Germany there is a specific clause in individual employment contracts which restricts the movement of employees to rival firms with the aim of preventing firm-specific knowledge from being transferred or used by an individual to set up their own business. See Mason and Wagner (1998b).

[4] This then raises the 'one size fits all' question of whether one dominant type of labour market and associated means of skill diffusion is adequate to realize high skills in all sectors of the economy.

access to the different sectors, initially determined by the ET system, is central to the kind of knowledge and skills workers may gain.[5]

A further aspect of these regimes concerns the way workers' identities and related aspirations and motivations are constructed—what in shorthand terms we may call the process of socialization. The acquisition of skills and the learning associated with the updating and development of new skills necessary to successful innovation cannot be achieved without the related motivation and aspirations. Here again different ET and labour market structures are likely to create different processes of socialization and hence identity construction. How these identities are constructed is crucial, for the institutional and networked processes of skill diffusion can only work if workers are willing to acquire and transfer knowledge between one another.

Finally, in contemporary labour markets workers tend to be mobile across occupations. Of specific interest in relation to skill diffusion are the informal rules and assumptions which govern promotion and career change,[6] especially where different kinds of skill are brought together in the same job because it is through new combinations of expertise that innovation is likely to be triggered (Schumpeter 1934).

[5] It is worth noting that this approach to skill formation and in particular, the way access to knowledge is structured within the labour market raises further questions about the adequacy of human capital theory. For the kinds of investments human beings are able to make by acquiring further knowledge will be determined by how different ET systems and labour markets are structured. Moreover, in addition to questions of access to knowledge there are also issues about the nature and quality of knowledge that different labour market structures demand. Human capital theory assumes a neo-classical labour market which is only differentiated according to the degree to which it is more or less impeded from working optimally by 'rigidities' such as trade unions. It also assumes that workers have the same opportunities and motivation to learn within the labour market, but when labour markets are differentiated by the way knowledge is structured and by socialization processes which can encourage or inhibit learning, then this assumption must also be taken with a grain of salt. The fundamental problem with human capital theory is that it is primarily concerned with demand and supply and how these can be brought into equilibrium according some variant of a perfectly competitive market (see Chapter 1). This enables the theory to concentrate on market rigidities and to consider the question of who should pay for training in the light of poaching but it wholly fails to consider issues of diffusion and how the demand for skills can be upgraded. Since it only recognizes individuals in the process of skill diffusion and assumes them to behave in precisely the same ways in all labour markets, it simply does not have the theoretical resources to deal with issues of culture, different kinds of knowledge, state formation and history, all of which need to be included in an understanding of skill diffusion.

[6] In economic terms these assumptions are of considerable interest, although rarely discussed, because they are likely to be based on untestable or difficult to test assumptions. While in Germany an engineering background is seen as central to a management role in manufacturing, this is not the case in the UK or USA where the notion of generic management still holds sway. In Singapore, the leading agency for economic development, the Economic Development Board, has a majority of engineers on its staff, rather than, as might be expected, economists.

An example of this kind of 'progression' concerns the assumption commonly found in Germany and Singapore that in manufacturing managers should have a sound engineering background (O'Sullivan 2000; Brown and Lauder 2001*b*). However, this kind of progression must also be related to socialization. Transferring skill sets from one context to another and integrating them with new skills to create innovation requires a degree of risk-taking, confidence, and the desire to learn which is either acquired or reinforced through a process of socialization (T. Rees 1998).

LABOUR MARKET REGIMES AND EXCLUSION

The role of gender has been integral to the workings of each of the labour markets regimes examined in this chapter largely by acting as a barrier to skill diffusion. However, women have been positioned differently in each of these labour markets. As Esping-Andersen (1999) has argued, the nature of labour markets with respect to women's participation is in part due to family ideologies and practices, welfare state provision in relation to child benefit supports and childcare and, we can add, ET systems. How the gender division of labour is structured with respect to state support for women's employment in each of these labour markets is also crucial to the nature of women's participation (Crompton 1999). Nevertheless, in each of the labour market types under consideration women have been used to introduce flexibility in one form or another to help cope with the fluctuations of capitalist economies. In terms of equity and security, the cost to women has been and continues to be high, but a further penalty has been incurred because of the barriers to skill diffusion that, often, have been part and parcel of this flexibility. Given that the nature and construction of these barriers varies according to labour market structure, the key role that gender has played in their functioning needs to be assessed.

However, there are other factors woven into the fabric of labour markets which will have a determinate effect on knowledge and skill diffusion. Of these polarization of income, and by implication skill, is particularly germane to some contemporary economies like that of the United States and Britain especially, although not exclusively, with respect to women. This issue will be dealt with separately because currently polarization constitutes a prominent threat to the flow of knowledge in these labour markets.

Finally, this chapter looks to the future and asks what impact national systems of skill diffusion may have on attempts to move production up the value chain. The higher up the value chain sectors of the economy can move, the more competitive they become. But such movement requires improvements in skill and innovation, hence skill diffusion becomes central in understanding this issue.

A COMPARATIVE ANALYSIS OF ET SYSTEMS, LABOUR MARKET STRUCTURES, AND SKILL DIFFUSION

Having considered the links between the ET system, labour market structure, and innovation, we will now examine each of the national case studies in terms of access to knowledge, socialization, the informal rules for transferring from one occupation to another, and social exclusion in terms of gender and poverty. We begin with the occupationally structured labour market typified by Germany.

THE OCCUPATIONAL LABOUR MARKET

In this labour market access to jobs is initially dependent upon gaining an occupational qualification. In Germany, what constitutes an occupation is determined by national ordinance on the basis of tripartite negotiations between trade union and employer representatives and the state. The very tight linkage between qualifications and occupation (Maurice, Sellier, and Silvestre 1986) reflects two principles: a commitment to a highly qualified and trained workforce and what may be termed equality of productive capacity (Streeck 1992; see Chapter 2). By this is meant that everyone has the right to an education and training to enable them to be productive. Consequently, everyone in Germany has the right to enter the Dual System of training in order to qualify for an occupation. Tied into this system of skilling are wage rates set regionally or nationally for most occupations (Hassel and Schulten 1998). There is some flexibility in what companies can offer in wage rates, although these are set by wage 'corridors'. Nevertheless, this system has produced low differentials in income (Streeck 1997), which have remained remarkably stable over the past twenty years despite major changes in the German economy (Prasad 2000). It is for this reason that trade unions in Germany see the issue of occupation construction and allied training as central to their mission.

In Allmendinger's (1989) terms, the links between the German ET system and the labour market are highly standardized and stratified. By standardization she refers to what employers can expect on the basis of type of training and credential. The effect is 'a smooth transition between the educational and occupational sectors, a transition that does not require repeated job shifts to achieve a good match'. In relation to skill and innovation there are four advantages to such a system. The first and most important in relation to skills diffusion is that skills acquired under each occupation will apply as much to the SME sector as to major multinationals. But how this training is delivered successfully so that apprentices are exposed to leading-edge practice is a key question to which we shall return. The second is that this system delivers consistency; employers have a strong idea of newly trained workers' capabilities. The third is that job stability can enhance innovative practice: one of the lessons learnt from the Japanese regarding continuous improvement is that a thorough and wide-ranging knowledge of the productive process is a prerequisite of innovatory practice. This presupposes the necessity for a relatively stable workforce. The fourth and related point is that poaching is less likely in a labour market in which there is a rough equivalence in skill and wages, thereby enhancing stability.

By stratification Allmendinger refers to the degree of differentiation between levels in the ET system and their relationship to the labour market. In Germany the school system is highly differentiated with different types of secondary school, leading, by and large, to different kinds of further education and training which track students into specific ranges of occupation in a highly segmented labour market. The consequence of this system of stratification for innovation and skill is once again to emphasize stability and continuity.

Within this structure the Dual System operates in such a way that it carries knowledge of leading-edge innovation to apprentices and to SMEs within manufacturing. While the majority of training contracts with the Dual System are with SMEs the role of the major leading-edge companies such as Daimler-Benz, Siemens, and BMW are crucial in disseminating knowledge of innovation.[7] There are several channels

---

[7] Interview with Prof. Wolfgang Streeck. It is worth noting that 65% of apprentices are trained in companies with less than 50 employees.

of communication. The first and perhaps most direct concerns the possibility of apprentices in SMEs spending some of their training in the leading-edge companies. This enables apprentices to carry the information regarding new innovations back to the SME. Beyond this, the role of the Chambers of Commerce as an intermediate institution within the Dual System is crucial. Although funded by employers, they occupy a position within the system in which they are legally charged to represent the interests of the economy in general rather than the sectional interests of employers.

As it was made clear to us, in our fieldwork, this position is only viable on the basis of trust. Chambers of Commerce are, as one interviewee put it, 'the seismographers and we are able to say what business wants . . . we are also the melting pot, we translate and we are in the middle of both sides; but we are on the side of the economy of course!'. In this role they are able to gather intelligence about innovations. They meet the managers of training in the leading-edge companies on a regular basis and exchange information on training needs. In addition, they have training advisers who visit firms. Part of their role is to convince firms of the need for training, but they also 'play the role of seismographer' bringing back information which can then either be incorporated directly into training programmes or form part of the nationwide debate about training needs. Perhaps as significant as knowledge of the skills needed for innovations is the transfer of new pedagogical techniques developed in companies like Daimler-Chrysler. These techniques are transferred not only into the Dual System but to those secondary schools which were likely to feed students into the Dual System. Clearly the process of consensus embodied in the German social market is integral to this system of skill diffusion. However, it seems to work best in manufacturing. In the banking system we were told that in the schools which undertake vocational training for the Dual System, the *Berufschule*, the IT hardware and software used was not up to date because of the expense.

Over and beyond the question of whether this system of skill diffusion can work well in all sectors of the economy, further fundamental questions have been raised about the rigidities of an occupational labour market. For example, Kern (1998) places some of the responsibility for what he sees as a crisis in basic as opposed to incremental processes of innovation in German industry at the feet of the occupational labour market, and indeed the Dual System which services its training needs. This is because occupations generate exclusive competencies which valorize knowledge and problem-solving in a specific domain but devalue or underestimate external knowledge. The consequence is that it is difficult to generate basic, as opposed to incremental innovation because the former requires the combination and exchange of different kinds of knowledge and understanding (Schumpeter 1934). What, potentially, exacerbates this problem is a set of training and labour institutions which socialize the individual into a specific craft or occupation which is reinforced by the stability of employment, status, and reward described above. These arrangements, it is argued, are well suited to incremental innovation and problem-solving but are inappropriate to a world where competitiveness is dependent on rapid changes in basic innovations.

There are three dimensions to this issue. The first and perhaps most crucial for this kind of labour market is whether it can develop flexibility within the broad system of occupational stratification or whether as Kern (1998) suggests it fatally slows innovation and skill diffusion. Our research in Germany suggests that the flexibility in combining new kinds of knowledge is available in the Dual System. New or changed ordinances, which effectively construct the occupations or 'professions', used to take up to ten years to be established, but now take one to one and half years. In the skills necessary for the new knowledge economy, for example, in information technologies, media, and design, thirty-one 'professions' and 60,000 places have been created since 1996.

In this period the number of new contracts signed for these 'professions' had risen by 50 per cent between 1998 and 1999. The new mechatronics ordinance, which combines mechanical engineering and electronics, provides a good example of combining different disciplines and greater flexibility. Indeed included in the list of occupational skills for mechantronics are inter-company and technical communication and the ability to read English language documents and communicate in English.[8] The need to introduce greater flexibility was a fundamental concern of the large industrial companies and again provides an example of how they influence the curriculum on the basis of their own innovation needs.

The second concerns the question of socialization and flexibility. Kern's argument would have far greater force if, indeed, those trained within an occupation remained within it. However, this is not the case.

---

[8] The skills demanded for this specific ordinance, 'Mechantronics Fitter (m/f)' introduced 1 Aug. 1998 are far wider than for what might normally be considered a technical education, including elements of citizenship, leadership, and sensitivity to the environment. It is an example of a technical training embedded in a concept of citizenship. See Green (1998).

Approximately half of all German men and 60 per cent of women currently have jobs which fit their prior vocational training (Witte and Kalleberg 1995) with a slightly lower proportion for those men who have been trained in the Dual System. The degree of exit from specific occupations is linked to age, as might be expected.

In terms of innovation a change of occupation may well bring with it the ability to combine new ideas, indeed in a flexible labour market it is the principle means by which new ideas are combined. But what is interesting about the Dual System is the platform for a career that it builds for the worker-citizen. As we have seen in the case of the mechantronics fitter's ordinance, more than just technical skills are involved in the training.

There are three further advantages of the dual-system occupational labour market which relate directly to the willingness of the labour force to embrace innovation. As was stressed in our interviews, it socialized young workers into the appropriate habits of work giving them a sense of direction and identity. It also provides a sense of pride and commitment in doing a good job (Fevre, Rees, and Gorrard 1999), which is essential if the economy is to trade on quality rather than price. Finally, it provides young workers with a sense of confidence. As Rosenbaum (1999) has put it:

In biographical studies of German youths, it is striking how apprenticeship certification gives a sense of purpose and confidence that work bound youth cannot easily get in the United States or Great Britain (Evans and Heinz, 1994). In a good labour market, youth are nearly guaranteed a job, but even in a bad labour market, German students still know they have qualifications. If they are unemployed they feel unlucky but not incompetent. (1999: 257)

This view is supported by Heinz (1999). In a study of the biographies of apprentices' transition to work, he found that 24 per cent of car mechanics opted to return to education with a view to gaining a degree. He shows that the motivation for this was not the threat of unemployment—only 4 per cent were unemployed—but due to a discrepancy between expectations developed during the apprenticeship and their work experience. In this case the Dual System served to raise their aspirations. In this respect the highly structured Dual System can be seen as a springboard for later flexibility.

These changes in occupation raise the further question of the informal rules by which workers can 'legitimately' switch from one occupation to another, which appears to be quite different in our comparator labour markets. Perhaps the clearest example of this concerns the qualifications required of managers in the different labour markets. In Britain and the United States the doctrine of the generic manager has taken hold (O'Sullivan 2000). According to this doctrine a suitable business school qualification enables the holder to manage any kind of organization. In contrast, in Germany this doctrine is only now gaining a foothold. Traditionally the basic or prior qualification needed for management is in engineering.

The German system of skill diffusion appears to be able to cope with the demands of flexibility in relation to intermediate technologies, a view also supported by Culpepper (1999), although there is clearly a question concerning the suitability of the Dual System for hi-tech production and the service sector.

Gender and The Occupational Labour Market

In order to understand the nature of women's relationship to the occupational labour market we should begin with some descriptive statistics. Of these, perhaps one of the most significant is that of participation in higher education. After all, it is through higher education that women can aspire to the ranks of professional and managerial occupations, traditionally the pinnacle of a male-structured labour market.[9] In Germany, a smaller proportion of women participate in higher education than in Britain. Approximately 42 per cent of women participate in higher education in Germany, whereas in Britain approximately equal proportions of women and men attend university. However, it is also the case that there are more intermediately skilled women workers in Germany. This is due, in large part, to the Dual System. While it is the case that traditionally, fewer young women than young men have participated, the share of female trainees had risen to 40 per cent by 1990 and has remained at that level throughout the mid-1990s.[10] However, the occupations that they are trained in tend to be heavily gender typed with the top five most 'popular' occupations being: hairdresser, clerk (retail trade), office clerk, doctor's assistant, and industrial clerk. Within the 'knowledge economy' professions, the percentage of women apprentices is 28 per cent of the total. Within this percentage Werner reports that:

[9] Although, the fact of women's participation may not lead to equal participation in the labour market or indeed empowerment (Jayaweera 1997).

[10] Ceedefop, 'Apprenticeship in the Federal Republic of Germany', 1997 <http://www.train-ingvillage.gr/etv/library/apprenticeship/country/d.asp>.

Female apprentices have a higher participation share in the communication service industry (67%) and in media and information services (88%). Other than that young females are represented to a higher degree is the less sought after trades such as such as photo media laboratory technicians and sales persons for audio visual media (68% and 63%). Their participation in information technology apprenticeships is on average 14 per cent (2000: 2)

It is clear that the gender stereotyping of apprenticeships remains a major barrier to skill diffusion even in the new largely service sector 'professions' and is a major concern in Germany (Klatt and Richter-Witzgall 2000). The problem is not merely that women are excluded from particular types of knowledge but that stereotyping inhibits progression up the credential ladder and hence the possibility of combining knowledge and experience in novel ways. Most of the above occupations tend to be 'dead end' with little possibility of progression. This is perhaps most clearly demonstrated by the male-dominated IT apprenticeships where 48 per cent have gained a university entrance standard (*Abitur*) or the equivalent (Werner 2000). In this respect entry into an IT apprenticeship can provide a springboard to higher qualifications. Given these data, A. Brown's (1997) optimistic view that as attempts are made to develop routes of progression between the Dual System and higher education systems women could benefit may be premature.

Traditionally, the chances of women entering the professions and or management have been lower in Germany than in Britain. However, in the period 1992 to 1997, the rate of growth of women's participation in these occupations was equally matched (EC 1999*b*: 60). Overall, though, as in Britain, women are heavily concentrated in a few sectors with approximately 65 per cent in both economies in health and social services, the retail trade, education, business activities, the hotel sector, and public administration. What is significant about these sectors is that they are confined to services which raise questions, to which we shall return, about the issue of low pay.

While there is an M-shaped distribution in Germany, that is to say young women enter the labour force, stay until they are married and then leave to raise children, re-entering in middle age when the children have grown up (Crompton 1999), women do not have the low skilled 'role of shock absorbers' to the same extent as in other labour markets, especially the internal market of Japan. In part, this is because they are likely to be more skilled and this is reflected in the spread of wages relative to men and, as we shall see shortly, in relation to the service dominated occupations in which they work. The role of 'shock absorber', until recently, has fallen to guest workers (*gastarbeiter*) (O'Sullivan 2000), while greater temporal flexibility has also been created through the use of non-standard working hours. Yeandle (1999) notes that three-quarters of west German employees' working hours do not conform to the morning to evening, Monday to Friday model. In the occupational labour market, the role of women is better understood in terms of a struggle centred on the traditional male breadwinner model which has been supported by all the parties in the social partnership. In particular, part-time work has not been promoted as both the social security system and career prospects militate against it. The trade unions have focused on full-time work, perhaps not surprisingly, since the traditional male preserve of intermediate manufacturing industries remains the motor of the German economy, while the aim for many feminists has been the full-time integration of women into the work-force (Pfau-Effinger 1999).

The impact of these policies can best be understood by comparing the flexibility of the British labour market with that of Germany. Overall, in 1997, 53.6 per cent of German women of working age were in the labour market, while 64 per cent of British women were in paid work. Even allowing for their respective unemployment rates (6 per cent in Britain, 10 per cent in Germany), there is still an appreciable difference in labour market participation. In 1994, in Britain, 55 per cent of women in employment were in part-time jobs, whereas the comparable figure for Germany was 35 per cent. However between 1994 and 1997, in Germany, the newly created jobs for women were all part-time, but the numbers involved amounted to just under 1 per cent per annum. In contrast, job creation in Britain was split between part- and full-time jobs, but again the percentage increases were small with roughly the same number of part-time jobs being created in Germany and Britain. Finally, in the same period there was an increase of between 8 and 10 per cent in temporary jobs for women in both economies (EC 1999b).

Given that the key relationship of women to the occupational labour market remains centred around the traditional male breadwinner model, the major issues regarding skill diffusion concern the way gender barriers block the dissemination of skills. However, given the shortage of IT skilled workers in Germany, as elsewhere, the issue of the supply of skills in relation to gender must also be of fundamental concern. Beyond these specific concerns there are more detailed questions about skill formation and diffusion in relation to gender and the German labour market that need to be raised. While Germany has an underdeveloped service sector judged by the standards of the Anglo-

Saxon economies (Esping-Andersen 1999), most of the job growth for women has been in this sector. The service sector is widely divergent and as we have already indicated, for areas like banking, our research suggests that the Dual System may not work well in providing the relevant skills. While the Dual System has been extremely successful in diffusing skills in the intermediate, mainly male-dominated sector, the major question confronting the Dual System now is to what extent it can be successfully applied to a service sector comprising a significant proportion of women.

THE INTERNAL LABOUR MARKET

Japan epitomizes the internal labour market model in the post-war era. The Koreans have followed the Japanese lead but with rather different results, it is therefore helpful to compare the two. The comparison is made prior to the Asian economic crisis of 1998. There is a discussion of the impact of the crisis on the Korean system of skill diffusion in the following chapter (also see Chapter 2).

What the Japanese have understood is that lifelong employment and learning go hand in hand. The key to the link between a job for life and learning is a reward system that is based on seniority and not on skills. Consequently, when fundamental changes are required in workers' skill sets, the combination of commitment to the company, rather than to a craft and to the rewards and status of that craft, generates flexibility in learning. Indeed Dore (1986) attributes Japan's successful response to the oil shocks of the 1970s to this system, arguing that by bringing lifelong employment and learning into harmony it provides a balance between security, flexibility, and the risks corporations need to take. Underpinning this economic logic is a high trust bargain between workers and corporations. Its linchpin is the stability employment offers in a highly uncertain world in return for commitment. In Japan, as in Korea, the socialization of the worker is undertaken by what might be considered strong and persistent forms of indoctrination. In Korea this has been accomplished by constant reinforcement of the company mission and likening the company to an extended family. This emphasis on loyalty and harmony is reinforced by single enterprise unions.

Since learning in the internal market is production-specific, the education and training systems are largely divorced. Education is highly standardized and stratified in the later years of secondary schooling, being concerned to develop the foundation for firm-specific training through a high level of general education for all. Consequently, in both Japan and Korea, there are highly centralized curricula focusing on a generic education. In addition, the socialization emphasized in schools is directly related to the social relations of production in both countries. Teamwork, communications, and collective problem-solving lie at the heart of these processes. The links between schools and higher education and companies are fundamentally concerned with the allocation, rather than the technical training of students, and depends on well-established reputations and networks. For example, entry to prestigious universities is dependent upon attendance at an equally prestigious high school. For those secondary school students entering the labour market, over 75 per cent are given access by their schools to specific firms on the basis of well-established networks (Rosenbaum 1999).

One of the advantages of training in the internal labour market being production-specific is that it enables the most to be made of human resources. Time and energy are focused directly on production, yet flexibility is built into the system, according to Koike and Inoki (1990), through the repeated transmission of new skills. This transmission is incremental and is aided by the culture and history of a corporation which enables the acquisition of the tacit knowledge necessary for skilled performances. In making these observations they rely on Polanyi's distinction between scientific knowledge and that of discrete things, times, and places. Both are necessary in the production process and are embodied in what Polanyi called personal knowledge. But as Koike and Inoki note acquiring personal knowledge requires interaction between teacher and learner to produce a skill that is often indefinable. As they describe it:

The colour of the fire for baking ceramics, the doctor's diagnosis of an illness, the condition of the cutting sensed by the machine tool operator are types of knowledge also having the property of incomplete expressibility through either words or pictures. (Koike and Inoki 1990: 44)

The issue of tacit knowledge and the institutional role in its transference is central to an understanding of how skills are diffused at the individual or micro level. In Germany this is transferred through the craft or occupational training and is built into subsequent on-the-job learning. A. Brown notes that 'coaching or supporting expertise is bedded in the structures of work' and that even 'formally skilled workers still required the explicit support and encouragement and advice from their peers' (1997: 10). In internal labour markets it is the company culture which generates the understanding of the tacit skills necessary to adapt to innovation. But the internal labour market also generates innovation through job rotation. In both Japan and Korea it is accepted practice to generate multi-skilled workers through a process of on-the-job learning through job rotation. Promotion is often based on skills acquired. In Korea, one of the leading *chaebol* we interviewed linked promotion to a ladder of modules that workers had to take successfully in order to be considered for promotion. In the broader context the significance of a flexibly skilled internal labour market based on a job for life becomes clear when placed against the demands made on workers for constant innovation within a zero defect production system.

In relation to skill diffusion there are several potential problems confronting the viability of internal labour markets. These can be divided into three broad categories: that relating to the internal labour markets of large companies, that which centres on the pivotal relationship between the large companies and the SME sector, and the role of women in providing flexibility within a system in which the internal labour market is largely, but not exclusively, based on the concept of the male breadwinner. In the case of the internal labour market of large companies, the potential threats to the system come from global competition, the continuing flat performance of the Japanese economy, and the changing social structure. At least one major Japanese electronics manufacturer has recently adopted a two-tier employment structure in which some are employed as prospective 'core' long-term workers and others are taken on only to meet current demand. There is no reliable data on how widespread this practice is, but there is a perception that it is increasing (Sakamoto-Vandenberg et al. 1998). Since this strategy is precisely that of the flexible labour market, the implications for skill diffusion will be examined when we look at the United Kingdom. Changes in the social structure of both Japan and Korea are also likely to pose a threat to the internal labour market. These have to do with changes in the aspirations of the younger generation who do not think they should stand in line for either pay or promotion. We saw earlier that job rotation was a key to continuous improvement, however in Japan, new employees trained as engineers tend not to be interested in learning shop-floor jobs, they want to be solely engaged with the advanced technology they have been trained to manipulate (Sakamoto-Vandenberg et al. 1998). This problem is in line with a more general trend in which the aspirations of the young are consistent with the perceptions of some senior managers that specialized professionals and most young recruits perform better in a merit pay system. The personnel manager of one major manufacturer had this to say about the changes in his company:

In the late 40s and 50s, the middle aged or experienced employees have been accustomed to the rich secure employment system, however the company is now restructuring the system in a way which affects them unfavourably. On the other hand, for younger people, they have already been unhappy with the pay system which is co-ordinated with the length of service rather than merit. Therefore, they may be happier if they are rewarded according to their performance regardless of age bracket. (Sakamoto-Vandenberg et al. 1998: 33)

Inevitably the internal labour market as practised in Japan and Korea presupposes a form of social discipline and economic stability which may be hard to sustain if younger workers will not defer to elders and especially in relation to career advancement.[11] Here the challenge of greater flexibility is not generated internally, as in the occupational labour market, but is generated by the societal modes of interaction underlying the labour market.

The second potential weakness of internal labour markets concerns the SME sector. For while skills may be highly developed within the large corporations, the crucial issue concerns the way skilling in the latter can generate commensurate levels of skills in the SME sector. In Japan there are three reasons why skill diffusion between the large corporate and SME sector appears to have been successful, when in Korea it has not. In Japan, there is a limit to the vertical integration within conglomerates. Since World War II considerable use has been made of the SME sector as a supplier to the corporates. The relationship between corporates and suppliers has not been solely based on price but also on mutual learning and development. Patchell and Hayter describe the relationship as follows: 'two firms are tied together by a learning situation, and the exchange of information in the relationship enables them to develop assets, whether those assets are considered human or physical' (1995: 344).

The result is a set of mutual dependencies between corporates and SMEs, which can lead to relationships that last for thirty years. In their study of the robot industry in Japan, Patchell and Hayter note that core and supplier firms engaged in a mutual exchange of personnel in order to upgrade skills, including new management techniques. This

---

[11] It should be stressed that there are differences between the labour markets in Japan and Korea. The Korean *chaebol* who have created internal labour markets are still family dominated and younger members of families tend to be promoted more rapidly into senior positions. Alongside them is a generation of senior managers and executives who were in at the beginning of the phenomenal growth of the *chaebol* and to whom younger managers defer in ways which would not be found in the West.

exchange is necessary, since engineers from both sectors collaboratively design product and processes.

These relationships generate further diffusion through the tradition of the *oyabun* or master craftsman which has persisted in modified form. According to Jones (1997) their workshops, which have persisted and thrived as suppliers to the conglomerates, have also been a source of training and career development. Once trained by *oyaban*, skilled workers could often be expected to set up their own workshop. It is an example of Streeck's (1987) observation that pre-industrial craft forms have remained a significant source of skill advantage.

If the links between the internal labour markets of the corporate and SME sector have been successful in diffusing skill because of the learning relationships between them, the same cannot be said of the relationships between the corporate and SME sector in Korea. There the links between the *chaebol* and SMEs have never been strong, leaving the latter underdeveloped in terms of innovation and skill (Lauder 1999). The reason for this lies in the recent history of Korean economic development. *Chaebol* are vertically integrated and are heavily dependent on imported parts and machinery. Consequently, the *chaebol* have looked overseas for the supportive role, which in Japan, is played by the SMEs. As Porter (1990) has noted, this has limited the capability for indigenous innovation. Interestingly, *chaebol* in their overseas operations in ASEAN countries are more likely than their Japanese comparator corporations to use indigenous suppliers for this reason, although the take-up rate is still small (Gamble et al. 1998). In Korea the state has sought to boost skill development in the SME sector for over a decade, and although this funding has been significant (Lauder 1999), the *chaebol* have effectively acted as a magnet attracting both human and financial resources away from the SME sector. Additionally, the prestige of the *chaebol* coupled to their policy of a job for life has meant that the middle classes have eschewed vocational and technical education for the higher education sector. The result has been considerable graduate unemployment. In effect the combination of the *chaebol* coupled to middle-class social aspirations has generated a misallocation of resources which the state has been unable to combat.

Gender and the Internal Labour Market

While there are clearly differences between the position of women in Japanese and Korean labour markets, the similarities are more

apparent. In both countries a male breadwinner model has predom-
inated (Cho and Chang 1994; Sako and Sato 1997). Perhaps the most
telling indicator of gender bias in this respect concerns participation in
higher education. The data on the rates of participation by women in
higher education in both countries have been low relative to Western
societies. For example, in Japan 34 per cent of women are enrolled in
higher education; in Korea the figure is 33 per cent, while in Germany
it is 42 per cent. In the United Kingdom the percentages are close to
parity (OECD 1997a).[12]

In Japan and Korea these low rates of participation are mirrored in
the proportion of female managers in firms of 100 or more workers. In
Korea, 4.1 per cent of managerial and administrative workers are women
(Jayaweera 1997). In Japan, while the numbers effectively doubled between
1982 and 1992, the total now also comprises 4.1 per cent of all managers
(Wakisaka 1997). The typical profile for women's labour force participation
remains M shaped. As Lam (1992) notes, many companies encourage
women 'to retire at marriage or childbirth through offering them special
allowances. Since the majority of women are assigned to unskilled or
assistant type jobs, the replacement of senior women by young school
leavers serves the purpose of reducing labour costs' (Lam 1992: 58).

This distribution in women's labour force participation is consistent
with a conservative view of their role in the family, but in the internal
labour market it has also generated flexibility. Higuchi (1997) shows how
women's accession and separation rates are far higher than those for
men. During a recession the workforce is not decreased by layoffs, since
that would challenge the commitment to lifelong jobs. Rather, early
retirement is encouraged. But alongside this strategy there is likely to be
suppression of the recruitment rate and this adversely affects women.
As he puts it, 'This kind of labour adjustment is likely to lead to massive
cuts in female employees' (34). With this kind of 'function' within the
labour market, it is hardly surprising that women are less likely to be
promoted, and receive less training (Wakisaka 1997). Women are not the
only form of flexibility available in the Japanese version of the internal
labour market (Elger and Smith 1994), although historically they have
clearly been a major factor in acting as 'shock absorbers' to sustain it
through periods of slump.

---

[12] The figure for Japan is taken from the *Statistical Abstract of Education, Science, Sports and
Culture* (MOESSC 1998a: 74). The data for Korea, Germany, and the UK are for 1995 and are taken
from *Education at a Glance* (OECD 1997a: 171). It should be noted that in Korea, parity between
males and females in the transition from high school to university is now being achieved (Paik
1998: 12).

In Korea, patriarchal assumptions have dominated the internal labour market even more than in Japan. For example, in Japan 87.5 per cent of men and 57.4 of women are economically active, but in Korea the corresponding figures are 72 and 43 per cent. The Korean figures need to be qualified, however, since they comprise a majority of non-paid workers in family businesses. It is estimated that these exclude 10.4 per cent of the workforce.[13] Lee Hye Kyung has suggested that the invisibility of women working in family businesses, predominant amongst the less educated and rural areas, is related to a patriarchal culture in which the man is traditionally seen as the provider: a fiction, she observes, that 'has to be maintained carefully for the peace of all concerned' (1994: 308). Paradoxically, the lower rate of female participation in the formal manufacturing and service sectors means that the kind of flexibility generated by low skilled women workers in Japan is less available to medium and large companies in Korea. Undoubtedly, a reason why they have not utilized women as 'shock absorbers' in the labour market relates to Korea's rapid expansion and consequently tight labour market in the 1970s and 1980s. However, there has been a pool of women seeking work. In 1992 the unemployment rate amongst women was 17 per cent. On average they were high or middle school graduates in their mid-thirties. Of these, 41 per cent desired part-time employment (Jeong In-Soo 1996). Arguably, institutional discrimination against these women is only part of the story. It is the case that across the board those graduating from high and middle schools are four times more likely to be unemployed than college graduates (Jeong In-Soo 1996), and this may well relate to the poor quality of non-academic tracks in secondary schools in Korea (Cheonsik Woo 1998).

However, in both countries there are major changes afoot in relation to women's participation, which are likely to challenge the character of the internal labour market. Women's participation in the labour market has seen a steady increase in both Japan and Korea, and this has been accompanied by equal employment opportunities legislation in both countries. Wakisaka (1997) reports that as a result of the passing of the Equal Employment Opportunities Law, 1985, in Japan companies started to recruit women graduates, and it is this which accounts for the doubling of women managers, although as we have seen they comprise, still, a small proportion of managers. She also points out that not all part-time women are used as part of the 'shock absorber'

---

strategy. The average length of service for part-time women increased from 2 to 4.9 years between 1970 and 1995. Moreover, part-time women employees can be divided between those who are considered core part-time workers who are highly skilled manual workers and those that are unskilled. Amongst full-time white-collar women workers double tracks have been developed, distinguished by those that seek a full-time career in paid work and those expecting to leave when they marry or have children. Those that opt for a full-time career are more likely to be more highly trained and promoted. However, as Wakisaka (1997) notes, this strategy is flawed, since women may and often do change their minds.

This latter strategy looks like an attempt to accommodate women within the demands of the equal opportunities legislation and the logic of the internal labour market in which company investment in training is seen as an integral part of the job-for-life bargain between capital and labour. Women, who may wish to interrupt their careers, clearly fit awkwardly into such an arrangement. The key question underlying this point concerns the significance of the patriarchal assumptions that have supported the internal labour market in Japan. The ability of knowledge transfer and skill diffusion to transcend the gender barrier will turn on how deeply rooted these assumptions are. It should be emphasized that patriarchy is not a necessary condition of internal labour markets provided the various institutional and social-psychological impediments to women's careers, such as lack of adequate childcare facilities, are removed.

In Korea, perhaps the most significant indicator of change in women's participation in the labour market concerns the near parity of progression rates between sexes from high school to university which have been achieved (Paik 1998). Of course, this development does not relate directly to the labour market. However, it should be seen against the background of a patriarchal society in which fees for university are privately paid and in which, as recently as 1987, 70 per cent of Korean women agreed with the statement, 'The husband should be the bread-winner and the wife should stay at home' (Kim Byong-Sub 1994). However, while the proportion of women attending university should be seen as a clear signal of change, the nature of future employment for many women in Korea will turn on the quality and status of vocational high schools, since unemployment of women vocational high school graduates is also high. This is a point to which we shall return in the next chapter.

THE GUIDED LABOUR MARKET

The Singaporean labour market may be described as guided for the following reason: skill formation in Singapore is central to its political viability as a city state, since the ruling People's Action Party has taken the view that rising prosperity for all can only be achieved through a process of moving the workforce up the 'value chain' of economic activities. Hence, the question of economic competitiveness and that of the role of the state in upgrading the skills of the workforce are understood in almost identical terms by all policy stakeholders in Singapore (see Chapter 2). This consensus is based on the view that economic development cannot be left to the operation of the global marketplace. As Philip Yeo, CEO of the Economic Development Board (EDB) has observed, 'our government has always been a development capitalist'.

In consequence, the Singaporean state has had a two-prong strategy for moving the demand and supply of skills up the value chain. It has identified and attracted MNCs with high skill demands to Singapore, and it has sought to coordinate the supply of skilled workers to meet the demands of MNCs coming to the city state (Brown and Lauder 2001b). In addition, it has picked indigenous 'winners' to meet its policy aims and sought to raise the skills of older workers with little education (Ashton and Sung 1994). Where demand has continued for low skill work, the state has sought to address this issue through the recruitment of guest workers. In times of crisis the state has sought to reduce the social cost to firms of employing workers. Finally, but by no means least, the state has applied a series of strategies in order to socialize and exercise control over the worker-citizens of Singapore. These measures have provided a highly motivated and compliant workforce which understands its position in terms of the basic tenets of economic rationality. It is for these reasons that we have termed the labour market in Singapore as 'guided' by the state.

In respect of skill diffusion, the guided market trades for its success on a series of linked intelligence gathering and dissemination exercises. At the highest level of decision-making, the Economic Development Board (EDB) plays a pivotal role through foresight planning that involves scanning the globe for companies, inventions, and people able to add value to Singapore's strategic initiatives in new or emerging spheres of economic activity. It has regional offices around the world which enable the EDB to develop personal contacts with key corporate personnel in order to build the trust relations which are often necessary before companies will commit to the inward investment deals that the EDB are interested in attracting. As in other countries, the EDB uses a range of incentives including cheap rents, tax breaks, cheap energy supplies, etc., but in Singapore these are invariably linked to a commitment to skills upgrading. Raising the demand for skills requires a corresponding supply of increasingly skilled workers. This is achieved through a sophisticated system of education and training in which there is, effectively, no distinction made between the vocational and other aims of education: everything is geared towards the economy (Ashton and Sung 1994). In seeking to tailor supply to demand, the Singaporean system can often work at short notice and in this sense is highly flexible. Again the 'one-stop shop' approach of the EDB is central. It can initiate new training programmes in advance of MNCs arriving in Singapore to fulfil its commitment to supply skilled labour. During the course of our research, the EDB was developing a strategy of attracting wafer manufacturers to Singapore. There was a shortage of wafer engineers, so the EDB arranged for physics graduates to take a bridging course which would qualify them within the year. The government would pay for the bulk of this training on the understanding that more workers would be trained than immediately necessary, using state of the art technologies sometimes provided by the MNCs, but enhanced by major government investments in tertiary education and training provision. The reason for training more workers than strictly required is to encourage the inward investors to expand their operations and to make it easier to attract other companies in the same sector to enter Singapore in an attempt to create industrial clusters.

The coordinating role of the EDB is only possible when there is an institutional framework of 'joined up' government that includes the education and training system, housing, land, and environmental agencies. This allows the EDB to offer a 'one-stop shop' approach, where the inward investor can deal with one person within the Board, responsible for overseeing the business start-up within Singapore. Once in the city state, the EDB works closely with companies to move production or service delivery up the value added skills chain.

Clearly, the ability of the EDB to deliver appropriately skilled and socialized workers to the MNCs is crucial. In order to understand how this is achieved, we need to provide some background before looking at the mechanisms by which supply is matched to demand. The issue here is not just technical but of how the motivation and socialization of workers is achieved (Brown and Lauder 2001b).

The Goh Report (1979) formed the basis for the competitive and selective structure of primary and secondary education. It led to the introduction of academic streaming at both primary and secondary levels so that 'for a child who is not meant for academic endeavours, streaming would help to ensure that he acquires basic literacy and numeracy, as well as preparation in training for a skill' (Yip et al. 1997: 17). It is worth noting here that assumptions about innate differences in ability were presented as a temporal issue; giving 'less capable' students the chance to develop 'at a pace slower than for the more capable' whilst also allowing 'a child every opportunity to go as far as he can'.

At the secondary level three streams were created: the Special, the Express, and the Normal. The Special route was offered to the top 10 per cent of students who were expected to be bilingual at first language level and sit the General Certificate of Education 'O' level after four years. Students on the Express course were taught in only one language and also sat 'O' levels after four years, whilst the Normal students sat a different 'N' level examination which reflected the less academic nature of their studies. There was also greater scope for these students to study vocational subjects of immediate relevance on entry to the labour market. The streaming of students was extended in 1984 with the intro- duction of the Gifted Education Programme (GEP) for the 'intellectually gifted' child, although less than 1 per cent of students have attended these schools. Along with this system of streaming is the principle of 'progression' based on the idea that Singapore cannot waste the talents of its people and given that intellectual maturation may vary, it is important to ensure that students always have the opportunity to advance through to university.

This system of streaming at secondary level articulates with three levels of tertiary education, the universities, polytechnics, and the Institute for Technical Education. Gaining access to university is the major prize and while demand is high the government have set a limit of 25 per cent of an age cohort. Supply is adjusted to demand for universities and polytechnics through the deliberations of the Council on Professional and Technical Education (CPTE). The role of the CPTE is to set quotas for courses in universities and polytechnics which match the anticipated demands for different kinds of workers. The priority is to ensure that there are enough technicians and engineers. The Ministry of Trade and Industry told us that at the secondary school level 'we don't care if you study literature, but you have to be good in math- ematics and science'. Rationing of places is combined with keeping the costs of science and engineering courses comparable with arts and business studies. Students are given a preference for what they would like to study at university and polytechnic, but this is strictly determined by school grades. 'Those who don't get their choice are allocated, especially to engineering.' These students 'are carefully monitored and given extra tuition'. The concern about training enough engineers at the tertiary level is not only motivated by an inherent global shortage which Singapore also tries to overcome by attracting foreign technicians and engineers, but from a belief that an education for economic life is best achieved through the Sciences rather than the Arts. As we were told by the Ministry of Labour, 'we are more worried about people adopting the softer options rather than engineers going into business. Doing Law, Arts, etc. . . . engineering degrees give you a lot of systematic analytical skills . . . an engineer is better than a business graduate at the first degree level. The engineer could go on to an MBA but the business graduate is not going to become an engineer.' Such sentiments are reflected in the proportions of university students studying engineering. In 1997 about 61 per cent of males and 28 per cent of females were studying engineering. The deliberations of the CPTE are informed by manpower planning (their term) forecasts. While these have tended to be inaccurate in Western economies (Klees 1986) and largely dropped as a result in favour of market mechanisms, Singapore can be much more precise about its forecasts because of the coordinating role of the EDB. The intelligence it gathers about the kinds of industries it is attracting or seeking to attract coupled to the flexibility in training that it enables, allows a far more accurate picture of the demand for skills to be developed.

Beneath the polytechnics is the ITE which runs a number of training centres with state-of-the-art facilities both as a way of making training more relevant to the needs of an advanced economy and to dampen the demand for university and polytechnic education. The aim is that an ITE training offers the best route to the real vocational prizes.

So far we have charted the way in which the supply of skills is matched to a system of continuous upgrading in the demand for skills at the macro level. We now need to turn to the way in which skills are upgraded at the micro level of educational institutions and firms. Again, the role of intelligence and coordination between the state, industry, and education are at the heart of this process.

The Diffusion of Cutting-Edge Skills and Ongoing Training

The framework for intelligence gathering and skills upgrading from cutting-edge MNC practice to tertiary institutions and SMEs is set by the state in the relationships it has established with MNCs. The state actively seeks the cooperation and expertise of MNCs at the highest level. The clearest example of this is that we were told that some of the CEOs of the *Fortune* 100 companies are invited to Singapore every year to discuss key strategy issues with respect to the city state's role in the global economy. The more mundane but nevertheless significant way in which senior managers of MNCs in Singapore are involved with the state's affairs is by being co-opted onto various advisory committees and government task forces. In return for this involvement managers give their time freely. When we asked the Director of Motorola University (Pacific Region) about why he contributed to the state in this way he replied wryly, 'flattery I suppose'! In fact the Singaporean strategy of co-option or perhaps more accurately incorporation of MNCs into the policy-making process does far more than merely make MNC managers feel good about the place. Rather it is central to the extensive involvement by the state in skills upgrading of the existing workforce as well as those engaging in initial vocational training, since this close cooperation between MNCs and the state enables a high degree of permeability between them. This process is aided by the recruitment of EDB staff into senior positions within MNCs,[14] thereby facilitating the dialogue between MNCs and the state. However, despite the excellent relations that have been established between the state and MNCs, the transference of innovation and skill from MNCs to indigenous SMEs has been less successful and has prompted a consideration of alternative strategies for upgrading the SME sector. This strategy, which is still in its infancy, is discussed in the next chapter.

In relation to initial vocational training, tertiary institutions form committees at the subject level to advise on both the type of skilled labour required and cutting-edge practice. The tertiary institutions can provide the appropriate training to meet the demand for cutting-edge skills because they are abundantly resourced, with for example, robots, cadcam equipment, and the like. What is required of these institutions,

---

[14] For example one of the human resource directors of one leading MNC that we interviewed had been an EDB officer with some responsibility for recruiting that company to Singapore.

therefore, is that their teachers are up to date. Here generous sabbaticals are provided either to work within client MNCs or to go further afield, wherever cutting-edge practice has been identified.

The close cooperation between MNCs and the state also enables the latter to play an active role in transferring leading-edge techniques and skills. For example, the Productivity and Standards Board is seeking to improve the utilization of labour through helping companies redesign their jobs to raise skill levels by introducing high-performance work organizations (the Job Redesign 2000 programme). This involves what may be considered a typical set of strategies used by the state to raise skill levels encompassing: *models* of high-performance workplaces that companies may emulate; *consultancy* work to help with job redesign; the *promotion* of the programme to help raise awareness, a *skills development* programme to help workers acquire the skills for redesigned jobs, and a *support package* of financial incentives and policies to 'encourage' firms to join the programme. Another programme designed to raise both the demand for and supply of skills is the Investors in People strategy, noted in the previous chapter, in which training to improve the use of human resources is substantially subsidized by the government. This programme is available to all companies in Singapore and operates with much the same kind of formula as the Job Redesign Programme.

The multi-pronged attempt to constantly raise all elements of skill amongst the workforce made possible by the close cooperation between MNCs and the state has a more profound underlying motive to do with the leitmotif of survival which dominates much of the state's rhetoric and is clearly designed to legitimize its economic and political strategy. Government officials often describe Singapore as 'Singapore Inc.' but the competition for Singapore Inc. is not with MNCs, rather it seeks to co-opt them in order to gain comparative advantage over its competitor nations.

The fundamental problem of Singapore's guided labour market concerns the nature of the socialization and education of the workforce in relation to future demands. Singapore's students have consistently been at the top of the IEA comparative studies' league tables in maths and science. However, there has been a concern that goes back to at least 1986 (Tremewan 1994) that the education system is turning out smart conformists who can follow manuals but can not think creatively. The Singaporean ET and labour market system has worked because of the discipline and indeed obedience of young people. Now they are being asked to question and take risks. It is a moot point as to whether the broad strategy of upskilling and skill diffusion can be sustained in the absence of the kind of social discipline that has been exerted hitherto. It can be argued that the level of coordination and the rapid responses and flexibility that the state has been able to create are a function of a highly centralized, hierarchical, system of governance: one that has also been able to exert considerable power in socializing 'smart conformists'. The problem then is whether the machinery of state which is so closely linked to a form of democratic authoritarianism could be undermined by its own desire to develop creative risk-takers.

The crucial question is whether the system of coordination and flexibility that is at the heart of the guided market can be sustained if the political character of Singapore changes, or to what extent the techniques and strategies that typify the guided market can be successful within a different political and economic context. This is an issue which is addressed in the following chapter.

Gender and the Guided Labour Market

While, initially, a policy of inviting guest workers to Singapore was designed to provide cheap semi- and unskilled labour, as Singapore has become more successful in moving up the value chain it has suffered an acute shortage of educated labour. It is in this context that the role of women is best understood. To the mid-1980s the relationship of women to the labour market was made problematic by the state's desire to control women's reproduction largely by discouraging working-class women (often Malays) from having large families while encouraging middle-class women to breed (Hill and Lian Kew Fee 1995). However, this led to a backlash with these women becoming better organized and more vocal in defending their interests (Tremewan 1994). Consequently, the government admitted these policies had been in error and have stepped back from seeking to regulate women in this way. The combination of the withdrawal of policies designed to regulate the population of Singapore and the shortage of labour has led to increased participation by women in education and the labour market. For example, the proportion of women in professional and technical work is 68 per cent of men in the same category, while the proportion of women in senior administrative and managerial positions relative to those of men is 19 per cent (Jayaweera 1997). This is a significantly higher participation rate than for their counterparts in Korea and Japan.[15] Participation in higher education is now effectively at parity with males with 49 per cent of women comprising the university population.[16] The situation is comparable in polytechnics, where 46 per cent of the sector comprises women. There is, however, a major difference with respect to the ITE sector where women comprise 28.5 per cent of the population, although they also comprise 44 per cent of graduates. The ITE sector mainly caters for those at the lower end of educational achievement, representing, approximately, the bottom 30 per cent of secondary school graduates. The low participation rates amongst women are likely to be related to issues of class and ethnicity, but it is difficult to gain a real insight into the processes involved. Critics of the Singaporean system argue that the PAP have historically 'managed' ethnic conflict in Singapore in favour of the Chinese, creating a Malay underclass in the process (Tremewan 1994). If this account is correct, then what the figures for the ITE may indicate is a legacy of this process with Malay women failing to participate in tertiary education. Certainly, the state has released figures, from time to time, showing the educational levels of the various ethnic groups to stimulate debate about its causes but to our knowledge, no origins and destinations studies have been undertaken which might give an overall picture of education achievement and occupational destinations by social class, gender, and ethnicity.

When it comes to the barriers to skill development caused by the gender typing of training undertaken, some of the vocational ethos which pervades education and training in Singapore serves to break down the gender typing seen elsewhere. For example, 24 per cent of those enrolled in engineering, 30 per cent of those enrolled in computing, and 64 per cent of those enrolled in science at university are women. Moreover, they are dominant in accountancy (64 per cent) and business studies (70 per cent). At the polytechnics they comprise 38 per cent of information technology enrolments and 30 per cent of electrical engineering enrolments. They also constitute just under one-third of students in mechanical and manufacturing programmes. Gender typing is, however, far starker at the ITE. Here only 13 per cent of those enrolled in engineering are women and 11 per cent in technical skills. The majority of women are enrolled in business and service skill

---

[15] These comparative data should be taken as indicative only, since there will be differences in the classification of occupations in the respective countries.

[16] The education statistics for Singapore are taken from the Ministry of Education website: <www1.moe.edu.sg/esd/esd/99> and refer to 1999.

programmes. Clearly, the close to parity enrolments at the university and polytechnic levels by women will provide the potential for a high skills gap in Singapore to be addressed. The state is now encouraging women's participation in education with considerable success. The major issue, now, is whether this educational equality at the upper levels will be translated into occupational equality.

THE FLEXIBLE LABOUR MARKET

In Britain, the dominant labour market structure can be described as one centred on flexibility. Elements of the internal labour market have been adopted from Japan but rarely with a commitment to a job for life. This internal labour market has been constructed in order to ensure continuity of expertise and learning for businesses. The percentage of workers in the internal labour market tends to be low relative to Japanese and Korean firms, while the numbers of casualized workers are correspondingly greater. Flexibility, therefore, centres on the ability to hire and fire rather than on multi-skilling (Brown and Lauder 1996). The education and training system reflects both the demand for skilled workers in the flexible labour market and the underlying ethos which makes it different from either occupational or internal labour markets.

In relation to the stock of skills Britain produces a significant proportion of well-educated graduates who, broadly speaking, are destined for the internal or core labour market, while also having a large tail of poorly qualified workers (see Chapter 2). These provide numerical flexibility by being hired at times of boom and fired in times of slump. This type of flexibility tends to polarize differences in labour market power and makes insecurity of work endemic since those with few or no qualifications have little control over their working lives. The link between the ET system and the labour market is that of 'choice'. It is a fundamental tenet of the system that the best way in which education and the labour market can be coordinated is through individual judgements about the worth of particular kinds of credential in the labour market. Individual choice becomes central to the type of post-16 education young people receive. In turn the educational market has responded by providing a myriad of routes and courses for students leaving secondary school. Consequently, there are few structured career pathways into the labour market, leaving socialization open to the specific influence of family, peers, and the school. The choice mechanism is significant in relation to skill diffusion because throughout the economy skill acquisition and diffusion rests primarily with individual social networks rather than with the web of institutional networks which structure careers, and skill acquisition and diffusion in the occupational and internal labour markets.[17]

Employers may take an interest in the general educational standard of those recruited into the internal or core labour market, but their focus will be on firm-specific training.[18] Fundamentally, the aim is to hire workers that 'plug in and play' and so the training is likely to be only on a 'need to know' basis. Where training exceeds that limited to being able to do the immediate job, it is likely that it is also seen as a defensive strategy against poaching.[19]

However, there is a further problem in the kind of internal or core labour market adopted in the United Kingdom. Companies like the intermediate manufacturer who we interviewed appeared to have been able to make a job for life commitment through a strategy in which many of the risks associated with a job for life were transferred on to suppliers. Increasingly firms in the United Kingdom appear to be dominated by a strategy of offloading risk, either to suppliers or by casualizing larger proportions of the workforce. At the extremes this means that the core of workers comprising the internal market is very small indeed, while the remainder are recruited through agencies

[17] The choice mechanism in the UK can be considered problematic in several ways. The first is that there are time lags between when an individual 'reads' the labour market for jobs in demand and when they qualify to undertake those jobs. Effectively jobs may have changed or no longer be there after the period of qualification. The second is that given the wide range of courses competitively on offer in further education colleges, universities, and New Start programmes, it is important that the links between these courses and the labour market are well established. In fact many appear to have a marginal relationship to the labour market and hence provide limited access to it. This involves economic costs in terms of matching individuals to jobs and psychological costs in terms of loss of confidence when a job considered appropriate to the training cannot be found.

[18] Several points arise from this. In economies with flexible labour markets the nature of the debate over ET is likely to be quite different, with employers commenting and criticizing from the touchlines as it were. Whereas in occupationally structured labour markets, there is likely to be a more consensual hands on approach to ET. In the UK the NVQ can be seen as a compromise between the interests of the state in the successful functioning of the economy and the sectional interests of employers. By having an externally validated and moderated certificate, the state seeks to ensure that skills can be transferred from one company to another. However, employers will structure the portfolios that comprise NVQs as specifically as possible to their needs so that these skills are not easily transferable, in order to prevent poaching.

[19] A Training Manager of a British intermediate manufacturer held out the possibility of a job for life which generated commitment amongst the workforce, however he reported high levels of poaching for managers and other graduates who have completed their training.

(Purcell and Purcell 1998). Such agencies cater for both the skilled and unskilled and provide a further example of where it is the individual who has to bear the cost of pension plans and forms of social insurance rather than corporations. The fundamental problem with this is that employers have little reason to invest in the training of their casualized workers and indeed the evidence suggests that this is the case (Arulampalam and Booth 1997). Moreover, despite some adoption of Japanese-style relationships between the large companies and SMEs, training within the SME sector in the United Kingdom is limited (Kitson and Wilkinson 1998).

There are several consequences for the development and transmission of knowledge in a flexible labour market of this kind. The first is that the transmission of tacit knowledge is limited to the internal market, since continuity within production is essential to its acquisition, reproduction, and modification. The second concerns the heavy reliance on the individual to acquire the appropriate motivation to gain new skills. The third is that a labour market which places responsibility on the individual for their skills and the costs of social insurance is not likely to engender qualities of commitment and loyalty which are so central to the occupational and internal labour market (Sennett 1998). Moreover, Fevre, Rees, and Gorrard (1999) in their study of training and labour markets in South Wales show that a culture has developed over time amongst workers which is highly sceptical of anything but on-the-job training tied to immediate tasks. The orientation of the workers in their study was largely instrumental in contrast to the German orientation to an intrinsic concern with the quality of work undertaken. These patterns of socialization are also consistent with the different approaches to competitive strategy in the two countries which will be described below. The fourth is that the predominant mechanism for skill diffusion is through 'job hopping' on the part of individuals and poaching on the part of companies. The fifth is that a significant percentage of the workforce will receive little training. In a casualized labour market in which the semi- and unskilled have to work long hours to earn something close to a living wage, the opportunities for upskilling become difficult. The final point concerns information rigidities (Brown and Lauder 2001a). Where workers are operating in an uncertain and low trust environment, it is likely that they will withhold key information for their own advantage, especially where it might be used to gain another job.[20]

[20] Clearly this is disadvantageous to the company currently employing such workers. If they then job hop and release the information, this may well 'socialize' the knowledge across the industry. However, if the knowledge is 'stored' as an insurance against unemployment and no job-hopping occurs the information is simply lost and no one gains.

This type of labour market may be successful under at least two kinds of competitive strategy. The first, typical of the higher end of the semi-conductor market, is where it is basic or breakthrough innovations that generate competitive edge. Here the erratic brilliance of an individual may be what is required. A similar observation might be made about work in the 'creative' industries like television and design where Britain is clearly competitive. The key question is, then, does this model of highly individualistic brilliance point to the future in most forms of production or is it unsustainable because innovation is a collective venture, depending upon breaking down information rigidities. If skill is defined primarily in terms of labour market power, the commitment to company-specific innovation is likely to be limited.

Finally, it is worth considering the informal routes by which individuals change occupation and seek promotion in the flexible labour market. The key mechanisms for doing this are the *curriculum vitae*, informal networks, and, increasingly, a battery of psychological tests used by recruitment agencies. The informal assumptions by which skill sets are brought into new combinations through individuals changing occupations are always open to question because their 'rationality' seems to be deeply embedded in specific national cultures. In Britain, in the past it was accountants who could use their training to become managers and senior executives, while more recently the trend has been to follow the American fashion for generic managers. In neither case is it clear how these forms of initial training can help to generate value added based on innovation, since generic managers may not have the intellectual expertise or sensitivity to understand their company's potential for innovation. It is more likely that they will seek to satisfy shareholders by making quick profits from takeovers and buy-outs rather than by adding value through innovation. Certainly this appears to be the lesson in all but the hi-tech sectors when British and American company performance is compared to, say, that of Germany (O'Sullivan 2000).

Gender and the Flexible Labour Market

In relation to women, the flexible labour market exemplifies many of the same characteristics as for men. On the one hand, the numbers of women in managerial and professional occupations is higher than in many European countries, including Germany. This is reflected in the greater participation of women in higher education. On the other hand, the bottom 10 per cent of women earn less than 38.5 per cent of the average for the EU. Equally the gap between men and women's pay is higher in Britain than the rest of the EU with women earning, on average, 34 per cent less than men's pay (EC 1999*b*).

The links between the ET system and the labour market for women mirrors the profile of men with respect to the distribution of credentials. Broadly speaking, there is a bi-modal distribution of credentials in which there are an increasing number of degree holders while at the bottom end there is a high proportion of women workers with few or no qualifications. For example, in 1997, 40 per cent of women had less than an upper secondary qualification, in comparison to Germany where only 20 per cent were similarly lowly qualified (EC 1999*b*). Much has been made, in Britain, of the trend by which women are outperforming men in secondary school examination results (Arnot, Weiner, and David 1999), but many young women are still leaving school with few or no qualifications and then participating in neither education or employment. The Social Exclusion Unit estimates conservatively that this applies to some 9 per cent of 16–18 year olds of whom the majority are women (Social Exclusion Unit 1999).

The distinguishing feature of the flexible labour market as developed in the United States and Britain is the polarization of income, with large numbers of low paid 'junk jobs'. While it is hard to argue that it is only relatively unskilled women that provide the necessary flexibility for this kind of labour market. They clearly make up a significant number of those at the sharp end in poor work, but it should be noted, also, that Britain has the highest number of young people, irrespective of gender, in the 16–18 age bracket in poor paying jobs (EC 1999*b*). That there should be such a high demand for poor work is not surprising, since with few market regulations and low social costs attached to hiring and firing, employers can make profit out of cheap labour rather than investment in technology (Brown and Lauder 2001*a*). The consequence is that a high proportion of British workers experience poverty and as we shall see this has a significant impact on their chances of gaining qualifications. Given that the issue of poverty and polarization of incomes looms large in flexible labour markets, we need to examine their effects on skill acquisition and diffusion.

POLARIZATION OF INCOMES, SKILL
ACQUISITION, AND DIFFUSION

The recent OECD report on *Poverty Dynamics in Six OECD Countries*
(OECD 2000*b*) estimates that in relation to income, pre-tax, and transfers, approximately 55 per cent of the British population experienced
poverty at least once in six years between 1991 and 1997, this figure was
reduced to 40 per cent after tax and transfers. These poverty levels are,
respectively, 18 and 20 percentage points higher than in Germany.

The reason why so many in a flexible labour market, like that of
Britain, experience episodes of poverty is that they earn wages close to
the most commonly used definition of poverty, half the average wage.
Goodman, Johnson, and Webb (1997) report that the heaviest concentration of incomes is around half the national average, in contrast to
thirty years ago when the heaviest concentration of incomes was around
80 to 90 per cent of the national average. Effectively nearly six million
workers, in Britain, have incomes in the range of 40 to 50 per cent of the
national average.

There are both demand and supply-side effects to having large
numbers of workers on low wages or in poverty. With respect to the
demand side, as was noted briefly above, both Hutton (1995) and Keep
(1999) have argued that with so many workers on low wages it is hardly
surprising that firms' dominant strategy has been to compete on price
rather than quality, simply because the latter cannot be afforded. The
difference between seeking to compete on price rather than quality is
that between producing a Ford Escort, rather than a Mercedes. In a
country with a large low-wage sector, Ford Escorts are likely to be
affordable in a way that Mercedes are not. But it requires far higher
levels of skill, which in turn create higher levels of profitability, to make
the Mercedes.

On the supply side, the crucial questions concern the influence of
poverty and low wages on skill acquisition and transfer and on the
social-psychological impact of low skill work on cognitive dispositions.
There is strong evidence of the connection between poverty, education,
and the labour market (P. Johnson and Reed 1996; Gregg, Harkness, and
Machin 1999). P. Johnson and Reed (1996), for example, show that 40 per
cent of sons, whose fathers experienced low income or periods of
poverty in the 1970s are likely to experience a similar fate themselves.
When the links between low income and educational performance are
set against the high demand for young cheap labour in Britain, it is not

surprising, as we have seen, that there is such a high wastage rate after the end of compulsory schooling.[21]

There are two further sources of evidence which suggest that the polarization associated with flexible labour markets is likely to reduce both skill acquisition and diffusion. The first concerns the work of Wilkinson (1996) who has shown that growing disparities in income lead to higher mortality rates and a series of problems for families at the bottom of the income parade. He argues that the latter have a clear influence on children's educational performance. Support for this view comes from Willms (1999) who, in conducting an international survey on adult literacy, found that when literacy was related to parents' level of education the steepest gradients were in countries with the most polarized incomes. Not surprisingly, therefore, countries like the Netherlands and Sweden had the shallowest gradients indicating high levels of literacy across the population.

The effect of a large sector of low skilled workers does not only have an impact on succeeding generations but on existing workers. Here, the work of Kohn and Schooler (1983) is of particular relevance. They have found that the cognitive complexity and responsibility associated with a job have an impact on individuals' values, conception of reality, and ideational flexibility. This research is all the stronger because it is longitudinal and they have been able to establish that while there is a reciprocal causal relationship between job conditions and the psychological dispositions they studied, the link from job conditions to psychological dispositions is strong. Consequently, there are likely to be social-psychological barriers to the upskilling of those in low skilled work.[22] The consequence is that the assumption at the heart of skill diffusion strategies in the flexible labour market, that it is through the mobility of individuals that skills are diffused, is likely to be false.[23]

The summary point to make about polarization is that it excludes people from the pathways and systems by which skills are acquired and diffused. The kinds of clear pathways found in the Dual System in Germany generating confidence in the individual and the system are

[21] The recent OECD report on the transition from education to work found that one year after the end of compulsory schooling about 26% of young people were not in education or in employment in Britain (OECD 2000c).

[22] Esping-Andersen notes that low skill service workers tend to be heterogeneous but not all such workers can be university or college students. The data suggest that however diverse this group is, it will include a sizeable proportion of long-term semi- and unskilled workers.

[23] There is a second point concerning human capital theory and in particular the pre-social assumption that human beings will always seek to upgrade their skills as a matter of self-interest. If Kohn and Schooler are correct, then this casts considerable doubt upon this key assumption.

simply absent or likely to be blocked in a flexible labour market like that of Britain.[24] Polarization is, therefore, a major impediment to a high skills strategy. Indeed, it generates paradoxical outcomes. On the one hand, more people are placed in work, albeit poor work. Consequently, the policy response is to create a working families tax credit for those in poor work. But such a policy merely reinforces a market strategy of competing on price, delivered through low labour costs. The only way a high skills strategy can work in a flexible labour market is if a sufficient income floor is placed beneath workers so that effectively poor work is priced out of the market. This could be done, for example, through the introduction of a citizens' wage (P. Brown and Lauder 2001*a*).

TRAINING AND SKILL FOUNDATIONS FOR MOVING UP THE VALUE CHAIN

The final issue that needs to be addressed concerns the role of national systems of skill diffusion in relation to competitiveness. Here the fundamental question is: To what extent do national systems of skill diffusion help or hinder moving up the value chain?

There are good reasons why companies competing on price may seek to upgrade their performance to compete on quality. In general terms competing on quality will bring higher profits and a more skilled workforce. In Britain there is a strong incentive, especially amongst manufacturers, to upgrade their strategy, since fluctuations in the exchange rate can have a substantial effect on price-led competition.[25] Competing on quality typically means introducing high-performance work practices, since these have been shown to generate higher value added products than other kinds of training and human resource practices. However, upgrading a company's performance requires the

---

[24] The contrasting point may be made that Germany has higher levels of unemployment than the UK, which will also serve to lower motivation. However, whereas in the UK the unemployed tend to have lower skills than those in employment in German, there is no difference in the skill levels between those with jobs and those without them (Freeman and Schettkat 1999). The often quoted solution to Germany's unemployment 'problem' of creating low skill service industry work would in this context be problematic, since those currently unemployed would be overqualified.

[25] Unfortunately, there are also strong disincentives to do with the risks involved in ascending the value chain, including the lack of low interest capital, the ability to break into the quality end of the market, and devolving power to the workforce. These risks seem to prevail over the advantages (see the following discussion).

diffusion of new process or key skills. This is because high-performance work practices are reliant on devolving the power of decision-making to teams, just-in-time production, and total quality management systems. In turn these require key skills like being able to communicate well, work in a team, use IT, problem solve, and have a sound level of numerical skills. These are not skills which are required in standardized systems of mass production, but they are central to high-performance systems. In other words, they require far broader levels of skill and systems of learning than those found in the varieties of standardized production.

Recent work by Cappelli (1999) and his co-contributors raises the possibility that firms will adopt different training and human resource practices when competing in the same product market. Indeed a clear example of this came from Daimler-Chrysler who told us that some of their plants maintained a variant of standardized mass production where others had adopted high-performance work practices. Nevertheless, even in their standardized production plants, Daimler-Chrysler allowed some worker flexibility and capability to be innovative.[26]

The key point here turns on training and skill diffusion systems which are sufficiently flexible to allow the possibility of different types of production. There is considerable evidence that the Dual System and occupational labour market provide for such flexibility (Mason, van Ark, and Wagner 1996). Similarly, an internal labour market should also provide the flexibility for varying modes of production. The reasons for this have to do with the 'overtraining' that these systems permit and their consequences for enhancing process or key skills. The problem-solving and innovation-making that overtraining permits are central to high-performance work systems. They presuppose allowing workers a degree of autonomy, initiative, and flexibility, which is precisely what studies of German productive systems by Mason and his colleagues have found. In fact, the Mechatronics Fitter ordinance we referred to previously covers the type of process skills necessary for high-performance work systems. Moreover, they may also provide workers with the confidence to take the kinds of initiatives a high-performance system requires.[27]

[26] Daimler-Chrysler maintained standardized mass production systems where their products were less customized and the workforce older.

[27] We should be careful not to make too much of this point, since Daimler-Chrysler reported to us that introducing high-performance systems has not always been straightforward due to what they perceive as their failure to train workers sufficiently well in process skills in some plants. Even with overtraining there are clearly other obstacles to overcome in introducing high-performance work systems. Overtraining is clearly a necessary but not sufficient condition in facilitating the move to high-performance work systems.

In contrast, in flexible labour markets like Britain's, training is far more likely to be 'just-in-time' provided so that workers are fit to do a specific job. This is because Britain, in contrast to Germany, is far more likely to compete on price rather than quality (Regini 1995).[28] What is clear, though, is that the kind of just-in-time training systems stand at a considerable disadvantage in providing a foundation for a shift to high-performance work practices. The micro comparative evidence furnished by the National Institute for Economic and Social Research demonstrates the disadvantage of British companies with just-in-time trained workers, when compared to their German counterparts. This evidence has now been supplemented by macro survey data published by the National Skills Task Force (2000). This shows a degree of inertia in adopting such practices in Britain. For example, in the survey conducted by Waterson et al. (1999), the majority of companies reported that they had either not adopted the key elements of high-performance practice or had only done so to a moderate extent. Companies which were seeking to move up the value chain clearly identified the process or key skills necessary for high-performance work practices, but many found that skill shortages were an impediment to moving. Moreover, approximately half the establishments with skills gaps acknowledged that these were partly due to their own failure to train and develop staff.

The implications of this research are that national systems of training and skill diffusion can have a significant impact on strategies to move up the value chain. This is not just a matter of a shortage of supply of skills, but the way in which individuals are trained. This is especially so in relation to the diffusion of skills. In the occupational and internal labour market there are mechanisms for diffusing best practice from leading-edge companies to SMEs, including those related to process skills but in a flexible labour market this is far more problematic. Moreover, the training systems which provide the foundation for process or key skills associated with high-performance practice are deeply embedded in the history, politics, and culture of a nation: a point we shall pick up in the conclusion.

---

[28] The distinction between competing on price rather than quality is a relative one (see Oulton 1996). However it helps to clarify a puzzle in the research. Gallie and White (1993) have found that in Britain all but semi- and unskilled workers have experienced an upgrading of skills. The notion of a significant upgrading of skills when there is a significant low skill sector in Britain appears paradoxical. Yet it makes sense if we understand that there are different types of training and hence skills upgrading depending on which type of competition firms enter, price or quality. Overtraining in the German system clearly allows for innovation, less so in the British just-in-time system.

CONCLUSION

There are three broad conclusions to be drawn from this chapter. The first is that while little attention has been paid in the past to the analysis of national systems of skill diffusion, it is hoped that the research reported here demonstrates the importance of this particular field of study. As with the closely related field of technological innovation, there are distinct systems of skill diffusion in the terms defined in this chapter. Reflecting on the comparative strengths and weaknesses of the different systems opens the way to considering the question of judicious importation to improve national systems. This is not necessarily by copying institutions or policies wholesale because, as noted below, they are deeply embedded in particular political and cultural contexts but by asking what the analogue to a particular policy in one framework might be in another. However, these systems of skill diffusion are not static and in the next chapter we shall examine them in relation to the global economy.

A second point related to intermediate institutions concerns their absence in flexible labour markets. In principle they can act as a conduit between cutting-edge MNCs and national companies and SMEs and it is difficult to see how the links between cutting-edge practice and SMEs can be made without them.[29] Job-hopping may have a limited role in the SME sector in the transference of knowledge and skills precisely because those with cutting-edge knowledge may be priced out of the SME market, unless of course they are in hi-tech start-up companies. There seems a clear role for institutions which can act to transfer the relevant knowledge of technology and skills.

The third point is that the Singaporean case, in particular, throws into sharp relief two of the key issues relating to initial training that aims to be at the cutting-edge. These have to do with how students gain access to what is often very expensive and sophisticated equipment and how this is to be resourced. In the occupational labour market, where training is shared between employers and the state education system, students gain access through the apprenticeships in plants and offices. As we have seen, this problem is not necessarily solved in the case of banking because the computer hardware and software which seem integral to training for banking are not of equal standard in the *Berufschule*

---

[29] This point did also apply to the internal labour market of Korea. However, given the fundamental changes afoot there, it may no longer. See the next chapter.

and the companies. In the internal labour market where companies undertake all the vocationally specific training the general point applies: students gain access to the latest equipment and related skills through the company. However, in a flexible labour market, it is a moot point as to whether students who typically complete much of their training at further education colleges get such access.

In broader terms, the research shows that different national systems have very clear strengths and weaknesses in diffusing specific kinds of skill. For example, the German occupational labour market, the Japanese internal market, and the Singaporean guided market are clearly superior to a flexible market in diffusing the skills necessary for intermediate manufactured goods, albeit in quite different ways. The flexible labour market appears much better able to handle diffusion in the hi-tech electronic sector.

Each of the above types of labour market and competitive strategy generate a potential and actual problems that need to be addressed. What is significant about many, but not all of these, is that they are generated by social forces outside ET and labour market systems or by tensions between systems of political control and the demands for new kinds of workers and skills. The issues of worker identity construction, socialization, and social control are never very far away because they underpin labour market structures and in particular the way skills are generated and disseminated within them. Perhaps the fundamental question which is posed by this research is whether the dominant ET, labour market, and competitive strategies described here are adequate to the kind of global competition that nations now confront. Ideally different kinds of labour market, and competitive strategy are required for different market sectors. Yet it will also be apparent how deeply rooted skill formation and skill diffusion are in national politics and culture. For example, the German occupational labour market and Dual System are intimately linked to a politics of equality of productive capacity and notions of the worker-citizen in which workers not only have rights in relation to being skilled but civic responsibilities which extend beyond their immediate workplace. In Japan the emphasis on teamwork, it has been argued, has its roots in pre-school education (Tobin 1999). In Singapore, it is difficult to divorce the specific techniques used to raise the demand and supply of skill from its particular kind of authoritarian democracy, geo-politics, and its small population. While in Britain, the individualism which characterizes skill formation and diffusion seems closely tied to the neo-liberal policies introduced in the 1980s (Lauder 1999). What appears clear is that any attempt to develop a skill diffusion strategy in Britain will be within the framework of individualistic assumptions developed in the 1980s and taken on board by the present Labour government. In this chapter we have looked at some of the key features of skill diffusion, in the next we assess the likely impact of global economic forces upon them.

Globalization, Multinationals, and the Labour Market

HUGH LAUDER, WITH YADOLLAH MEHRALIZADEH

INTRODUCTION

One of the major claims made for the current development of the global economy in relation to the production of goods and services is that multinationals are a conduit for the transfer of technology and with it, skills. In this chapter we shall look at the competing hypotheses regarding the impact of globalization on the different types of ET and labour market systems in Germany, Korea, Singapore, and Britain. This also involves looking at skill transfer and the development policies of multinationals. In the final section of the chapter we report on the impact of multinational ownership on 'key' skills training and application in one major British subsidiary of a foreign multinational. It can be argued that key or core skills, those relating to teamwork, communication, problem-solving, and the use of IT, which are required for high-performance workplaces provide a litmus test of the convergence thesis. If the impact of globalization is that these skills are transferable across national borders, then the convergence thesis will have passed a particularly stringent test.

COMPETING HYPOTHESES CONCERNING GLOBALIZATION

In order to locate the issue of skill transference and diffusion within the global economy, we need to locate it within a theoretical framework. Here there are two broadly competing hypotheses that we can entertain. They are as follows:

(1) *There will be a greater convergence in education, training, and labour market structures over time. Consequently, national systems of skill diffusion will also converge. This process will facilitate the global transfer of skill, just as it has technology.*

This 'convergence' view has gained popularity for at least two reasons. The first concerns some of the general and unique features of this phase of global economic integration. These include for the purposes of our discussion: (1) deeper and wider integration of national economies through trade, direct investment, and other capital flows; (2) the enormous cost, risk, and complexity of technology in many strategic or leading sectors; (3) the digitalization of the economy combined with the movement of markets from geographic to cyberspace; leading to (4) space–time compression in information and decision-making (Kobrin 2000).

These factors would certainly provide a prima facie case for thinking that the forces for convergence are powerful. The combination of free capital flows, the expense and complexity of technological development, and the compression of space–time would all suggest that speed in the transference of skill is of the essence in order for technology to be developed and utilized. Consequently, it might also be expected that the ET and labour market system which can deliver the most efficient and flexible diffusion of skills is likely to be adopted in all nations. However, what this hypothesis lacks is a political economy which explains what the levers of change are which would bring about such a convergence. As it stands, convergence, according to this hypothesis, is merely a matter of technical rationality or economic imperative. The problem with such a determinist view is that, as we have seen in the previous chapters, there are clearly several capitalisms with distinct ET and labour market systems and accordingly, several ways of achieving competitiveness: there is no economic logic to which all nations should necessarily conform. This then brings us to the second reason for the popularity of the convergence thesis.

One of outcomes of the Asian economic crisis of 1997/8 is that we are now far more aware of what could be called the imperialist tendencies of shareholder capitalism (Dore 2000; Dore, Lazonick, and O'Sullivan 1999). Central to this view of capitalism is the dominant belief that the business enterprise makes its best social contribution, as well as serving its own purposes, if it is run to maximize shareholder value—a concept in which, for quoted companies, the share price plays a major role. Competitive discipline is exercised on quoted companies through shareholder activism which responds to instances of managerial delin- quency, through the substitution of voice strategies for exit strategies. These include takeovers forced on companies by an oligarchy of powerful fund-holders. However, in relation to investment in capital and skills, the key feature of shareholder capitalism is its short-termism, which demands that shareholders achieve constantly high returns on investment over relatively short periods of time.

The role that this form of capitalism is playing in seeking to drive national economic systems towards global convergence became clear during the Asian crisis when the Washington–Wall Street axis first mani- fested itself (Wade and Veneroso 1998). The arguments of Wade and others in this respect will be revisited when we examine the impact of globalization on the system of skill diffusion in Korea. However, the key point for now is that the hypothesis that convergence will be driven by the imperialist tendencies of shareholder capitalism provides one high- profile explanation of the political mechanisms that could bring about a degree of convergence. So there are both technicist and political explanations underlying the convergence hypothesis. But it will also be clear from what has already been said that there are countervailing forces which have led to an alternative hypothesis:

(2) *The global economy will exert a limited influence, at best, on national ET and labour market systems and hence on national systems of skill diffusion.*

The reasons in support of this hypothesis are threefold. First, training systems are embedded in national norms, practices, and legal frame- works and are not amenable to rapid change. There are instances in related areas of the economy where national practices appear to be stronger than the apparent imperatives of economic rationality. Two observations from a related field would back up this view. In the United States knowledge of best practice high-performance systems of HR management derived from Japanese lean production models is wide- spread yet many firms even within the same industry operate with diverse systems of management (Capelli 1999). Equally, research reported by the National Skills Task Force (2000a) shows that the adoption of such best practices system in the United Kingdom has been slow and uneven (Waterson et al. 1999). These examples suggest that national economies are not as permeable as advocates of convergence would suggest. A similar point can be made with respect to ET systems in Europe (Green, Leney, and Wolf 1997).

Secondly, national ET and labour market systems may not have the capacity to diffuse skills imported by multinational companies. In order for nations to take advantage of foreign direct investment two conditions need to be obtained: MNCs need to establish plants overseas that utilize a range of skills. The concern is that the overseas plants are frequently 'screwdriver' assembly plants with little capability or commitment to research and development. Over and above this, however, MNCs need to be embedded in a network of local suppliers and education and training establishments, if the benefits of skill transfer and diffusion are to be captured. In developing countries these conditions need to be supplemented by the relevant communications infrastructure. Where these conditions do not exist, what we are likely to see, at best, is the development of high skill enclaves (Kobrin 2000).

This brings us to the third issue: for the convergence hypothesis to gain any real purchase we should be observing a fundamental shift in the organization, culture, and vision of corporations, operating in the global economy from MNCs rooted in the national culture of their origins to truly transnational corporations. In an extensive analysis of the behaviour of American, German, and Japanese MNCs, Doremus, Keller, Pauly, and Reich show that so far MNCs have remained rooted in their national contexts. The reasons for this concern the different national systems of corporate governance, finance, and innovation, which they describe as 'remarkably enduring' (1998: 138).[1] Their findings are summarized as follows:

MNCs based in these three leading home markets continue to govern and finance themselves quite differently. Although there are some changes at the margins, there is scant evidence that basic patterns of corporate control, which is what governance and financing are ultimately about, are shifting fundamentally. (Doremus, Keller, Pauly, and Reich 1998: 138)

---

[1] With respect to high skilled work in relation to Japanese and Korean MNCs, see Munday, Morris, and Wilkinson (1995). Also Jung (1999), who compares the strategy of leading Korean electronics manufacturers in Europe. He describes their European operations as Fordist screwdriver plants that are disembedded—he notes, for example, how frequently one manufacturer has relocated plants in order to reduce labour costs. He argues that this 'fragile Europeanization' was intensified by the Asian crisis.

If these are the hypotheses concerning the effects of globalization, what can our High Skills data tell us about them? We begin with the skill diffusion system of the occupational labour market, as represented by Germany.

GLOBALIZATION AND THE GERMAN OCCUPATIONAL LABOUR MARKET

The Dual System of training and its relationship to the occupational labour market is at the heart of the wider consensus politics of co-determination between trade unions, employers, and different levels of the state that have made post-war Germany such a success. For example, wages are intimately linked to the construction of professions within the Dual System and the latter are co-determined by trade unions, employers, and the state—at various levels. The strong influence that has been exercised by the trade unions has meant that the polarization of wages, which has been a feature of the British and American economies, is unknown in Germany (Prasad 2000). Now, however, German companies have become part of the global economy with a vengeance buying up major companies in America and Britain (Meyer-Larsen 2000), while at the same time resisting similar levels of investment in Germany. The cost to German companies of taxes paid in social protection and training are high and the general question that needs to be addressed is whether the leading German corporations will continue to pay such a high price for social consensus. Since the Dual System is at the heart of this system of co-determination, secession by the leading companies from the consensus politics of the past is likely to threaten the Dual System.[2] As we saw in the previous chapter, the role of the leading companies in promoting innovation and skill diffusion is central to Germany's competitiveness in intermediate manufacturing goods. The key question, then, is whether these leading-edge companies see sufficient advantage in maintaining the Dual System to outweigh the costs they have to bear.

---

[2] There is also an internal threat due to unemployment. Here the argument is that Germany needs to introduce a flexible labour market to create cheap service sector jobs to mop up the unemployment. However, reducing the costs of employment threatens Germany's ability to compete using highly skilled workers because it will enable the option of making profit out of cheap labour. It is also the case that those currently unemployed would be overqualified for such jobs, see the previous chapter. In contrast to the UK, the policy of having high employment costs has clearly paid off in terms of investment in capital equipment. See Prasad (2000).

Our research suggests that these companies remain committed to the Dual System and moreover are seeking to replicate it when they establish plants overseas.[3] For example, we were told by Siemens that they were establishing a joint training system, with Lufthansa, in China according to the principles of the Dual System. Lane (1998) in her discussion of the relative embeddedness of leading-edge companies in the United Kingdom and Germany also found that German firms have tried to re-create the high skills produced by the Dual System overseas. Where these attempts have not been made, their overseas ventures have either been unsuccessful or have caused concerns about the lack of a skilled workforce.[4] The drive by German firms to re-create the foundations for their success overseas attests to the more general point made by Doremus et al. (1998) that by and large multinationals seek to reproduce the strategies that have made them successful in their home countries. Perhaps one of the most interesting insights into this process also came from the director of human resources of a renowned German company that had a British subsidiary. Since the British firm had been taken over, there had been a major debate as to the nature and quality of its training between the two companies.

Part of the problem, as the director of human resources perceived it, concerned the British national qualifications structure which she described as 'incredible' because of the variety of courses, often based on a modular structure. This enabled the development of knowledge in breadth but not in depth. As she commented: 'In our country we don't like this idea because we say there is a craft and that these requirements are needed.' This comment was very much tied to a view of specialism. In her view workers needed: 'key qualifications (skills), they have to know how to learn, how to change' and 'they have to have the qualification of a specialist. Both because tomorrow they will be another specialist and then they will know how to adapt and how to learn. They have to have both.'

While we did not probe this point, it could be argued that underlying this view is a cultural assumption about the socialization of workers into achieving the highest standards possible. Specialization in one area and the social status accorded it in Germany teaches workers the standard required for specialization in another area. Certainly the British company had taken on the message that breadth needed to be enhanced by depth of specialization. Yet if the argument

[3] Interviews with Daimler-Chrysler, Siemens, and another leading German MNC.
[4] This point was also made to us by the Minister for Education and Culture, Baden-Württemberg.

about the deep-rooted cultural assumption underlying the German view of specialization is correct, then a fundamental change in culture as well as training techniques would be required in order to bring British workers in this company up to the standard expected of their German counterparts. In this case a European apprenticeship scheme had been developed by the German company in order to enhance cross-cultural understandings between workers in the two countries but also by implication, to attempt to transfer German training practices and assumptions to the British subsidiary. Certainly there was no doubt in her mind that workers in Britain came to Germany to learn. This generated greater mobility of skill between countries and hence greater flexibility in how the company uses it because, as she observed, 'they have to multiply their knowledge to their people at home'.

As with her counterparts in other leading-edge manufacturers, the combination of competitive advantage that German skill formation and diffusion delivered coupled to the costs of exit from Germany made her confident that her headquarters would remain there. She pointed out that design and engineering contributions could be bought from India or California, but the development of corporate strategy and coordination would remain in Germany. This view was echoed by *all* our interviewees in Germany who recognized that German intermediate manufacturing competitive advantages was based on the training of their workforce. As the Executive Vice-President, Human Resources of a leading motor manufacturer put it, 'Chryslers may be engineered in America but not Mercedes.'

In this context, consideration of Kobrin's (2000) point about the electronic compression of space and time is worth revisiting. For it can be argued that the Internet is as much a force for national skill development as it is a vehicle for global convergence. German Mittelstand engineering firms have developed techniques for supervising and servicing plants around the world. Local firms simply hook their machinery onto the Internet and diagnosis and remedy are supplied from Germany.[5]

In the case of skill diffusion, it is clear that the leading-edge intermediate manufacturing companies in Germany have much to gain from its continuation. When this is placed alongside the normal economic and political costs of exit and the additional start-up costs of establishing a culture of training overseas, it is clear that there are strong countermanding forces to those of globalization to keep leading-edge

---

[5] Reported in the *Financial Times*, 17 Feb. 2000, p. 17.

German companies within the Dual System.[6] It is also the case that where they establish plants overseas they seek to replicate, as far as possible, the German training system.

It should be noted, however, that all those we interviewed had a vested interest in 'talking up' the prospects for the Dual System. Since the Dual System is at the heart of the wider consensus politics of co-determination, to question its prospects and in particular, the role of the leading-edge companies in it, is to trigger political reservations about the entire system of co-determination. Therefore the positive commitment to the Dual System expressed by the leading-edge MNCs we interviewed in Germany may reflect these political sensitivities. On the other hand, those that we interviewed were at the cutting-edge of discussion about the Dual System, and we were prepared to take their opinions at face value. It is possible that the Dual System and the wider system of co-determination will adapt and survive as it has to date. An alternative possibility is that leading-edge MNCs will seek to retain the Dual System because they see it as central to German competitiveness, while attempting to disengage it from the costly wider system of industrial consensus politics. It might be concluded, however, that the evidence on this issue is so equivocal that the most prudent conclusion to be drawn at this stage is that how the leading-edge corporations will act with respect to the Dual System remains an open question.

GLOBALIZATION AND THE KOREAN INTERNAL LABOUR MARKET

In late 1997 the Korean economy went into a tailspin as the result of a major run on its currency, the won. The IMF was called in to 'bail out' the economy and in return for the series of negotiated packages which were provided demanded a major restructuring of the economy.[7] While there is a major debate as to the causes of the financial crisis in Korea,[8] there is agreement amongst protagonists that a crucial element of these packages was:

---

[6] There are further advantages to the Dual System. For example, it enables much greater reliability in terms of recruitment of good quality staff, since firms where apprentices are employed do not have to take them on when their apprenticeship is complete (Acemoglu and Pischke 1999).

[7] There were seven rounds of renegotiation between Dec. 1997 and Oct. 1998.

[8] See e.g. the special issue of the *Cambridge Journal of Economics*, 12 (1998).

A conspicuous American agenda to open up the Korean economy to foreign investment. This was contained in the restructuring and reform measures' clauses ... it called for ... the schedule allowing foreign entry to the Korean financial sector, including allowing foreign firms to establish bank subsidiaries and brokerage houses ... liberalising foreign investment in the Korean stock market ... and increasing foreign ownership in firms. (Mathews 1998: 752)

Mathews, who is a supporter of the IMF package, glosses these stipulations by saying: '*These matters are not normally the subject of IMF agreements and they reflect a clear concern by the American sponsors of the IMF, who wanted a substantial opening of the Korean market to United States investors as a quid pro quo for the bailout*' (1998: 752, emphasis added).

The motives behind the White House–Wall Street–IMF axis for seeking to use the currency crisis as a way of opening up the Korean economy are debatable. Some would see this as prompted by an ideological conviction that globalization will only bring the substantial benefits predicted by economic orthodoxy if it is accompanied by what is considered to be 'the one best system': shareholder capitalism.[9] In Korea all those we interviewed, without exception, took a different position. For them this was an exercise in American economic imperialism. As a leading economist for one of the *chaebol*, who had been trained in the United States, explained it, America has lost the global competition for manufactured goods and was seeking to make good its consequent balance of payments problems by gaining access to the Korean financial sector. In this way American companies could introduce key elements of shareholder capitalism through the control of finance while repatriating profits, thereby achieving American ideological, national, and corporation goals.

Alongside opening up the financial sector, the Korean government also set about rationalizing the *chaebol*. The argument for doing so was that their massive debt to equity ratios had led to overproduction and when demand slumped they were crucially responsible for the financial crisis. Rationalization took the form of reducing overstaffing by making workers redundant so that wages in the manufacturing sector fell by 2.6 per cent in the first quarter of 1998, by 3.9 per cent in the second, and 10.1 per cent in the third (*Korean Economic Bulletin*, May 1999); selling off parts of the *chaebol*, either as stand-alone units or to foreign interests; and swapping parts of their business with each other (known

---

[9] For a broader view which places the Asian crisis firmly at the feet of what he describes as an American economic and military empire, see C. Johnson (2000).

as the Big Deal) in order to create better synergies.[10] In addition, governance and financial structures were changed to enhance management transparency.

This process of rationalization led to an increase in unemployment of 5 per cent by the end of 1998, from just under 3 per cent to over 8 per cent. With the Korean economy now growing strongly again, unemployment has declined, but it is predicted that there will be at least one more major bout of unemployment as the *chaebol* continue their process of rationalization.[11] Officially, it is law that workers cannot be made redundant unless the firm they work for is in serious financial difficulties. However, we were told by a senior *chaebol* manager that his organization had found a way around this law and that others would follow.

Three factors in the above account are crucial to understanding why the skill diffusion system in Korea is in a process of major reconstruction. As was noted in the previous chapter, skill diffusion centred on the internal market created by the *chaebol*. A key element of the internal market was the idea of a job for life, which in turn was dependent on a strategy of long-term investment with the aim of securing market share. In this sense the Korean economic strategy resembled Japanese strategies of market share in contrast to the Anglo-Saxon aims associated with short-term shareholder capitalism. However, this system, at least in the form which had been so successful prior to 1997, is now dead as is the system of skill formation and diffusion that accompanied it. The *chaebol* have significantly reduced, and will continue to reduce, the number of workers that they employ, thereby depleting the numbers who can be exposed to the rigorous training systems they have developed. This has major consequences for skill formation and diffusion, since the SME sector is chronically underskilled and despite successive government's best efforts does not appear to have a capacity for generating and transferring skill (Lauder 1999).

In addition, the notion of a job for life is also under threat. This is due to the introduction of foreign banks into Korea who will operate according to the rules of shareholder capitalism and in part through the introduction of more foreign firms who do not adhere to the philosophy of a job for life. While the impact of a significant foreign presence in the banking sector remains to be seen, the effects of foreign 'hire and fire' strategies were already making themselves felt in late 1999. For example,

---

[10] The ceiling on equity ownership by foreigners was lifted altogether in June 1998 (*Korean Economic Bulletin*, May 1999).

[11] Interview with one of the 'big five' *chaebol*.

we were told by senior executives in two of the leading *chaebol* that the practice of American firms paying above Korean rates for skill meant that they had to follow suit. The issue they were wrestling with was how to reconcile these new labour market practices with Korean values. As one of our interviewees put it, they regarded American business practices as inhumane.

At the time of the last round of interviews (Autumn 1999) not all *chaebol* or their subsidiaries took the view that the principle of jobs for life was coming to an end. For example, the executive vice-president of one highly successful construction company, which was to be sold as a stand-alone company, independent of its parent *chaebol*, felt there was little pressure to move away from the jobs for life philosophy because his company was successful.

That said, it was clear that the Korean government was anticipating a shift from a jobs for life system to one in which workers would experience bouts of unemployment. For this reason work has begun on developing what is called a productive welfare state (*DJ Welfarism*, Presidential Committee for Quality-of-Life 2000). The concept of a productive welfare state seeks to integrate the three primary sources of collective welfare in a society, the economy, the family and its networks, and the welfare state. In doing so, it emphasizes the way in which these institutions can support individuals in making a contribution to society. Not surprisingly, issues of skilling and re-skilling loom large in this project. As the introduction to this document puts it:

Providing a means for . . . workers to be re-employed is viewed by the concepts of productive welfare as an obligation of the Government . . . Embracing everyone in society into the realm of productivity assures a higher degree of social integration across all socio-economic strata. (Ibid., p. ix)

The concept of the productive welfare state is significant for two reasons: it is an example of joined up thinking. Programmatically it seeks to develop policies that link market, family, and state. And, it sees neither the economy nor the welfare state as reified spheres, independent of the rest of society. It is a form of inclusive thinking that overcomes the standard Western dichotomy of state and market. In this respect it is an attempt to transcend the competing ideologies of left and right in the West that have turned on whether the state or the market is 'better' at providing goods and services. While state officials emphasize that such a welfare state could not afford to compensate workers in the way that European states do, nevertheless a commitment to some form of safety net, closely allied to retraining, is now part of the government's agenda.[12] It is made clear in the *DJ Welfarism* document that this concept is a response to the crisis of 1997/8. When the crisis hit Korea, the government responded by funding training programmes for those who had been made redundant. What was an *ad hoc* response has become a central feature of the redefinition of the state's role.

The logic of the development of the productive welfare state is fairly clear, since it has the backing, in principle, of both capital and labour. For capital, a job for life in the *chaebol* also frequently included subsidized housing. In essence the *chaebol* provided many of the major elements of a welfare state for their workers. However once this practice was threatened, workers' compensation for the risks of capitalist life had to be provided by other institutions, a welfare state being the most obvious candidate. The same logic applies to workers.

Trade union officials were sceptical about the government's intentions. There was a concern that if growth picked up, the productive welfare state would slip down the order of priorities. They also expressed concern that this would in effect be a 'neo-liberal' welfare state in which the safety net for workers would be minimal. With respect to the reconstruction of skill formation strategies, the union movement had had little time to consider their role. In discussions with them, it became clear that they did not see a Dual System of the German kind, in which they would have a key role to play as central to their strategy.[13] They pointed to a rather different example of dock workers where the union trained the workforce, and it was suggested that one possibility might be for the unions to take over training. But this possibility was not entertained with any great conviction as far as we could tell. Indeed, it is highly unlikely that either employers or the state would grant unions a monopoly on skill development. Part of the reason for this would be that, as a matter of fact, unions would have to cooperate with employers, since it is the latter that develop the technology and practices which require the skills. In this respect, the only two options are either for employers to take sole responsibility for training workers or for some form of shared commitment.

The overall conclusion to be drawn from this episode in Korea's political economy is that the financial crisis of 1997/8 has raised a series of major questions about the ability of the ET and labour market structure to continue to provide anything like an effective system of skill

---

[12] Director, Presidential Committee for the Quality of Life, Office of the President of Korea, reporting directly to the President on a blueprint for a welfare state.

[13] An attempt had been made to introduce elements of the Dual System into Korea, but it had failed. See Ashton, Green, et al. (1999).

diffusion. As the internal labour markets of *chaebol* shrink fewer workers will gain the training and pass on the practical know-how of tacit knowledge that characterizes markets of this kind. At the same time the links between the formal education system and the SME sector are tenuous while the SME sector remains recalcitrant to ongoing training and skill diffusion. There is a consensus that the *chaebol* were an impediment to the recruitment of skilled personnel within the SME sector, but even if their influence on the labour market is diminished questions remain as to what will be put in their place.

Woo (1998) and Woo and Lee (1999) argue that ET policies governed by the need to produce skilled workers quickly and in quantity now need to give way to policies that emphasize quality. They have two things, in particular, in mind: an emphasis on creativity and initiative and a far more sophisticated vocational secondary and tertiary education sector that can supply the SME market. Both require greater funding as well as institutional change. In turn this would require a re-vitalized SME sector which could utilize and pay for the greater skills emerging from the ET system, as envisaged by Woo and Lee. The hope would be that were these developments to take place the attractions of going to university would be reduced, thereby alleviating the pressure on a higher education system governed by the dictates of what the Koreans call 'exam hell'.

The global economy in the form of short-term investments in nations like Korea coupled to the influence of the Washington–IMF axis has clearly had a major impact on the national system of skill diffusion in Korea. The question now is how Korea will respond to the fundamental changes that confront it. Again, one thing is certain, if the views of those we interviewed have any force: shareholder capitalism with its casual system of hire and fire and extremes of poverty and wealth are not seen as an option. They also took the view that in terms of productivity there was a considerable cost in relation to the loss of loyalty, the development of new skills, and institutional memory to giving up a commitment to jobs for life. Whether and how a 'third' way between the old system of *chaebol* dominance and shareholder capitalism can be found remains to be seen. As a guide to thinking in Korea, it is worth quoting the former commercial attaché to London who was instrumental in helping to bring Korean investment to South Wales. When we asked about the possibility of adopting a neo-liberal response to globalization by introducing a flexible labour market, an idea which was prominent in public debate in Korea at the time, he replied, 'we owe our working classes too much to do that', and he reminded us that modern

Korea was at best three generations old. The memories of the feats of the earlier generations were still very much alive precluding the type of response to workers that we have seen in America and Britain during the 1980s and 1990s.

GLOBALIZATION AND SINGAPORE'S GUIDED LABOUR MARKET[14]

In order to understand the Singaporean state's response to globalization, it is important to appreciate its strategic economic position in South-East Asia. While globalization allows, in principle, for the free flow of goods, services, and funds, national competitiveness is often seen in regional terms. This is certainly the case in Singapore where economic survival is seen as dependent upon 'outsmarting' its neighbours. Singaporean policy-makers note that on their borders there are countries with a plentiful supply of cheap labour, and they recognize the modernizing ambitions of Malaysia. Against this background the Singaporean state is attempting to effect a fundamental shift from an economy based largely on the manufacture of intermediate electrical goods to one founded on knowledge-intensive manufacturing and service industries. It is an attempt to transform Singapore from a 'paradigm of late industrialization through learning' (Amsden 1989), based on borrowed technologies, technical training, rule following, and worker discipline to a paradigm of a knowledge-driven economy with its emphasis on innovation, research, technopreneurialism, and self-management, as previously outlined.

The shift to a knowledge-driven economy represents an extension rather than a retreat from the state's role in economic development. The underlying principle of economic development remains: that Singapore delivers higher income and well-being to its citizens through the upgrading of skills. The financial crisis in Asia, which hit Korea so hard, also exposed an underlying problem in Singapore: other regional economies had been upgrading their skill base in order to compete for the manufacture of intermediate goods, while at the same time experiencing a significant decline in the value of their national currencies, making Singapore look increasingly expensive. It is recognized that the only way to sustain Singapore's drive towards a high skill

---

[14] This section draws upon Brown and Lauder (2001b).

economy is to: (1) make it the 'virtual hub' of the region by ensuring that MNC regional head offices remain or are attracted to the city-state rather than to its neighbours; (2) lock foreign MNCs into Singapore by creating a research and design capability which cannot be easily transplanted elsewhere; and (3) to develop indigenous hi-tech industries based on local research.

The success of this strategy will depend on the development of exportable service clusters including headquarters services, logistics, communication and media, R & D, education, and health-care. These include the management and distribution of financial services, information technology (IT) services, e-commerce, and direct marketing. The development of an International Business Hub focusing on these service clusters is anticipated to generate a large proportion of 'skilled' jobs (EDB 1998).

Indicative of Singapore's current skill formation strategy is the Industry 21 (I 21) initiative launched by the EDB in 1998. It is anticipated that knowledge-driven industries under I 21 will contribute 40 per cent of Singapore's annual GDP and create 20,000 to 25,000 jobs every year over ten years. Of these two out of every three jobs will be for knowledge workers in the manufacturing sector and three out of four in the exportable services sector. 'I 21 aims to develop Singapore into a leading competence centre for knowledge-driven activities, as well as strengthening its claims as a hub for company headquarters and product charters' (EDB 1998). A key part of the investment in the social and economic infrastructure, especially for the IT, communications, and media sector is Singapore One, which is a broadband network across Singapore, capable of delivering interactive multi-media applications including access to the Internet and e-commerce.

It will be readily apparent that the response made by Singapore to the demands of globalization is state-led. 'Singapore Inc.' may be transforming itself into 'Singapore Unlimited', but this does not signify the rise of the virtual state as characterized by Richard Rosecrance (1999). A more accurate description is of Singapore as a 'one nation, dual economy' (Brown and Lauder 2001b). Here the state performs a *vital* role in Singapore, at the same time as performing a *virtual* role in the region. The development of an 'external wing' began in the early 1990s with the Singapore government acting as an outward investor in the region. This took the form of joint ventures with regional governments, MNCs, or Government Linked Companies (GLCs). The virtual role of the state has become increasingly important in its 'developmental' capacity given limitations of land and labour within Singapore. This approach allows the central economic planning agency, the Economic Development Board (EDB), the flexibility to encourage the development of a business hub or advance manufacturing in Singapore at the same time as participating in setting up low-skilled operations elsewhere within the region, or as we were told, 'you keep the brains here, export the brawn'.

The emphasis on developing an indigenous hi-tech, high skill capability is associated with the long-standing problem of what is seen as an over-reliance on foreign MNCs, who have failed to transfer technology and skills in the way expected (Ashton, Green, et al. 1999). The development of knowledge-intensive activities in manufacturing and service sector clusters is now part of an attempt to attract businesses to set up headquarters operations in Singapore to help extend the global reach of indigenous businesses and workers. The development of 'indigenous capability' in more knowledge-intensive manufacturing and services therefore depends in part on rooting the MNCs core value added activities such as R & D, design, marketing, and business services in Singapore. As we were told at an interview with the National Science and Technology Board (NSTB), 'when you say indigenous capability, what we mean is that Hewlett Packard, Singapore will not be able to do it elsewhere, the ideas, the decision-making, are all from here. Benefits will be stable, they will not just move their operations away because this is the source of new ideas.' Global networking is seen as essential for ideas, capital, technology, resources, and markets. This policy is reflected in the creation of new 'research' universities in niche areas such as business studies, life sciences, etc., to be run by world-class universities in these fields such as INSEAD for management and Johns Hopkins University for Life Sciences.

In addition to locking the knowledge-intensive operations of MNCs into Singapore, the government is keen to develop indigenous hi-tech industries and services. In contrast to much of the debate in Britain and the United States, Singapore views the need to create national corporate champions as central to its survival because Singaporean champions would put the city-state on a more secure economic footing while enhancing its growth potential. Singapore's virtual involvement in the regional economy is a way of developing its own World-Class Companies (WCCs) and Local Enterprises (LEs). The EDB has identified approximately 300 promising LEs to 'accelerate their growth' by offering financial assistance, resource support, image building, technology acquisition, strategic alliances and business partnerships' (EDB 1998). But this approach is seen to depend on innovation and knowledge-driven entrepreneurial activities which have not been a characteristic feature of the country's skill formation strategy to date.

This strategy raises a fundamental question about the type of worker-citizen that is needed for the new knowledge economy driven phase of Singapore's development. As the Committee on Singapore's Competitiveness has put it:

To develop into a knowledge economy, Singapore should be an open cosmopolitan society, attractive to global talent and connected with other global knowledge nodes. There should be a critical mass of Singaporeans who are risk-taking entrepreneurs, innovators and arbitrageurs. Together with the global talent, they will move Singapore ahead in the Information Age. (1998: 6)

In the context of this strategy, Singapore finds itself with a major shortage of hi-tech skills. In the short term the state's 'foreign talent scheme' designed to attract high skill workers to undertake professional, managerial, and technical jobs which cannot be filled by Singaporeans provides an answer. However, it is acknowledged that a more profound response is required.

It is not simply a question of a linear progression with an increased number of employees requiring technical and graduate level education and training. The change is both quantitative and qualitative. The workforce must be willing to update their skills on a regular basis and to become lifelong learners. But there is equally a need to have a workforce that is more creative, proactive, and which has people with good problem-solving skills. As David Lim Tik En, Singapore's Minister of Defence has noted:

In a global economy, we can stay competitive if we accumulate knowledge and use it to innovate. We have done well for the first part—accumulating knowledge. Our past emphasis on education and skills upgrading has given us a head start. But the second part requires a different ethos. Being innovative is not the same as being productive. It requires that we go beyond applying set rules and proven formulae. We have to invent new ideas from our existing pool of knowledge. We have to think outside the box. (1998: 62)

Thinking 'outside the box' requires a change in mindset from the smart conformists Singapore has excelled at producing (see Chapter 3). This change in mindset is central to a new model of the worker-citizen in a broader sense. There is a recognition that it is impossible to create a more innovative workforce based on a system of rote learning and close supervision. Regulation increasingly has to be 'self-imposed' as a part of 'responsible' rather than 'disciplined' activity. It is not by chance that the notion of 'emotional intelligence' (Goleman 1996) has been officially sanctioned with the publication of a series of books on various aspects of emotional intelligence at work and in everyday life, which can be purchased from the government bookshop. More of the in-employment programmes run by the PSB, such as People Developer, aim to improve the quality of human resource management and training in companies, while CREST (Critical Enabling Skills Training) attempts to develop non-technical skills designed to create a workforce able 'to continuously adapt to change, learn new skills and meet the challenges of the knowledge age' (PSB 1998).

Reforms in the education system also centre on developing problem-solving, self-management, and interpersonal skills. 'As people are our only resource, we must develop the potential of our students to the fullest. Our curriculum must be responsive to current and future needs of our nation. Our students must be creative problem-solvers, constantly seeking ways to improve what they do and with a lifelong quest for learning' (quoted in MOE, Singapore 1998: 30). This has led to the introduction of the Thinking Schools Initiative (noted in Chapter 2), which is aimed at 13 and 14 year olds in the Express and Normal Academic streams. It is not intended for less academic students found in the Normal Technical stream, although some of these students are following this programme.

There is also a policy to reduce curriculum content by 30 per cent to allow for more project work and teamwork in order to develop a broader range of skills (Gopinathan 1999). Change in university entry requirements are also being introduced to reflect the shift away from rote learning and the production of a nation of 'great copiers' in a system 'drowning in information, gasping for knowledge'.[15] It is proposed that by 2002 A-level grades will account for 75 per cent of the entry criteria to university, with the introduction of the American Scholastic Assessment Test (SAT) (to be modified for Singapore students) accounting for the remaining 25 per cent. There is also the possibility of bonus points being awarded for extra-curricular activities, although the exact basis on which such awards are to be made remains unclear. By 2004 A-level grades are set to decline to 65 per cent of the entry criteria as 10 per cent will be awarded for project work.

Alongside these initiatives, the Ministry of Education has introduced a programme of National Education about which they say:

Our education system should not be judged solely by the number of A's our students get in major national examinations, nor by the high standing of

---

[15] Interview with the Ministry of Education, Education Technology Division.

our students in international comparisons of science and mathematics achieve-ments. Equally important is the quality of the people the education system produces—their integrity and character, their attitude towards work, their ability to be team-players, and their sense of responsibility and commitment to society. (MOE, Singapore 1998: 58)

The need to inculcate a sense of what it means to be Singaporean reflects the increasing problem of finding a new balance between greater personal freedom in what people think and do and a concern to maintain social discipline and cohesion.

It will be evident that these changes not only raise questions about Singapore's skill formation system but also its ability to diffuse skills. If greater creativity and initiative also implies greater individual autonomy for workers, the highly centralized system of skills diffusion which has the EDB at its heart may also be threatened. Clearly, it is the way that the Singaporean state responds to the challenges of the global economy that is crucial to its survival. However, the mechanisms of a high skills strategy based on overseas MNCs and social control which assures investors that Singapore is a stable well-ordered society will have to change. In doing so, it will remain an open question as to whether Singapore will be able to 'grow its own' MNCs under conditions of far greater social freedom.

GLOBALIZATION AND BRITAIN'S FLEXIBLE LABOUR MARKET

The British response to globalization can be characterized as funda-mentally neo-liberal, albeit with some modification by the Labour government (P. Brown and Lauder 2001*a*). For the labour market this has meant creating flexibility (see Chapter 3) by removing impediments, either such as those created by social regulation or through the strength of trade unions, so that workers can be easily hired and fired. In this type of labour market, it is, therefore, not surprising to see a wide dispersion of wages with extremes at either end of the income continuum or parade. Such a labour market can be viewed as one element of a strategy to entice foreign direct investment into the country. Its purpose is to make labour easily available under two key conditions which are considered central to any rational response to globalization. The first concerns the idea that there is now a *global auction* for foreign direct investment (P. Brown and Lauder 2001*a*) in which, all other things being equal, MNCs will invest in countries where costs, including labour, are cheaper than elsewhere and returns higher.[16] By removing significant forms of worker protection, employers can drive down wages so that they become globally competitive. The second idea concerns changes in technology and demand. Here it is argued that the combination of globalization and the advent of new technology will bring about rapid shifts in demand. Companies that can relatively easily hire and fire workers will be able to adapt more quickly to these changes in demand. Consequently, while workers may have to change jobs more frequently, their periods of unemployment will also be limited. Where workers once had trade union protection and support from the welfare state, now their only defence against exploitation is the knowledge and skill they possess.[17]

There is a further element to this response to globalization which concerns the question of ownership. It is assumed that ownership in terms of country of origin is irrelevant to an economy's well-being. Indeed given that MNCs dominate the global economy, the idea of corporations who act as national champions is obsolete. As such, the demand for skills will be entirely determined by the corporate sector. Given these assumptions, it follows that the fundamental task of the state is to raise the knowledge and skills of the workforce because it is only through raising skill levels that workers can achieve higher incomes.

In the case of Britain, there is a further issue that is relevant. This concerns the decline in manufacturing over the past thirty years and in particular over the past fifteen years. During the Thatcher era, the attraction of overseas MNCs, especially from Japan, was seen as a way of importing knowledge of best practice which would once again make Britain's manufacturing sector competitive. Eltis and Fraser articulated the thinking behind the attraction of foreign direct investment as follows:

The presence of some of the best Japanese companies in an industry creates a clear challenge to remove known inefficiencies. . . . Britain is therefore finding out that the ideal way to remedy industrial weaknesses is to get the world's best into the economy, and to learn from them with the greatest possible rapidity. (1992: 18–19)

---

[16] In the West MNCs often pay above the minimum but then often apply pressure to their suppliers to reduce costs.

[17] For a discussion of the fundamental changes in rules of engagement, eligibility, and wealth creation under globalization, see P. Brown and Lauder (2001a). It should be noted that in the USA and UK there is minimal protection in the form of a minimum wage, but in the UK it leaves 4.2 million workers earning poverty wages.

In particular what these authors and others thought Britain required was to learn about the Japanese mode of production (Elger and Smith 1994), which emphasized continuous improvement, just-in-time inventories, and jobs for life (see Chapter 3). Underlying this form of production were 'process' or key skills based on teamworking, problem-solving, communication, and IT skills. These skills were necessary because under the Japanese mode of production a degree of power was devolved to teams to engage in a constant process of innovation and improvement. It was this form of work organization which was considered to have given Japan such a competitive edge over much of the rest of the world in manufacturing.

More recently, some of these ideas have been embodied in the concept of high-performance work practices (Capelli 1999; Appelbaum et al. 2000). These practices are based on the idea of a high degree of team autonomy in decision-making and the skills described above in order to 'permit front-line workers to participate in decisions that alter organisational routines' (Appelbaum et al. 2000: 7). It is assumed that this form of work organization taps into the crucial implicit knowledge front-line workers have in order to innovate, while giving workers a stake in what is produced through the decisions they make. The weight of opinion is that this form of organization is necessary to enhance productivity and competitiveness and indeed Appelbaum et al. (2000) take this further in arguing that it is the shift to high-performance work systems, in manufacturing, which accounts for the accelerated increase in American productivity between 1995 and 2000.[18]

If corporations take on the idea that high-performance work practices are essential to raising productivity—and this is certainly a central assumption underlying the reports of the National Skills Task Force (2000a, b) in Britain—then it can be assumed that workers' wages would rise commensurate with their increased skills and productivity. In one sense, this view supports the idea that there is a natural progression towards employers demanding higher skills. Hence the task of governments is merely to supply, through the education and training systems, appropriately qualified workers for high-performance systems (see Chapter 1).

---

[18] The evidence from Capelli (1999) is at odds with this. It is not clear that American manufacturing has changed work practices to the extent argued by Appelbaum et al. (2000) (see also Knauss 1998). The situation is probably uneven in the USA. However, given the large markets and economies of scale that can be derived from them, in the USA, standardized systems of mass production can still produce 'efficient' outcomes, that is productivity may remain high with a relatively low skilled workforce.

However, in our view there is a tension if not outright contradiction between the response to the global economy, as exemplified by the flexible labour market, and the development and application of key skills in corporations that seek to develop high-performance work practices. It is this tension which we will sketch out in the remainder of this chapter.

HIGH-PERFORMANCE WORK PRACTICES AND KEY SKILLS

In this section we explore the hypothesis that there is a tension between the neo-liberal response to globalization and the development of key skills through a case study of a leading manufacturer in southern England. However, before doing so we should discuss the conceptual issues relating to key skills. Of particular relevance is the current debate concerning the question of whether key skills are generic, occupationally specific, or organizationally specific. Key skills such as teamwork, communication, and shared problem-solving require a range of social and personal skills, experience, and understanding. For example, teamwork cannot be effective unless the members of the team are prepared to understand one another's point of view, to listen to what they have to say, and to respect and trust their opinions. However, teamwork may operate quite differently according to context. Teams may be structured internally in different ways (Cressey and Kelleher 1999) so that there can be either a team leader or a partnership based on an equal say in decision-making. Likewise teams may relate to the occupation into which members have been trained or the broader organization to which they belong in different ways, with some given a high degree of autonomy and others less. How teams are structured and relate to the broader occupational and organizational context may in turn determine the way they interact.

There are two research traditions that can be drawn upon to find answers to the central questions of how key skills function in an organization and the degree to which they are organizationally or occupationally specific or generic or some combination of these. The first seeks to address these issues inductively by starting with qualitative observations of the way workers in specific organizations use key skills (Thurly and Lam 1990; Stasz 1997). The second begins from a rich social theory of learning known as situated cognition (Rogoff and Lave

1984; Collins, Brown, and Newman 1989; Gott, 1989; Lave and Wenger 1991). This theory is derived from the work of the Russian psychologist of learning, Vygotsky. Intrinsic to his theory is the notion that social experiences shape the ways that individuals think and interpret their world. Thus, individual student cognition occurs in a social situation, and is inseparable from it. Vygotsky (1978) asserted that skills have a social systemic nature and hence cannot be divorced from the context in which they are learned.[19]

Both research traditions have yielded considerable insight into the central questions regarding key skills. The Stasz study found that key skills vary within the job context which reflect the nature of occupational training. They also found that employers do not necessarily understand the key skill requirements of their front-line workforce, and hence they may lack effective strategies for developing key skills.

Thurly and Lam in their study of the development of the skill formation of electronic engineers believe that skill development is, in significant ways, organization specific.

the skill formation process and the learning associated with it [is] a by-product of the task organisation system in which the work role is located . . . the structure of the socio-technical work (task) organisation actually experienced by individuals is one of the main determinants of the skill formation process. Other crucial determinants are the culture or values dominant in the task organisation and the rewards and reactions related to learning, the perceptions and expectations of the individuals concerned on the relevance of learning to the work role; the learning skills and capacity of those individuals and finally, but not least, the degree of identity felt by them in their work roles (1990: 12)

The insights of the situated learning theorists chime well with this conclusion. The exercise of key skills requires judgements to be made both about technical work processes and other colleagues. These standards of judgement cannot be made independent of context and will be determined collectively by the history and culture of an organization. Similarly, as was seen in the previous chapter, the ability to constantly adapt is partly a function of the repeated transmission of new skills. This transmission is incremental and is aided by the culture and history of a corporation which enables the acquisition of the tacit knowledge which includes standards of judgement necessary for skilled performances (Koike and Inoki 1990).

---

[19] It should be emphasized that key skills can be used differently according to the type of production being used. In low skill production the rhetoric may be about key skills, but they are more likely to be used for surveillance and control purposes (see Mehralizadeh 1999).

The following case study will, therefore, focus on the significance of an organization's history and culture for the transmission and application of key skills.

THE CASE STUDY

The overarching question in relation to this case study concerns the issue of whether key skills can be transferred within companies from one country to another. If they can, then it follows that there will be convergence at least in this aspect of training and production.[20] The case study was conducted in a large plant of a company that was a subsidiary of a German manufacturer. The recent history of the company had been turbulent. In the early 1980s this long-standing British company was effectively bankrupt and was sold off to another British manufacturer that had expertise in a quite different economic sector. The late 1980s saw it enter into a partnership with a prominent Japanese manufacturer who made the same type of goods but by the early 1990s it had been bought by the German company. It had recently created a new settlement with its workforce which guaranteed a job for life in return for a high degree of flexibility, on the lines of Japanese companies.

The study concerned an investigation into the nature and use of key skills at the plant in relation to recruitment, training, and application on the shop floor. Data were principally gathered through interviews with some shop-floor observation. Interviews were conducted with the German parent company, senior management at the head office of the British company, the managing director and personnel manager at the plant, along with the training manager, trainers, apprentices, and ex-apprentices (workers). By interviewing this group we were able to triangulate the views on training and the role of key skills in the plant.

The issues raised by the changes in ownership in relation to key or process skills were put into context by the plant management:

On a fairly simple level, clearly there were large numbers of people over a long period of time who had some contact and direct involvement in visiting Japanese assemblies, so there were obviously skill benefits out of that. But

---

[20] It should be emphasized that this test is of one company taken over by a foreign company. The possibility of transferring key skills may be quite different where an MNC establishes a greenfield site and recruits labour that is new to the industry. This is a strategy frequently adopted by Japanese companies.

probably much more significant than that is what it drove us to do for ourselves in the area of TQ, and out of that a general understanding of technology principles and then a lot of focus on training in specific technique, process, and process management.

It was also observed that:

We were brought face to face with the gap between the Japanese manufacturing industry and the UK and we recognized that we had to invest a lot in this kind of process thinking and the total quality ethos and so on. I don't feel that the restructuring of training in our company was influenced by the Japanese. We recognized there was a big gap to be covered here and we had to think hard about how we were going to set about doing that. So our investment in training and development of this process knowledge within the business had a tremendous amount of effort put into it ... that's significant and that's why the conversation in terms of development of people is very much in the action just now. What we got from Japan was that we need to look at process, you draw people out so that they understand what happens before they get it and after they get it and therefore we were doing lots of process learning across the breadth of our business and probably we spent too long in that mode because we were confronted with German industry and we realized too that in German industry they have people with lots of expertise, really deep knowledge about metal forming and you drill right down into the total technicalities of metal forming, in perhaps quite junior management positions.

When asked how they are going about addressing getting the greater depth and whether that was being done with their German counterpart or on their own, we were told:

First of all there's not been any massive import of training or skill development infrastructure from Germany. There has been strong encouragement and saying, 'look you don't have enough people and you are missing out in terms of business, the quality of product, technical expertise, the competency of the quality of the product is not high enough', therefore you need to do something about it. So we got a strong leadership thrust. In terms of the delivery of that, once again we are turning our minds as to how we are structurally organized to do that. We have got some exchanges, so we've got an understanding of what the issue is. It's more about getting people to understand what the issue is, what the gap is, and what needs to be done.

In discussing the importance of so-called soft skills–teamwork/communication in the training that they offer, a plant manager said that

There's talk about total quality leadership, that's a bit about making sure we don't lose the openness to process thinking that we really got from the Japanese. We really don't want to lose that because that was an important learning for us, getting people engaged in process improvement, learning about the process, leading and motivating others, getting the best out of people, tapping into people's knowledge that they keep bottled up. It's really important to us and we don't want to lose that.

Clearly the association with Japanese and European companies had prompted considerable reflection on training and in the case of the Japanese relationship on process or key skills in relation to workers' tacit knowledge. However, it was also clear that they felt it undesirable to simply import training techniques from their overseas counterparts. The question then is what happened on the ground as a result of these deliberations.

Training school managers at the plant were committed to the importance of key skills:

These soft skills never came into my apprenticeship. You were trained to do a job and you got on and did it. Improving learning performance? What the hell was that? Problem solving? Well everyone does that anyway don't they. These are formal training actions to show people, so that's different.

Another staff member noted:

Any job has changed. If you look at this company it is not just about engineering, we can train them but in the past it was just working toward engineering. The modern world now is not just about that. It is changing in terms of technology. We need to bring everybody not just our apprentices up to speed. With these sort of [key] skills and training we bring them up to speed as people not just as engineers (Engineering Trainer).

Similarly, most of the apprentices seemed to fully understand the varied significance of key skills:

If this company is to be competitive, they need these skills. I say without developing these key skills it is very difficult to be competitive with other companies (Technician Apprentice).

We do key skills everyday, it is hard to prove it on paper, if you walk around the office with the assessor and you can say yes he is doing that, now with this interview we are doing a key skill talking with someone who we don't know. Generally, this company is going to prepare workers for unknown situations and help people to understand each other and then get profit from it (Engineer Apprentice).

It helps you to be confident at work, it teaches you to work with people whether you like or dislike them (Business apprentice).

This company needs these skills, because they want to produce better products and facilitate the work. And also in your career you need these skills (Business Apprentice).

However not all apprentices understood the reasons for learning key skills:

I really do not know why they need them, that is a company idea. They emphasized key skills which I think are not very important for my career (Engineer Apprentice).

We did a week away of team-building, work with others, IT, and communication. At college we really done too much on how to work with each other in terms of ways of supporting and helping people at work (Technician Apprentice).

When one of the shop-floor managers was asked about the importance of team-building and problem-solving skills in work, he commented:

We really need these skills, because we have teams which have regular sessions every week or month which will discuss the progress and problem they had, so all our workers and manager should learn these skills.

So far it seems that among the apprentices key skills are regarded by most involved as being vital to production. However, while shop-floor managers took the same view, ex-apprentices differed. While one saw them as essential in order to:

make the company speed up production, maximize efficiency, if everybody works with each other the jobs get done quicker and save lots of money.

The majority interviewed took a contrary view:

Key skills actually are not helpful as much as the company thinks. Everything in key skills you can learn on the shop floor with little training. You can learn how to communicate, when to communicate, with whom to communicate. The only part of key skills which is important is IT which helps us. Without knowledge of key skills you can go to the shop floor and do your work. In the case of team-work it is the same, definitely when you go to the shop floor you have to be a member of a team, so they help you to know what's your responsibility and how to communicate with other people.

Key skills are not as important as much as the specific training we received in engineering.

The disagreement over the significance of key skills also extended to the manager who had responsibility for liaising with the local education system:

Key skills are very vague, what are the skills. We have got a debate [amongst managers] like communication, teamwork, a whole list of different skills are required or claimed they are required. When we talk to other companies, they say we think we need these skills.

She went on to say that the issues concerning the nature and teaching of key skills had arisen since they started seeking to introduce the new apprenticeship scheme. Other managers had questioned both the relevance of the criteria for key skills as derived by the NVQ because they did not fit in with the plant's production process and the relationship between the new apprenticeship and what could be learned at school. She also commented on the experience of apprentices when they come to industry.

It seems to me to be going back to doing as they are told. Do we still need key skills? We have got various levels of debate about what is actually needed. It is a huge debate about what kind of skills we actually need. They [managers] were coming around to looking much more at going back to the traditional skills.

She went on to say that senior managers wanted transferable skills, key skills in NVQ, GNVQ tailored to the company skills which focused on creativity, taking responsibility, and thinking skills. Whereas some trainers wanted to go back to what they knew best—training in the way they had been trained. For this reason younger trainers had recently been recruited from the shop floor.

In terms of the reality of key skills on the shop floor, she said that

I think probably they need some of the old skills, not all of them. The old skills in terms of doing as they are told, I think quite a lot of people prefer to do things they are told but there is . . . a lot of debate about whether some things trainees are taught are actually required.

There are several issues that arise out of the disagreements about the nature and significance of key skills within this plant.[21] First, key skills were, primarily, taught at a local further education college, and it may be, as some of the ex-apprentices commented, that they had little relevance to what was required on the shop floor. The suggestion here is that key skills can only really be taught in context as situated learning theorists would claim. Secondly, however, it could be argued that for key skills to be applied successfully a highly stable culture is necessary in which shared meanings and understandings as to what key skills are and how they can be applied, can develop. What is clear from this case study is that no such shared understandings existed across the plant, let alone the company.[22] The explanation for this may well be found within

[21] This debate about the importance of key skills is not unique. The same outcome is reported by Stasz (1997) and Dench, Perryman, and Giles (1998).

[22] Other research on this plant had observed that the autonomy given to teams was relatively underdeveloped. It may therefore be that key skills were less important on the shop floor for this reason. This would point to a lack of trust by management. However, the lack of trust by management may also have to do with the constant change of ownership and management's concern that if they risked losing the reins of power it would look bad in the eyes of new owners.

the constant change of ownership that this company had experienced. While, no doubt, these rapid changes produced an equally rapid learning curve as described by senior plant managers, this learning was not translated through the organization.

In turn, this case study raises wider issues about not only ownership but relatedly the type of corporate control that is exercised. As described above, Germany, Japan, and Korea, for example, have exercised a form of 'patient' capitalism in which long-term employment and the settled cultures which accompany it have been made possible by low-cost, long-term investment. In contrast, the shareholder capitalism of Britain and the United States has demanded high and rapid returns which have often been acquired through takeovers, mergers, and buyouts, rather than through value added production. The consequence has been that companies within the United Kingdom and United States have been subject to frequent changes in ownership and control within the past fifteen years (P. Brown and Lauder 2001*a*). Under these conditions it is possible to hypothesize that Germany, Japan, and Korea have seized the competitive advantage in intermediate manufacturing goods precisely because their systems of corporate control and financing have allowed for stable ownership and production. In contrast, Britain and America have gained competitive advantage in areas where constant job-hopping and workforce turnover are not an impediment, and as we have seen in the previous chapter may in the hi-tech electronics industry be a positive advantage.

This case study illuminates the competing hypotheses regarding globalization by demonstrating how difficult it is to transfer and establish key skills across national contexts. However, this issue has often been seen as a function of national and organizational cultures where the argument advanced here is that it is also a function of ownership and ultimately corporate governance. If this argument is correct, it raises important issues about the viability of shareholder capitalism as a system of corporate governance in countries whose competitive advantage rests on the manufacture of intermediate and hi-tech goods through high-performance systems. It gives some credence to the view, for example, that the dual system will continue to be supported by the leading edge corporates in Germany because a Mercedes might be assembled elsewhere, but it can only be designed and engineered in Germany.

In broader terms, the response of the United Kingdom to globalization raises several problems. The first concerns the assumption that the demand for skilled labour will increase as educational and training standards rise. However, when this is linked to the policy of attracting foreign direct investment, the evidence of the past twenty years suggests that this assumption is questionable. Much of the work done in foreign-owned industries is low skill and few backward and forward linkages which would 'embed' foreign investment in the United Kingdom and raise skill levels have occurred. For example, in South Wales, one of the major recipients of foreign direct investment, there has been little attempt to coordinate foreign investment with the development of an indigenous supply chain nor with a strategy of raising skills. The fundamental concern has been with job creation because 'the most significant factor is economic activity rather than productivity. Economic activity would certainly reduce our GDP gap [with the rest of Britain] far more significantly than productivity.'[23] This policy view is well supported by the research which shows that while Britain has attracted some 10.6 per cent of the world's foreign direct investment and has created 400,000 jobs in thirteen years,[24] the majority of the investment is in the low skill sector (Barrell and Pain 1997). These general findings are confirmed for South Wales (Munday, Morris, and Wilkinson 1995). Labour market flexibility may help to attract foreign direct investment but on the basis of cheap labour rather than skilled labour.

The problematic nature of a strategy that links foreign direct investment to labour market flexibility is further highlighted by the Asian crisis of 1997/8. The consequence has been that Japanese and Korean companies have mothballed, exited, or forestalled further investment plans. Market flexibility may have led to easy entry into the United Kingdom but equally it allows for easy exit. When these issues are placed in the wider context of the links between ownership and skill formation, it suggests that the Singaporean emphasis on 'growing your own' MNCs may be a better way of using the money currently employed to attract and subsidize foreign direct investment.[25]

CONCLUSION

In relation to skill diffusion, there seems less evidence of convergence through globalization and, in particular, through the agency of MNCs

[23] Interview with the Welsh Development Agency.

[24] *The Independent*, 10 Oct. 1998.

[25] The Labour government is clearly trying to develop indigenous high skills work. However, it is still very much within a neo-classical framework, emphasizing state intervention on the grounds of market failure (see HM Treasury 2000). It also seems that lessons about the significance of developing indigenous capability are being learned in Wales as a result of the Asian crisis. See Munday, Pickernell, and Roberts (1999).

than might have been predicted. There are several reasons for this. First, each country has its own regulatory regime with respect to skill formation and MNCs work within these regimes. Secondly, MNCs still retain much of their higher skilled work in their country of origin. Often this is because the particular national systems of skill formation and diffusion provide, as in Germany or Korea, until 1997/8, significant competitive advantage. The way the state is positioned with respect to its history, culture, and politics and to its competitive relations to other nations is clearly a key factor in the way strategies for high skilled work are developed. This is perhaps most clearly seen in Singapore where the strategy of becoming a virtual hub is an attempt to establish its pre-eminence as the high skilled nerve centre of the region.

Finally, this chapter has pointed to the wider imperialist forces at work in shareholder capitalism and the implications this may have for convergence in skill diffusion.

The overall conclusion to be drawn in relation to the impact of globalization on skill diffusion is that we are in a period of transition the outcomes of which, in each of the cases examined, remain open. Much will depend on how the state in each of our comparator countries responds to the global pressure points that they now confront. This is the subject of the concluding chapter.

5

Globalization and the Political Economy of High Skills

PHILLIP BROWN

INTRODUCTION

Prosperity and social justice depend on the creation of a highly skilled workforce. This view represents the first commandment in what has become a secular religion throughout the developed world. In Asia, Europe, and North America we found evidence of how far-reaching and deep-seated such ideas have become among the movers-and-shakers of national policy-making. In albeit different ways, the knowledge economy has come to symbolize the global, technological, and social transformation of the late twentieth and early twenty-first century. Few of those we spoke to would deny that the commodification of knowledge has long been a feature of industrial capitalism. As Schement and Curtis have noted in the United States, 'capitalism provided the incentive to convert information into a commodity. Commodification, in turn, affects technology and labor. Though it never went unopposed, the tendency to commoditize information was apparent at the birth of the republic; and, by 1889, was clearly a vital part of American business' (1998: 143). But what is seen to distance knowledge-driven business today from its earlier incarnations is the sheer scale and speed of the knowledge enterprise.

Throughout the last century industrial capitalism depended on knowledge and skills, but their application was restricted to a relatively small cadre of managerial, professional, and business elites. Today it is argued that the demand for high skills has been extended throughout the whole economy. Economic competitiveness can no longer rely on an occupational elite but must harness the talents and skills of all. Thus, the secular religion of 'high skills' promises more than wealth creation, it promises opportunities for all to get a good education, a good job, and earn decent wages. This offers a solution to income polarization given that if everyone can get the skills that employers want, this will be reflected in rising wages, especially for those currently at the wrong end of the earnings curve. The political economy of high skills is, therefore, intimately related to the political legitimacy of governments and the goals of collective purpose, that include issues of social justice, equity, and social cohesion. So what does our analysis tell us about the potential of knowledge-driven economies to unite the historical foes of economic efficiency and social justice?[1] Is a high skills society a feasible political goal?

In answering these questions, there are a number of concluding comments to be drawn from our analyses: first, those who seek simple answers are destined for perpetual disappointment. High skill formation is as much an art as a science. We are able to outline most of the basic ingredients, but this does not amount to a recipe for success. The application of a universal law, as advanced by some human capital theories, serves only to hinder rather than facilitate the development of viable skill formation strategies. There are powerful societal effects that need to be taken into account. This is why the problem of policy importation, in contrast to the importation of electrical appliances, rarely boils down to a simple matter of changing the voltage. It almost always involves changing the circuits. Alternatively, we should reject the contention that policy importation is destined to fail because of the unique constitution of societies. The spread of Fordism from America in the early part of the twentieth century and the spread of Japanese lean production techniques in the 1980s, along with the growth in

---

[1] How this question is answered will depend on how economic efficiency and social justice are understood. From the view of the employer, efficiency is likely to be couched in terms of enhanced profitability. This can be achieved through reducing the size of the workforce, cutting training budgets, or alternatively through investments in employee training leading to improved productivity in the medium term. When based on downsizing and cost-cutting, it may be efficient for companies but extremely inefficient from a societal view. Equally, neo-classical economists may well view the growth in income inequalities in the 1980s and 1990s in America and Britain as a reflection of a more just society as these inequalities are taken to reflect the 'true' market value of labour rather than national bargains that are seen to have little moral justification. Alternatively, if social justice is understood in terms of equalizing opportunities to compete for academic credentials and good jobs; as the 'equality of productive capacity' (Streeck 1992), and as giving people a right to participate within their society even if they are not actively involved in the labour market, it will lead to a quite different answer.

privatization that began in the United Kingdom under Margaret Thatcher, all demonstrate that there is considerable potential to import other approaches, but they clearly need to be adapted to local circumstances. If the transfer of high skill policies is to have any chance of success, it is necessary to avoid 'policy prejudice', where certain aspects of national systems are 'cherry picked' because they conform to the political predilections of the importer, whilst ignoring other aspects of the skill formation process which may be less politically palatable, but decisive to successful policy transfer.

The volatile nature of global capitalism has taught us a different kind of lesson: that what many commentators regard as 'best practice' is always contingent. It is subject to the vagaries of global market sentiments. In the late 1990s skill formation debates focused on what could be learnt from Japan and the Asian tiger economies. The Asian financial crisis, along with impressive growth in the American economy, turned the debate full-circle inviting a reinterpretation of the advantages of Anglo-American capitalism. The advocates of the free market regained the ascendancy, supported by powerful allies including the World Bank, OECD, and the International Monetary Fund. But despite much talk about the new economic paradigm in the United States, it is based on very shaky foundations that are unsustainable in the medium term (C. Johnson 2000; Krugman 1999). If the United States economy moves into a recession or if there is a collapse in United States share prices, perceptions will change again.

With respect to skill formation strategy, hindsight appears safer than foresight. But foresight is vital because national skill formation policies cannot be delivered just-in-time. New areas of economic activity give rise to new knowledge requirements. These take time to develop in the form of education and training programmes, and this is before anyone enrols on any of these programmes. Successful skill formation inevitably involves a balancing act between meeting the immediate 'needs' of the economy at the same time as fashioning the system for the medium term.

Secondly, the political economy of high skills has been obscured by the obsession with global competitiveness. We live in an age mesmerized by league tables on economic growth, per capita income, productivity, academic results, and most crucially who is 'number one' in the competitive premier league. This is macho economics with a vengeance. In the discourse of high skills there has been a tendency to use economic competitiveness as a shorthand for both questions of economic efficiency and social justice. It is assumed that high skill economies will be at the top of competitive league tables because competitiveness is seen to depend on highly skilled labour. Never far behind is the 'stick' of poverty, unemployment, and national decline. A feature of contemporary debates about global knowledge-driven capitalism is the view that competitor nations are ready, able, and willing to exploit uncompetitive economies with overgenerous (*sic*) welfare provision, unless the principles of fiscal rectitude and market policies are followed. There is certainly an element of truth in respect to financial rectitude as global financial markets are always looking to cash-in on governments that do not conform to the market's criteria of sound government, including interest rates, inflation figures, taxation, and public spending. It is, however, worth remembering that those who live in the developed world now confront the same competitor nations as a century ago with few exceptions. There have been changes in national fortune, such as the decline of the British empire that previously gave it control of one-third of the world's surface. But Britain remains an affluent economy, at least four times richer today than at the beginning of the twentieth century (Halsey 2000).

Despite the mantra of 'competitiveness', the gap between the richest and poorest nations has increased. Landes has found that the difference per head between the richest and poorest countries 250 years ago was around 5 to 1 whereas today it is 400 to 1 (Landes 1998*a*: p. xx). In a context of knowledge-driven capitalism, it is also worth noting that although the developed nations represent 21 per cent of the world's population, they account for approximately 84 per cent of expenditure on education. Competitive pressures have increased, but this is not unrelated to the way MNCs are seeking to maximize profits based on 'shareholder' value (Dore 2000; Lazonick and O'Sullivan 2000), rather than the immanent danger of the developed economies being trounced by emergent industrial competitors.

We have also shown that there are different ways to be competitive. There is a mixed economy of competitive strategies within as well as between national economies. All countries have some companies that compete primarily on price rather than on quality, although the preponderance will vary significantly between countries.[2] However, there is little doubt that the discourse of competitiveness has limited public

---

[2] In the USA and Britain, for instance, vast swathes of the service sector are based on price competition because of family self-servicing (Gershuny 1978; Esping-Andersen 1999). In other words, when it comes to eating out, cleaning, laundry, childcare, home repairs, there is always a calculated trade-off between doing these things oneself or paying someone else to service these needs.

debate, most notably in Britain and America. The danger is that people are being duped into believing that nation states have no choice but to pursue the neo-liberal agenda driven by the internal logic of global capitalism (Hutton 1997; Elliott and Atkinson 1998). Peter Drucker has reminded us that the basic assumptions about reality that inform the social sciences often have different consequences to those of the natural sciences.

Whether the paradigm states that the sun rotates around the earth or that, on the contrary, the earth rotates around the sun has no effect on sun and earth. ... But a social discipline such as management deals with the behaviour of People and Human Institutions. Practitioners will therefore tend to act and to behave as the discipline's assumptions tell them to. (Drucker 1999*b*)

Social research shows that people do not always conform in the way Drucker assumes, but there is little doubt that dominant assumptions including those about economic competitiveness, globalization, human nature, economic efficiency, and social justice, do have an important impact on the way we understand the social world, our place within it, and the scope for progressive change. Indeed McNeill and Bockman noted that the way in which the Asian financial crisis unfolded was, in part, 'determined by how it [was] perceived and understood by powerful economic and political actors outside the region' (1998: 1529).

Thirdly, our analysis suggests that there is scope to unite economic efficiency and social justice. It is important to recognize the possibilities as well as the limitations of skill formation policies. The potential for a greater share of the working population to 'develop' themselves through their employment; to derive innate satisfaction from what they do; to work in new and constructive ways with others that may extend beyond national boundaries; the entry of women into arenas of education, training, and employment previously restricted to men; the expansion of tertiary education and training that offer opportunities to social groups excluded from higher education in the past; and the development of lifelong learning strategies are all in the main positive developments. But there are losers and we should not shy away from highlighting their plight.

We reject the prevailing political consensus in Britain and America that market capitalism is leading to a high skill economy that will deliver prosperity, opportunity, and social cohesion. This win–win scenario exaggerates the social benefits of knowledge-driven capitalism. This book has shown that free market policies in respect to education, training, labour markets, and the workplace are a limited strategy for raising skill levels throughout the economy (Crouch, Finegold, and Sako

1999). It does not result in high skills or low skills for all, but a bi-skills economy with enclaves of knowledge work alongside large swathes of low waged, low skilled jobs. The polarizing tendencies of the marketplace are also amplified through economic globalization and technological innovation (Esping-Andersen 1999). Equally, relying on 'supply side' market reforms is a strategy that is especially vulnerable to the ebb and flow of employer demand, as the incentive to upgrade skills and increase wages depends on labour shortages that force employers to make jobs more attractive. The 'flexible' labour market significantly limits the development of high skilled work because there is little incentive for employers to increase the demand for skilled labour.

Hence the question of social purpose must not be lost. Technology and economic organization do not define social purpose, they represent the means to achieving our individual and collective goals. Throughout the book we have used the concept of a 'high skill society' to reflect both the social foundations of skill formation and the societal goals that underwrite skill formation policies. Equality of opportunity, for instance, cannot be taken for granted as a source of economic competitiveness, but rests on a societal commitment to equalizing life-chances regardless of social class, gender, race, or religion. The creation of a high skills society depends on building the societal capacity that harnesses social and economic institutions to the upgrading of skills as a source of efficiency, justice, and social cohesion.[3]

However, there is little doubt that this understanding of a high skills society will need to be extended in the future. The definition of high skilled work cannot be restricted to the skills applied in the formal economy of waged work. It implies that those involved, for instance, in unwaged childcare can be well educated and engaged in skilled work even if it is unpaid, likewise those who are 'unemployed' may use periods without waged work to upgrade their skills or to participate in voluntary work of a skilled nature (Rifkin 1996). There also needs to be a recognition that a significant minority of jobs will remain low skilled at least in the sense that they require little formal training, although they may depend on good social and communication skills. This does not preclude the possibility of widespread prosperity, but this cannot be based solely on the market value for waged labour. The social dividends from improvements in productivity need to be spread widely throughout society based on some form of a carer's income, basic income, or citizen's wage (Brown and Lauder 2001a).

[3] This can also be understood to involve the struggle for collective intelligence (Brown and Lauder 2001a).

Fourthly, smart economies require smart government. And smart governments understand that there are different ways of being smart depending on historical conditions and a nation's position in relation to the global economy. Our analysis shows that the way national debates about high skills are constructed reflect the historical, social, economic, and political circumstances in that country. Equally, the forces of global capitalism are posing a challenge to all national systems, but these challenges take different forms in different national contexts.

The strategic role of government is far removed from the image of the 'command' economy where the state controls all areas of the economy and educates and allocates labour according to the requirements of a five-year plan as epitomized in the former Soviet Union. What smart governments understand is that markets do not exist in the abstract, but are embedded within social and economic institutions that can be shaped in different ways to achieve improvements in productivity and economic growth. In Singapore this involves the state holding both employers and trade unions at arm's length to ensure that sectional interests are not permitted to override the national commitment to skills upgrading. In Germany there are legal requirements that under-write a social partnership between employers, trade unions, and the state, with a high degree of devolved power to the regions. The social partnership, through the Dual System and regulatory framework, have structured the demand for labour in ways that increase the proportion of jobs that require training and pay decent wages. We have seen that human capital theory gives scant attention to this societal context, but it is these differences that are of the utmost importance. 'If we learn anything from the history of economic development,' writes David Landes, 'it is that culture makes all the difference' (1998a: 516).

Our analysis suggests the need for sophisticated forms of social, polit-ical, and economic organization that shape markets according to national settlements. Skill formation can therefore be understood as a manifestation of societal goals delivered through social and economic means. This is why we have insisted on a holistic definition of skill formation outlined as the seven C's (see Chapter 1).

THE FUTURE OF SKILL FORMATION: PRESSURE POINTS AND TRADE-OFFS

Global capitalism at the beginning of the twenty-first century makes all forms of prediction a precarious business. There is little doubt that the emphasis that governments now place on the skills, knowledge, and insights of the workforce reflect a genuine recognition that human labour is a vital ingredient to lifting productivity as well as spreading prosperity. But for reasons outlined in this book, it is difficult to predict what the impact of globalization, new technologies, and changing work practices will ultimately have on the shape of national skill formation policies. This is especially true for Germany, Japan, and Korea as these countries all confront serious challenges to their existing models of skill formation. These are the countries that have tried to maintain a commitment to competitiveness, skill upgrading, and narrowing income inequalities during the 1980s and 1990s. If these countries fail to develop a new balance between efficiency and justice in a global knowledge-driven economy, the prospects for the development of high skill societies looks bleak.

This remains to be seen, but what is clear is that the future of skill formation policies will be shaped by the way countries respond to a number of systemic 'pressure points'. These were identified in all our comparator countries and they converged around issues of globalization, skills upgrading, social inclusion, and 'model' workers of the future. These have been examined to various degrees throughout this book, but they now need to be brought together in order to assess the future prospects for a high skills society in each country.[4]

The term 'pressure point' is not necessarily synonymous with 'contradiction'. Each of the pressure points may involve contradictions such as between the forces of global capitalism and a commitment to economic nationalism (Reich 1991; Brown and Lauder 2001a), that depends on 'walled' economies insulating companies, workers, and governments from international competition and the vagaries of global financial markets, but this is not inevitable. They are not used in a Marxist sense of inherent contradictions of capitalism between, for instance, capital and labour. However, what these pressure points do inevitably involve is conflict and political struggle that nation states attempt to manage.

A brief examination of these pressure points in this conclusion is useful because it offers an insight into the 'possibilities' for high skills in different societies. These need to be analysed alongside the 'limitations' that can take various forms, including political inertia or low

---

[4] Systemic pressure points are not necessarily seen to be the key issues by all stakeholders in all countries. Indeed, the nature of the 'problem' was often contested. Gaining a sense of how the pressure points were understood in different national contexts was central to understanding the possibilities and limitations of change.

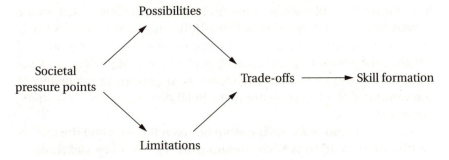

Fig. 5.1. Pressure points, trade-offs, and skill formation policies

educational standards, that may blunt (or undermine) the post-industrial possibilities for a high skill society.[5] These possibilities and limitations involve 'trade-offs' between competing vested interest groups that will shape the policy framework on the basis of politically negotiated settlements, such as the 'social partnership' model in continental Europe, or through the assertion of naked political power, characterized by British politics in the 1980s, that left enduring issues of conflict and opposition unresolved. The study of pressure points and trade-offs, therefore, enables us to define the parameters for the reformulation of skill formation policies (see Figure 5.1).

THE IMPACT OF GLOBALIZATION

The first pressure point concerns the implications of economic globalization for national skill formation policies. At the same time that nation states share an understanding of knowledge-driven global capitalism, within which the quality of human resources has become paramount, the question of the 'commanding heights' (Yergin and Stanislaw 1998) is subject to significant differences in national response. The issue of the commanding heights concerns the relationship between the role of government and the marketplace in a context of economic globalization. It turns the spotlight on the political economy of each country and

---

[5] This part of the analysis can be both descriptive and prescriptive. The descriptive part of the analysis involves specifying the limitations and possibilities for change as revealed within each national context, whereas the prescriptive analysis draws on the comparative analysis to specify the post-industrial possibilities for progressive change, even if these are not on the political agendas of the nation in question.

how the state, employers, and the trade unions are 'positioned' in the formulation of skill formation policies. If the quality of a nation's workforce is as important as is now commonly assumed, the question of whether the competing interests of government, employers, and the trade unions can be managed to ensure an upgrading of the quality of the workforce is a key pressure point in all developed and developing countries.

An examination of the relationship between the state and the market can be used to address such questions as: How do key stakeholders define national goals and priorities in terms of skills formation? Is skill formation policy based on a social partnership, state directives, or adversarial market relationships? How do stakeholders represent the opportunities and threats that globalization harbours for social justice and economic competitiveness? Is globalization seen to facilitate or threaten skill formation strategies? It is this final question that is of particular concern here.

In Britain we have seen that the interests of employers play a vital role compared with the trade unions in shaping skill formation policy, whilst the government has a highly circumscribed role in industrial policy.

Britain's success in the knowledge driven economy of the future is ultimately down to business. But Government has a critical supporting role to play. The present Government will not resort to the interventionist policies of the past. In the industrial policy making of the 1960s and 1970s, to be modern meant believing in planning. Now, meeting the requirements of the knowledge driven economy means making markets work better. (DTI 1998a: 11)

The policy framework of the Labour government has not fundamentally changed from the gospel of market competition espoused in the 1980s. Indeed, much has been made of the virtues of global capitalism and being *governed by the market*. Globalization represents an extension of 'free markets' beyond the national context that are seen to allow a market friendly strategy to reap the benefits of globalization in the form of inward investment and new business opportunities for British companies. In this context the impact of globalization has been to reinforce the direction of skill formation policy, and there is to date little sign of a radical change in approach, although market policies in education, training, employment, and business organization continue to be contested by the trade union movement and centre-left commentators.

In the United States the virtues of being *governed by the market* are extolled with even greater vigour than in Britain. This is hardly surprising given that the deregulation of global financial markets is the true lasting legacy of Ronald Reagan and Margaret Thatcher. As Reagan noted 'we meant to change a nation, and instead we changed a world'. In the 1990s sustained economic growth, soaring stock market prices, and 'full employment' in some parts of the country silenced critics of economic globalization and the free market. But even when the American economy is sluggish, it is extremely difficult to challenge a political culture that sets stringent limits on the powers of federal government to intervene even in the areas of education and training that are administered at the state level.

This is significantly different from the social partnership model which is upheld in most of the countries within continental Europe, where there are legally binding commitments on employers and trade unions to negotiate agreed settlements (Streeck 1992). In Germany, high skills are not viewed as a political aspiration but the established foundation of the social partnership between employers, trade unions, and government. In this context globalization is not seen as a spur to upskill, but as a threat to the social partnership within which the Dual System of training performs a pivotal role.

Therefore, in Germany a high skills strategy is seen as crucial to the future of the 'social partnership' between government, employers, and the trade unions. In a society based on such a partnership the prospect of social and economic polarization presents a serious threat (Martin and Schumann 1997). The state needs to find ways of responding which will keep the basic partnership in place, although this is by no means an easy task (Streeck 1997). It certainly cannot be achieved without considerable government action, since the legitimation of the social partnership involves more than a semblance of substantive justice (Habermas 1988). This has led key stakeholders in Germany to shape their response to global economic forces to maintain a *market consensus*, which, on the one hand, recognizes the need to play by the rules of international competition, but on the other, to avoid the kind of market competition within society which can lead to greater inequality and social polarization. The 'trade-off' in persisting with a market consensus approach is presented in terms of the exclusion of the unemployed, uncompetitive wage costs, and inflexibility within the Dual System to meet the changing needs of German companies. However, seeing the trade-off in these terms might have more to do with ideology than solving the problem of exclusion. As we saw in Chapter 3, the skills of those unemployed in Germany match the skills of those in employment, and under these conditions, creating low skilled service work would be problematic. Moreover, it could open the path for German employers to take the route of making profit out of low skill rather, than, as now, out of a combination of technology and skill.[6]

Japan and the Asian tiger economies have all been characterized as models of the 'developmental state' (C. Johnson 1982; Castells 1996). This, as we have seen, involves the active intervention of the state in key areas of social and industrial policy as a way of accelerating economic growth and widespread prosperity. Skill formation was identified as a major part of their developmental strategies. The liberalization of international trade in the 1980s and for much of 1990s permitted Japan and the tiger economies to win a competitive advantage in many overseas markets including car production, electronics, household appliances, and ship building. The Asian financial crisis in the late 1990s marked a decisive moment in shaping skill formation in the future, but our investigations highlight both a high degree of uncertainty about the direction of change and significant variations in circumstances in Japan, Korea, and Singapore.

In Japan and Korea, global financial capitalism is having a profound impact on the developmental state. The institutionally embedded practices that enabled Japan to enjoy rapid economic growth and a high degree of equality in earnings is going to be difficult to maintain unless the country can pull out of its sluggish economic performance at the beginning of the twenty-first century. The trade-off is clear. The state can try to maintain its commitment to efficiency and social justice by attempting to reform rather than transform existing practices or else it can fully embrace the market and 'shareholder' capitalism that would have a positive impact on the sentiments of international financial markets at least in the short term. There seems little doubt that the extent to which the Japanese government will attempt to 'govern the market' (Wade 1990) will decline.

The impact of the Asian financial crisis in Korea has been far more serious than in Japan. Before the crisis Korea appeared to be swimming with the tide of globalization as the leading *chaebol*, including Samsung, Daewoo, LG, and Hyundai, were all developing impressive globalization strategies that were intended to turn them into the world's leading companies. This led to substantial borrowing on international financial markets resulting in enormous debt with the precipitous fall in the value of the Korean Won. The subsequent intervention of the International

---

[6] Germany provides an excellent test case when compared to the UK of the hypothesis that the possibility of cheap labour reduces employers' incentives to invest in technology and skill in order to add value (see Prasad 2000).

Monetary Fund was premissed on a 'structural adjustment' of the Korean economy, that included trade liberalization, labour market deregulation, reductions in social spending, and overhauling of its banking system. The transformation of the banking system that involves alliances and buyout of Korean financial institutions by overseas investors, along with the sale of various companies controlled by the *chaebol* to foreign companies, will inevitably change the relationship between the state and the market. However, market deregulation is highly unpopular and is being vigorously contested by the trade union movement. The Korean government has not embraced market capitalism and is seeking to find a middle way between the developmental state and the free market. The trade-off in this case is yet to be defined. Koreans cannot return to the old *chaebol*-dominated way of running the economy, yet an alternative third way has still to be articulated.

Singapore has fared much better that Japan and Korea in being able to combine global capitalism with the developmental state. This is because Singapore has had to operate within international markets for decades. Being able to attract foreign multinational companies has been the linchpin of its competitive strategy. The absence of its own large companies has enabled the government to develop a highly effective civil service which has distanced itself from both employers and trade unions in the 'national interest' (Ashton and Sung 1994). Moreover, the image of a small country 'surviving' against the odds has played an important role in moulding a political consensus in Singapore based on social inclusion and the upgrading of the skills of the workforce (Low 1998).

In Singapore the state continues to operate in a 'developmental' capacity. This includes scanning the global marketplace for MNCs who are using state of the art technologies as a way of pursuing a general process of skills upgrading and enhancing national prosperity. But 'Singapore Inc.' has transformed itself into 'Singapore Unlimited' (Mahizhnan and Lee 1998) based on what can be called a 'one nation, dual economy' model (Brown and Lauder 2001*b*). Here the state performs a *vital* role in Singapore at the same time as performing a *virtual* role in the region. The development of an 'external wing' began in the early 1990s with the Singapore government acting as an outward investor in the region. This takes the form of joint ventures with regional governments, MNCs or Government Linked Companies (GLCs). The virtual role of the state has become increasingly important in its 'developmental' capacity given the limitations of land and labour within Singapore. It gives the state scope to encourage the development of value added business services and advanced manufacturing in Singapore, at the same time as facilitating foreign MNCs to set up low skilled operations elsewhere within the region. But it is also being used to give regional and global scope to Singaporean businesses to develop into World-Class Companies (WCCs).

UPGRADING THE SKILLS OF THE WORKFORCE

The second pressure point deals with the issue of whether nations are likely to be successful in developing the societal capacity for skills upgrading. We have argued that none of the countries included in our investigations are characterized by a low skill equilibrium (Finegold and Soskice 1988). In all countries there is high skilled employment in at least some sectors of the economy, and a growth in the demand for highly skilled employees. However, in most if not all cases there were also large numbers of jobs where the incentive to upgrade skills was missing. This suggests that there is a serious mismatch between the rhetoric of 'high skills' and the realities of policy implementation, unless the institutional mechanisms, along with the ethos of skills upgrading, are put in place.

This pressure point therefore raises the issue of how to coordinate education and training, labour market, R & D, and industrial relations policies and practices to develop the societal capacity for skills upgrading. It raises the question of how the supply and demand for labour are coordinated to encourage skills upgrading, and whether existing skill formation systems are structured in ways that inhibit skills upgrading. As previously noted, the societal capacity for skills upgrading will depend on the historical context in which the political economy of skill formation has developed in each country. This raises the question of whether the upgrading of skills throughout the whole economy will be easier to achieve in some countries rather than in others.

This pressure point has received considerable attention throughout this book given that it offers an excellent focus for examining the effectiveness of skill formation policies in practice. In Britain there is a policy commitment to raise skills levels, but in a historical context characterized by serious inadequacies in technical education and training, along with low employer commitment to training, especially in small and medium-sized companies. In many sectors of the economy, employers are reluctant to invest in new technologies or to upgrade the skills of the workforce, recognizing that it is still possible to make good profits through competition on price rather than product or service innovation (Keep 1999). This will make it difficult to embed skills upgrading when skill formation is based on a voluntary code of practice, given that employers have also resisted what they see as state interference in commercial decision-making. The final report of the National Skills Taskforce in England (DfEE 2000b) reaffirms the question of skill formation as a supply-side issue that needs to be geared to meeting the perceived needs of employers. This historic trade-off between government and business will continue to leave large numbers of those entering the labour market better qualified but unable to find suitable employment.

The dominance of business interests in American politics is even more in evidence. As in Britain the supply and demand for labour is left to the marketplace. The focus on the supply-side is warranted because it is assumed by government and business leaders that the demand for high skills is buoyant and because government should not try to shape industrial policy, including the demand for skilled labour. Closing the gap between efficiency and justice depends on the performance of the economy. Upgrading the skills of workers paradoxically depends on the inefficiency of labour shortages, although even here there has been a tendency for America to hire skilled workers from other countries rather than to meet such shortages by adopting a planned approach to skill formation. Nevertheless, when labour shortages exist there is the potential for employers to improve working conditions and wages as was the case at the end of the 1990s. But this has done little to overcome the problem of low waged, low skilled work in the United States. The huge inequalities in living conditions, health, education, and employment opportunities that now pertain make it difficult to predict a decisive political shift in the direction of a high skill society. The election victory of George W. Bush will further weaken the powers of the federal state to act as a 'strategic trader' in the interests of the American workforce as a whole. The joker in the pack is the fortunes of the US economy. A serious recession in America, possibly triggered by a collapse of share prices on Wall Street, is perhaps the only prospect for a fundamental rethink of how to reunite efficiency and justice in the interests of social cohesion.

Germany comes closest to our model of a high skills society given that it has a large proportion of its workforce in employment with relatively advanced training. The Dual System of apprenticeship in German has been used as a way of linking training to earnings and the labour market. We have shown that the assertion that the Dual System is too rigid in a context of rapid innovation has been exaggerated as companies have introduced ways to significantly compress the time it takes to get new areas of training officially ratified, facilitated by the Chambers of Commerce and a close working relationship on skills issues between leading-edge companies and trade unions. However, the image of the Dual System as inflexible remains, and it has been increasingly related to growing concerns about labour costs. There is a distinct possibility that Germany will move in the direction of flexible labour markets and shareholder models of financial management that now dominate global financial markets. German companies are increasingly looking to reduce their costs by establishing production outside the country. Equally, whereas German companies have being acquiring foreign competitors for decades, the organization of corporate finance within Germany has made it difficult for foreign competitors to take over indigenous businesses. This seems to be changing, suggesting that German workers will be increasingly forced to work under shareholder rather than stakeholder models of business. If this were to happen on a large scale, it would undermine the Dual System and with it the incentive for employers to train across the economy. If this happens, the long-standing link between economic efficiency and social justice will be broken along with the prospect of creating a twenty-first century high skills society.

As noted above, what will happen in Japan depends on whether the 'internal labour market' (see Chapter 3) remains intact. The internal labour market has provided an important link between the supply and demand for skilled labour. This is not based on the education system being tailored to meet the needs of employers, but rather the educational system is charged with supplying an educated population with good generic and transferable skills that can be developed within the company. Given a commitment to jobs for life and linking earnings to years of service rather than simply skill and occupational grade, there has been an incentive to develop the skills of employees. The close collaboration between the large corporations and the small and medium-sized companies that supply them has also led to the diffusion of 'good practice' in respect to skills training, but this should not be exaggerated. A majority of the workforce, including virtually all female employees, have not been part of the internal labour market. There are large numbers of make-work jobs in the service sector that offer little opportunity for skills upgrading that are preferred to unemployment. The future of the internal labour market is also in doubt as companies seek greater 'numerical flexibility' to meet the volatile nature of product markets. This has led to a re-evaluation of life-time employment practices and seniority pay. Young workers are also challenging the extensive control that the large corporations exert over workers and their families (Dore 2000). If the internal labour market were to give way to a more 'flexible' labour market structure, the coordination of the supply and demand of labour for skills upgrading would be undermined.

To repeat a familiar trend, the situation in Korea is even more precarious. What we have said for Japan equally applies to Korea. However, the supply chain (this can also be viewed as a skills chain) that has been a feature of industrial organization in Japan is not as tightly established in Korea. There has been a long-standing problem of developing high skilled small and medium-sized companies as the *chaebol* have monopolized the funds for new investment. Equally, the pressures to restructure the employment relationship within the *chaebol* are in many respects more urgent in Korea. The main problem in Korea is now the demand for labour, let alone skilled labour. At the same time Korean students are leaving university with little prospect of finding professional or managerial employment.

In contrast the Singaporean approach is based on 'top down' co-ordination of both the demand and supply of labour, which navigates a process of skills upgrading through strategic inward investment in high skilled manufacturing and exportable services clusters (e.g. wafer fabrication, precision engineering, international business services, education, and health care). Yet the rapid economic development of Singapore has highlighted the problem of how to lift the skills base, when approximately one-quarter of the workforce have no more than primary level education (Gopinathan 1999). Another problem is that in order to upgrade the skills of the workforce the government has to constantly address the enlightened self-interest of companies with reference to new market opportunities in Singapore. This is relatively easier to achieve when companies can see the benefits of production or service delivery at a reduced cost and in close proximity to emerging markets, but the same logic does not apply so readily in the case of research, design, and development, where proximity to regional markets is less compelling. The MNCs are reluctant to diffuse state of the art technologies for the purposes of domestic skill development. Much of the research and development undertaken by the MNCs remains close to the 'home' base. Singapore has the added problem of a weak research infrastructure. But unless it can develop its R & D capability, it will become more vulnerable to regional competitors such as Malaysia who are continuing to upgrade their skills base into technical areas with lower wage costs.

OPPORTUNITY AND SOCIAL INCLUSION

Knowledge-driven economies are associated with polarization and inequality rather than convergence and equality. How societies tackle the problem of social exclusion and the positional competition for education, training, and jobs is therefore an important pressure point for all countries (see Chapter 1). This is based on the contention that the competition for professional, managerial, and technical jobs is a vital part of understanding national skill formation strategy. It is inevitable that not everyone will find high skilled employment. Equally the ET system will continue to be used as a screening device to decide who are the winners and losers in the competition for the credentials required to enter good jobs. So how is this competition organized given the competing interests of individuals and parents who want to maximize their chances of winning a competitive advantage; employers who want a supply of appropriately qualified and trained recruits; and governments that require an efficient and legitimate system of allocating educational and labour market opportunities?

This will include an analysis of whether this competition is based on 'merit' or the 'market' (P. Brown 1995; Lauder et al. 1999). The former involves a significant role for the national or local state as it attempts to reduce the impact of class background, gender, ethnicity, or race on the outcome of the competition for a livelihood. Alternatively, where it is based on the wealth and wishes of parents, emphasis is placed on market forces deciding how students are to be educated with little attempt on the part of the state to intervene in this competition.

The organization of positional competition will reflect the power of the middle class and social elites in each society. It concerns the way the state attempts to regulate 'talent' and student aspirations, especially those from middle-class backgrounds. How then does the state try to regulate and legitimate restrictions on access to university education? One of the most striking features of the last thirty years has been the expansion of the middle classes and their expectations of higher education and a high skilled job for their children. Therefore the regulation of talent is not only a question of how youth are 'warmed up' to strive for educational and occupational success, but how they are 'cooled out' given the rising aspirations of parents and siblings. A related issue is whether the demand from employers is able to absorb the growing numbers of higher education graduates entering the labour market. Are there enough high skilled jobs to meet the aspirations of students, and if not, how does the state address the question of 'over-education'? This is an issue that has affected all the countries that we have studied, however, its impact has been most dramatic in Korea because of the high numbers of unemployed graduates.

The structuring of opportunity is also closely linked to the issue of social exclusion. Whereas the former focuses on the way the competition for education, training, and jobs is organized, the question of social exclusion focuses on the circumstances of the losers. Are the losers still able to gain access to good quality education and training, and are there decent jobs for them, even if they are not highly skilled? Or do they confront a polarized labour market which may force them into casual jobs or long-term unemployment? As we have seen the question of social exclusion is central to skill formation because it enables us to gauge whether national governments are serious about lifting the skills base of the whole society. Here it is recognized that the linear upgrading of skills is politically inspired rather than technologically determined.

Increasing unemployment due to international competition for low skilled work, technological innovation, and economic slowdown have all made the question of social exclusion increasingly problematic, especially when public expenditure is under pressure. This pressure point therefore involves an analysis of national priorities, such as whether the government gives priority to reducing unemployment or maintaining welfare budgets as opposed to reducing the tax burden on the wealthy. But what it also highlights is a trade-off between skills and employment that is increasingly difficult to avoid.

This pressure point highlights serious problems in the skill formation strategies of Britain and the United States. Empirical evidence on employment, income, and life-chances in both countries shows a significant divide, if not a chasm, between the work rich and work poor. Substantial numbers of children in both countries live in conditions of poverty, excluded from gaining the qualifications that would permit them to compete in the market for jobs. Decades of sociological research have taught us that poverty activates hungry stomachs and dulls inquisitive minds. Poverty and social disadvantage are closely correlated to educational failure and subsequent unemployment

(Halsey, Heath, and Ridge 1980). Income polarization and poverty will make it more difficult for the daughters and sons of the disadvantaged to compete with their middle-class contemporaries. This is because market rules of competition reinforce the advantages of those from privileged backgrounds and the longer the competition lasts, for instance, to postgraduate university study, the more it benefits those with the financial resources to stay in the competition (Hirsch 1977). This should not obscure the significant gains made by middle-class women in both societies. There has not only been an impressive improvement in academic performance, but they are infiltrating areas of professional and managerial employment that were previously the preserve of middle-class men.

In both countries the trade-off between employment and skills has decisively been won by those who argue that any form of economic activity is preferable to unemployment and the receipt of welfare benefits. This trade-off will result in a large proportion of low skilled, low waged jobs remaining a permanent feature of the employment structure, unless a serious recession obliterates vast numbers of these jobs in the service sector (Esping-Andersen 1999). This has not prevented social exclusion, as there are significant populations of working poor (those in employment but also able to obtain a living wage), and others who are defined as economically inactive and living on 'thin air'. There is little prospect of things improving for the socially excluded as they are held responsible for their own circumstances, unwilling to grasp the opportunities for training and employment that now exist. The emphasis is on a 'culture of dependency' which assumes that the socially excluded have developed an unhealthy dependency on state support which inhibits them from investing in their human capital or from looking for work.

In Germany income differentials slightly narrowed during the 1980s given a strong commitment to maintain social cohesion through instituting a correspondence between ET and a highly segmented labour market based on the principle of 'equality of productive capacity'. This meant that the German education system, although highly differentiated on the basis of academic attainment, has not led to income polarization because the Dual System ring-fences jobs for those with the appropriate qualifications rather than being part of a hierarchy of jobs that allowed the better qualified to trade down until they found employment, pushing other labour market entrants with inferior (i.e. vocational) qualifications further down the occupational pyramid. National agreements on occupational earnings attached to the training system also inhibited the race to inequality. But this infrastructure of high skill formation in Germany is under threat for the reasons already mentioned. This includes the problem of maintaining a broad-based commitment to the Dual System that may be more difficult as the proportion of jobs in the service sector expand, and the impoverished state of the economic infrastructure in the former east Germany.

The commitment to high skill employment throughout the economy also involves a trade-off between skills and employment. Relatively high unemployment in Germany has been blamed on the exclusionary tactics of German trade unions preserving the vested interests of members by keeping both skill and wage levels high, at the expense of the unemployed Germans who have, so the argument goes, been priced out of the market. Despite generous welfare provision for the unemployed the costs to the public purse are a source of heated debate and there are now government attempts to create more flexible work conditions at the low skilled, low wage end of the labour market to reduce unemployment.

Japan and Korea have also attempted to combine rapid economic growth strategies with relatively narrow income disparities. This is based on the male breadwinner model that has excluded large numbers of the women from the labour market or else female employment has been treated as an interim measure between leaving full-time education and getting married and having children. There are signs that the exclusion of young women from elite routes through education into the labour market is changing, but as shown in Chapter 3, a great deal of ground remains to be made up.

Equality of opportunity within the education system has been an important part of skill formation strategies in both countries. This typically involved a high degree of social mix especially during the early years of education and an emphasis on collective achievement rather than an overriding concern with the education of an elite. But there was also intense competition to gain access to elite universities as these fed the internal labour markets of the major corporations in both countries. There has been a long-standing concern about the hot-housing of students and fears that many of them were 'burnt out' by the time they reach university. The creation of 'smart conformists' able to pass examinations but lacking the creative problem-solving and entrepreneurial skills that are now required by employers is one of the negative consequences of this system to which we will return in a moment. Of more immediate concern is the fact that both countries are attempting to introduce parental choice in where their children are schooled along with greater 'diversity' in educational provision. This could be read as the first stage in the marketization of the education system, but the societal commitment to equality remains strong despite growing pressures from the middle classes to reproduce social advantages for their children (Dore 2000).

The economic problems that have beset Korea since the late 1990s have brought the problem of social exclusion into focus given rising unemployment without a developed welfare state. The question of unemployment is part of a major national debate about how the country should respond to its economic crisis and the need for widespread corporate downsizing advocated by the IMF. There are plans for the development of a 'productive welfare state' that would give the country the 'flexibility' to restructure employment without devastating the lives of millions of individuals and their families. If this fails to materialize, poverty and inequality will exclude millions of Koreans from being able to compete in the positional competition for real vocational prizes: those jobs that remain part of the internal labour market.

The robust performance of the Singapore economy has continued to offer education, training, and a living wage to virtually all Singaporeans, although the use of 'guest workers' as in other countries including Germany is relied on to undertake the low skilled, low waged jobs that Singaporeans are not available for or willing to contemplate. The vast majority of these workers are required to leave Singapore after two years.

What distinguishes Singapore from the other developmental states is that it has a pattern of income inequality more akin to the United States than to Korea or Japan (Low and Liang 1999). In Singapore there has been little attempt to restrict the pay of 'symbolic analysts' working for MNCs (Reich 1991). Equally, the government has been committed to equality of opportunity not equality. This commitment to rewarding male and increasingly female talent is reflected in the incomes of government officials.[7] However, the Singapore government has maintained a high degree of social inclusion because it has succeeded in 'raising all the boats'. Full employment has enabled virtually everyone to have a job if they entered the labour market. Through a process of

---

[7] Figures compiled by the World Competitiveness Report, 1996 show that the political chief executive in Singapore is compensated to the tune of US$812,858, this is over twice the amount paid in the USA, Japan, Germany, and the UK. Cabinet ministers in Singapore received US$574,476, legislators US$65,174, and senior civil servants US$292,714, these figures compare with an average salary of US$14,459 for manufacturing employees. On the World Competitiveness Report's Altruism Index, which is the salary of the political chief executive divided by that of manufacturing employees, the ratio is 56.2 for Singapore, 6.2 in the USA, 8.2 in Japan, 8.4 in Germany, and 5.3 in the UK (Low 1998: 214).

skills upgrading and productivity improvements significant wage increases have been achieved across all the major industrial sectors. Coupled with significant increases in the value of real estate spread throughout the population, widespread social exclusion has been avoided despite the scale of inequalities (Chua 1995), although the educational performance of Malays is a matter of concern. There is a relatively low rate of personal tax in Singapore (28 per cent) and the absence of a Western-style welfare state, but there is a significant redistribution of income based on the Asian proverb 'it is better to teach them to fish than to give them fish' (Government of Singapore 1991: 118). This has been used to legitimate major investment in housing, health care, and education based on co-payment to maintain a sense of contribution rather than simply one of 'rights' to services.

Chua Beng Huat suggests that 'for the first 25 years of rapid economic growth, the rate of upward mobility has been very rapid across the entire population. This was largely because of the relatively homogeneously "poor"—not only in wealth but also in education attainment' (1999: 216). But a class structuring has been developing in Singapore despite efforts by the government to use social and economic policies as a way of correcting some of the fragmentary consequences of market capitalism. This he suggests has become more conspicuous with the rise in consumer spending, especially in terms of housing and cars.

The impact of socio-economic inequalities on Singapore's commitment to meritocratic competition does present a major challenge to its skill formation strategy. The ideology of meritocracy is deeply ingrained in Singapore as it tries to keep alive the 'Singaporean dream' of social improvement for oneself, one's family, and the society as a whole. When meritocracy is able to operate in a context of economic growth and full employment, it can be seen as both a neutral way of judging contestants and to lead to greater equality of outcome, in the sense that more middle-class jobs are created. The problem today is that meritocratic competition operates in a different labour market context. There is more inequality between occupational positions, along with problems of unemployment or underemployment, which greatly exaggerate the consequences of success or failure in the competition for credentials. The more the stakes are seen to increase the more intensive 'positional' competition between individuals, families, and social classes will become. There is a real danger of growing rigidity in Singapore's class structure unless it can find ways of limiting the competitive advantage of middle-class families in the competitions for certificates and jobs. Equally, more conspicuous educational, social, and economic inequalities may make it harder to convince all sections of society to maintain the social discipline that has been a key feature of Singapore's skill formation strategy.

CHANGING MODELS OF THE WORKER

The final pressure point focuses on the way social, political, and economic change has challenged existing models of the 'worker'. This pressure point highlights the nature of the relationship between the individual and society. Changing models of economic efficiency have placed more emphasis on key skills including communication, team-work, problem-solving, and creativity. There is also more emphasis on individual initiative and self-reliance that challenges the routine, rule-following behaviour demanded by most employees in Fordist factories and corporate bureaucracies.

In all countries this debate included the issue of 'employability'. The volatile nature of consumer markets, the challenge to assumptions about lifetime employment, and the pace of technological innovations with built-in occupational obsolescence that demand regular periods of retraining, have all served to bring the issue of employability to prominence. It has highlighted the balance of responsibility between the individual and the state. Most notably in Britain and America employability has signalled an attempt to shift the responsibility for employment from government to the individual. The 'skills nexus' limits the responsibility of the state to provide education and training opportunities for individuals to compete for employment. But because skills are acquired by individuals and subject to the vagaries of the market-place, success is seen to rest with the individual. Social discipline has also become more than a question of getting a job and staying in it, but of developing the 'emotional intelligence' including commitment, perseverance, interpersonal empathy, and networking skills, to remain employable in the external labour market.

This emphasis on employability not only raises questions about the skills and attitudes of the new 'model' worker in Britain and America, but it can also lead to some unintended trade-offs that have implications for the relationship between productivity and skill formation. There is increasing empirical evidence in Britain that the knowledge workers of the future—graduates leaving university—are taking seriously the idea that they will have portfolio careers involving regular changes in employment. The problem this poses for companies is that if they invest in the initial training of these graduates how are they going to develop their commitment to the company, previously secured through bureaucratic career structures? The idea that this is not a problem for companies based on a 'plug-in and play' model of the inter-changeability of skilled labour is far removed from the realities of most businesses. Equally when employability involves a shift in responsibil-ities for employment away from companies to individuals, there is little incentive for individuals to invest time and energy developing knowledge, skills, and know-how that are non-transferable to other companies or that are not seen to add value to one's curriculum vitae. But improvements to productivity are frequently context-specific and involve the utilization of skills including local knowledge, skills, and know-how that are not easily transportable.

The focus on employability also encompasses the issue of entrepre-neurial skills that are frequently linked to creativity and risk-taking. When it comes to developing creativity and self-development, Western countries are seen to have a distinct advantage given systems of educa-tion that to varying degrees celebrate individual achievement and diversity at least among the higher educated. In America, Britain, and Germany the main issue is not one of individualization (Durkheim 1933; Beck 1992), but of social cohesion. It is the problem of how to balance individual freedom with the teamworking skills required in the workplace and the need to strengthen the social bonds between the individual and society. Companies have recognized the need to develop mission statements and corporate cultures as a way of trying to unite their workforce in a common cause. Governments have renewed their interest in moral (civics or citizenship) education as a renewed attempt at nation-building (Green 1990). But whether this has any chance of redressing the tidal wave of market individualism is to be doubted, yet as R. H. Tawney observed, in devaluing human cooperation Western societies have 'shot the bird that caused the wind to blow, and now have to go about their business with an albatross round their necks' (Dennis and Halsey 1988: 223).

The re-engineering of the model worker also involves challenging existing assumptions about the nature and distribution of human capa-bility. In Western countries it has been assumed that there is a limited pool of ability (Halsey, Heath, and Ridge 1980) that must be nurtured to fulfil the most demanding roles in the division of labour, whilst the majority are capable of little other than menial and routine employ-ment. It is also assumed that most workers have little commitment to their work and therefore should not be trusted with discretion or given responsibility (P. Brown and Lauder 2000, 2001a). Any serious approach to high skill formation has no chance of making progress unless these assumptions are challenged. The same is also true of established assumptions about the sexual division of labour that restricted the perceived competence of women to the nurturing of children, providing rest and recreation for the male breadwinner, or being engaged in 'caring' roles in the labour market (Crompton and Sanderson 1990). Likewise, in the United States the fact that Herrnstein and Murray's (1994) *The Bell Curve* became a bestseller reminds us that racial assumptions about intelligence remain deep-seated in Western culture and raise far-reaching political questions about the position of African-Americans in education, training, and employment.

In Japan and the Asian tiger economies, there have been vociferous calls for students and workers to show greater personal initiative and creativity (Green 1999a). In Singapore, for example, the 'Thinking Schools, Learning Nation' initiative introduced in 1997 represented a change in the pedagogical balance, away from the rote learning of content to the acquisition of process skills, which are the foundations of lifelong learning. 'There is no need to fear that we will blunt our competitive edge when we concentrate on much more than merely academic achievement. More and more, we will need our workforce to think, to be creative, to be self-reliant yet able to work in teams, to communicate clearly.'[8] The problem this poses for Asian countries such as Singapore is that creativity, self-reliance, and empowerment are seen to go together with Western individualism. This may seriously weaken the social cement that many believe to be crucial to the economic success of Japan and the Asian tigers.

But this is to pose an intriguing question for comparative analysis, because the relationship between social cohesion and economic competitiveness is historically variable. What is required in past conditions of industrial production may be different from what is required in the knowledge-driven economy. In the past social cohesion was a source of productivity gain when it contributed to a workforce that was committed, disciplined, hardworking, and able to accurately learn and copy routine ways of doing things (Amsden 1989). However, if people are expected to be creative problem-solvers, self-managers, enterprising, and lifelong learners, it involves more than a change in mindset. It involves institutionalized relations of trust (Fox 1974; Baron, Schuller,

---

[8] Mr Wee Heng Tin, Director-General of Education (Ministry of Education, Singapore 1998: 11).

and Field 2000), which assume a high degree of individual discretion and freedom that have been largely absent in Japan, Korea, and Singapore. Therefore, the question is: to what extent will these countries require wholesale changes in their social and political institutions to generate the kinds of workers they now believe to be essential to economic competitiveness? We are not in a position to answer this question, but as the developed Asian economies loosen the reins on individualism they confront an important challenge if they also seek to maintain a national commitment to equitable redistribution and social cohesion. How this challenge is met in the coming years will have a decisive impact on the future of skill formation in these countries.

CONCLUSION

This book has attempted to show that the study of skill formations stands at the heart of the social sciences. It requires a multidisciplinary approach, since an understanding of skill with all its social, political, cultural, and economic ramifications is beyond the grasp of any single social science discipline. Its study is critical because it is poorly understood, yet it has become a central plank in national political debates about economic competitiveness, globalization, and social justice. Much of the contemporary debate has confused or conflated questions of social purpose (political aims) with the means of how they can be met. This confusion is premissed on an evolutionary model of technological progression in which technology is the motor of social progress and the main problem confronting societies is seen to be one of upgrading the supply of skilled labour, a view that is rejected in this book.

The study of 'high skills' offers a way of reconnecting to questions of political economy. A return to questions of political economy is timely because it encourages greater clarity on issues of purpose (ends) and how to achieve them (means). However, a high skills society is not an end state that is ever achieved, but rather is an ideal at the centre of debates and political struggle over the production and reproduction of the societal capacity for high skills. Clearly some societies are closer to that ideal than others, but the skill formation strategies in all these societies hang in the balance. Of course this is where the analysis begins because even if we could agree that a high skills society is the best means for achieving economic and social progress, there is the question of how to create and re-create, in the face of the challenges posed by globalization, the appropriate social, cultural, and economic conditions. This is why the main question addressed in this book concerns the prospects for high skills societies through a detailed assessment of alternative national strategies. Our conclusion is that the possibilities are encouraging, the dangers are real, but the reality is messy. We hope that we have given the reader a sense of all three.

Appendix: List of Organizations Interviewed

FEDERAL REPUBLIC OF GERMANY

Organizations

Badin-Württenberg Ministry of Education and Culture
Bayerische Landesbank
BMW
Brandenburg Ministry of Education and Culture
Bundes Institut für Berufsbildung, Berlin and Bonn
Bundesvereinigung der Deutschen Arbeitgeberverbande
Bund-Länder-Kommission fur Bildungsplanung und forschungsforderung geschaftsstelle
Chamber for Industry and Craft in Potsdam, Brandenburg
Daimler Benz
DGB
Federal Ministry of Education, Science, Research and Technology
Hamburg Ministry of Education, Training and Youth
Hotel Vier Jahreszeiten
Ifo Institute for Economic Research
Industrie und Handelskammer—Region Stuttgart
Max Planck Institute for the Study of Societies
Max-Bravergestamtschule, Comprehensive School, Hamburg
Oberstufenzentrum 1 Technik (OSZ: Training Centre), Potsdam, Brandenburg
OSZ II (Wirtschaft und Verwaltung), Potsdam
OSZ III (Gesundheit/ErnahrungHauswirtschaft), Potsdam
Phillips, Hamburg
Siemens

Staatliche Gewerbeschule Informations und Electrotechnik, Chemie und
    Automatisierungstechnik, Hamburg
Staatliche Gewerbeschule Metalltechnik mit Technischem Gymnasium (G17),
    Hamburg
University of Hamburg
Wissencraftzentrum

FEDERAL REPUBLIC OF SOUTH KOREA

Organizations

Association of Korea Commercial Education and Association of Korea
    Commercial High School Principals
Daewoo Corporation
Daewoo Motor Co. Ltd
Dokok Elementary School
Dongyang Technical College
Hilton Hotels Group
Kangham Technical High School
Kongju National University
Korea Chamber of Commerce & Industry
Korea Education Development Institute
Korea Institute for Youth Development
Korea Labour Institute
Korea National University of Education
Korean Confederation of Trade Unions
Korean Development Institute
Korean Educational Development Institute
Korean Educational Development Institute, Vocational-Technical Education
    Research Centre
Korean Manpower Agency, Ministry of Labour
Korean National University of Education
LG Executive Offices
LG Semicon
Management, Innovation Dept., Samsung
Ministry of Education
Office of Planning for LWR Project
Office of the President
Policy Office, Federation of Korean Trade Unions
Presidential Commission on Industrial Relations Reform
Samsung Electronics, Management Innovation Dept
Samsung Fire and Marine Insurance

Samsung Global Management Institute
Samsung Securities Ltd
Sejong University
Seoul Girls Commercial High School
Seoul Hilton
Seoul National University
Seoul Polytechnic
Sheraton Walker Hill Hotels
Small & Medium Industry Promotion Corporation
Song Jun Argricultural High School
Soo-Do Technical High School
Yangjae High School
Yeong Deung Po Girls' Commercial High School

SINGAPORE

Organizations

Anderson Secondary School
Bedok South Primary School
Boon Tong Kee Pte Ltd
British Council
Cable and Wireless
Council for Professional and Technical Education
Department of Business Policy, National University of Singapore
Development Bank of Singapore
Economic Development Board
Henderson Secondary School
Hong Kah Secondary School
Hong Kong and Shanghai Banking Corporation Limited
Hong Kong Bank
Institute of Policy Studies
Institute of Technical Education
LG Electronics
Matsushita Electronics
Ministry of Education
Ministry of Labour
Ministry of Manpower
Ministry of Trade and Industry
Motorola Electronics Pte Ltd
Nanyang Girls' High School
National Computer Board

National Institute of Education
National Science and Technology Board, National University of Singapore
National Trades Union Congress
National University of Singapore
Ngee Ann Polytechnic
Oriental Hotel
Philips Consumer Electronics
Philips Electronics Asia Pacific Pte Ltd
Productivity and Standards Board
Resource Development Government Agency
Sheraton Towers Hotel
Siemens Microelectronics
Singapore Government Department of Statistics
Singapore Institute of Labour Studies
Singapore Polytechnic
Temasek Junior College
Temasek Polytechnic
Teradyne Singapore Ltd
Victoria School
Woodlands Secondary School
Xinmin Secondary School
Yishun Junior College
Zhonghua Secondary School

BRITAIN

Organizations

Centre for Labour Market Studies and Leicester University's School of
    Education
DfEE
Ford Motor Company
National Skills Task Force
Panasonic European Television Division
QCA
Samsung Training Centre
Welsh Development Agency

The subsidiary of a German Manufacturer,
    Head Office, the Plant Management,
    Apprentices Workers (ex-apprentices)

JAPAN

Organizations

Central Council for Education, Tokyo
Centre for National University Finance, Tokyo
Chuo University, Tokyo
Curriculum Planning Office
Daiichi Junior High School, Tokyo
Educational and Cultural Exchange Office
Education Promotion Society for Special Schools
Hitotsubashi University
Hosei University
Institute for International Policy Studies
Japan Institute of Labour
Japan Society for the Promotion of Science
Japan Women's College of Physical Education
Karikusa Gakuin, Tokyo
Kobe University
Kyoto Women's University
Matsushita
Meiji University
Ministers' Secretariat
MITI
Monbusho, Tokyo
Nagoya Institute of Technology
Nakano-Machi Kindergarden, Tokyo
National Institute for Educational Research of Japan
National Institution for Academic Degrees
NIKKOKYO (Japan Senior High School Teachers and Staff Union)
NIKKYOSO (Japan Teachers' Union)
Nissan
Ohasshi Seisakusho, Precision Engineering Company
Osaka Prefecture Board of Education
Osaka Prefectural Imamiya Sogo Senior High School
Osaka University of Education
Poole Gakuin University
Primary and Secondary Education Dept.
Research Institute of Democracy in Education
Senri Senior High School, Osaka
Tokyo Metropolitan Board of Education
Tokyo Metropolitan Harumi Sogo Senior High School
Tokyo Metropolitan University

Waseda University
Yodogawa Technical High School
ZENKYO (All Japan Teachers and Staff Union)

UNITED STATES OF AMERICA

Organizations

American Federation of Labor and Congress of Industrial Organizations
American Society for Training and Development
Institute of Educational Leadership, Washington, DC
National Association of Manufacturers
National Center on Education and the Economy, Washington, DC
National Governors' Association, Employment and Social Services Policy
   Studies Division
Office of Public Leadership
US Department of Education
US Department of Labor
Woodrow Wilson Center

REFERENCES

Abramovitz, M. (1989), *Thinking about Growth* (Cambridge: Cambridge University Press).

Acemoglu, D., and Pischke, J.-S. (1999), 'Beyond Becker: Training in Imperfect Labour Markets', *Economic Journal*, 109 (Feb.) 112–41.

Albert, M. (1993), *Capitalism against Capitalism* (London: Whurr Publishers).

Allmendinger, J. (1989), 'Educational Systems and Labour Market Outcomes', *European Sociological Review*, 5/3: 231–50.

Amano, I. (1997), 'Education in a More Affluent Japan', *Assessment in Education: Principles, Policy and Practice*, 4/1: 51–66.

Amsden, A. (1989), *Asia's Next Giant: South Korea and Late Industrialization* (Oxford: Oxford University Press).

Appelbaum, E., Bailey, T., Berg, P., and Kalleberg, A. (2000), *Manufacturing Advantage: Why High-Performance Work Systems Pay Off* (Ithaca, NY and London: Cornell University Press).

Archibugi, D., and Michie, J. (1997) (eds.), *Technology, Globalization and Economic Performance* (Cambridge: Cambridge University Press).

Arnot, M., Weiner, G., and David, M. (1999), *Closing the Gender Gap: The Post War Era and Social Change* (London: Polity Press).

Aronowitz, S., and DiFazio, W. (1994), *The Jobless Future: Sci-Tech and the Dogma of Work* (Minneapolis: University of Minnesota Press).

Arulampalam, W., and Booth, A. (1997), *Labour Market Flexibility and Skills Acquisition: Is There a Trade-Off?* University of Essex, Institute of Labour Research, Discussion Paper No. 97/13.

Ashton, D., and Green, F. (1996), *Education, Training and the Global Economy* (Aldershot: Edward Elgar).

—— and Sung, J. (1994), *The State, Economic Development and Skill Formation: A New East Asian Model?* Centre for Labour Market Studies, University of Leicester.

—— Felstead, A., and Green, F. (2000), 'Skills in the British Workforce', in F. Coffield (ed.), *Differing Visions of a Learning Society*, ii (Bristol: Policy Press).

Ashton, D., Davies, B., Felstead, A., and Green, F. (1999), *Work Skills in Britain*, SKOPE, Warwick University.

—— Green, F., James, D., and Sung, J. (1999), *Education and Training for Development: The Political Economy of Skill Formation in East Asian Newly Industrialised Economies* (London: Routledge).

Auerbach, J. A., and Belous, R. S. (1998) (eds.), *The Inequality Paradox: Growth of Income Disparity* (Washington, DC: National Policy Association).

Ball, S. (1998), 'Big Policies/Small World: An Introduction to International Perspectives in Education Policy', *Comparative Education*, 34: 119–30.

BankBoston (1997), *MIT: The Impact of Innovation*, Special Report, BankBoston Economics Department.

Baron, S., Schuller, T., and Field, J. (2000) (eds.), *Social Capital: Critical Perspectives* (Oxford: Oxford University Press).

Barrell, R., and Pain, N. (1997), *The Growth of Foreign Direct Investment in Europe*, National Institute Economic Review, 160 (Apr.).

Beck, U. (1992), *Risk Society: Towards a New Modernity* (London: Sage).

Becker, G. S. (1964), *Human Capital* (Chicago: University of Chicago Press).

—— (1996), 'Nobel Lecture: The Economic Way of Looking at Behaviour', in R. Swedberg (ed.), *Economic Sociology* (Cheltenham: Edward Elgar).

Bell, D. (1973), *The Coming of Post-Industrial Society* (New York: Basic Books).

Bendix, R. (1956), *Work and Authority in Industry: Ideologies of Management in the Course of Industrialization* (New York: John Wiley).

Berger, S., and Dore, R. (1996) (eds.), *National Diversity and Global Capitalism* (New York: Cornell University Press).

Bernstein, B. (1969), 'A Critique of the Concept of Compensatory Education', in *Class, Codes and Control*, ii (London: Routledge & Kegan Paul).

Bernstein, J., Rasell, E., Schmitt, J., and Scott, R. (1999), 'Tax Cut No Law for Middle Class Economic Wives' (Washington, DC: Economics Policy Institute).

Best, M. (1990), *The New Competition: Institutions of Industrial Restructuring* (Cambridge: Polity Press).

Birdcall, N., Ross, D., and Sabot, R. (1995), 'Inequality and Growth Reconsidered: Lessons from East Asia?', *World Bank Economic Review*, 9/3: 477–508.

Birke, B., Blumberger, W., Bremer, R., and Heidegger, G. (1998), 'Enhancing Vocational Programmes in Austria and Germany', in J. Lasonen and M. Young (eds.), *Strategies for Achieving Parity of Esteem in European Upper Secondary Education* (Institute for Educational Research, University of Jyväskylä, Finland).

Blackmore, J. (1997), 'The Gendering of Skill and Vocationalism in Twentieth-Century Australian Education', in A. H. Halsey, H. Lauder, P. Brown, and A. S. Wells (eds.), *Education: Culture, Economy and Society* (Oxford: Oxford University Press).

Blackwell, B., and Eilon, S. (1991), *The Global Challenge of Innovation* (Oxford: Butterworth-Heinemann).

Blair, M., and Kochan, T. (2000) (eds.), *The New Relationship: Human Capital in the American Corporation* (Washington, DC: Brookings Institution).

Blair, T. (1999), Bournemouth Party Conference Speech, 1999 at <www.labour.org.uk>.

Block, F. (1990), *Postindustrial Possibilities: A Critique of Economic Discourse* (Berkeley: University of California Press).

Bourdieu, P., and Baltanski, L. (1978), 'Changes in Social Structure and Changes in the Demand for Education', in S. Giner and M. Archer (eds.), *Contemporary Europe: Social Structure and Cultural Change* (London: Routledge).

—— and Passeron, J. C. (1977), *Reproduction: In Education, Society and Culture* (London: Sage).

Braverman, H. (1974), *Labor and Monopoly Capital: The Degradation of Work in the Twentieth Century* (New York: Monthly Review Press).

Brown, A. (1997), *Becoming Skilled During a Time of Transition: Observations from Europe*, Department of Educational Studies, University of Surrey, Guildford.

Brown, P. (1987), *Schooling Ordinary Kids: Inequality, Unemployment and the New Vocationalism* (London: Routledge).

—— (1995), 'Cultural Capital and Social Exclusion: Some Observations on Recent Trends in Education, Employment and Labour Market', *Work, Employment and Society*, 9: 29–51.

—— (1999), 'Globalization and the Political Economy of High Skill', *Journal of Education and Work*, 12/13: 233–52.

—— (2000), 'The Globalization of Positional Competition?', *Sociology*, 34: 633–53.

—— and Lauder, H. (1996), 'Education, Globalization and Economic Development', *Journal of Education Policy*, 11:1–24.

—— —— (1997), 'Education, Globalization and Economic Development', in A. Halsey, H. Lauder, P. Brown, and A. Stuart Wells, *Education, Culture, Economy and Society* (Oxford: Oxford University Press).

—— —— (2000), 'Human Capital, Social Capital and Collective Intelligence', in S. Baron, J. Field, and T. Schuller (eds.), *Social Capital: Critical Perspectives* (Oxford: Oxford University Press).

—— —— (2001a), *Capitalism and Social Progress: The Future of Society in a Global Economy* (Basingstoke and New York: Palgrave).

—— —— (2001b), 'The Future of Skill Formation in Singapore', *Asia-Pacific Business Review*.

—— and Scase, R. (1997), 'Universities and Employers: Rhetoric and Reality', in A. Smith and F. Webster (eds.), *The Postmodern University?* (Buckingham: Open University Press).

Bynner, J., and Parsons, S. (1997), *It Doesn't Get Any Better: The Impact of Basic Skills on the Lives of 37 Years Olds* (London: Basic Skills Unit).

Capelli, P. (1999) (ed.), 'Introduction', in *Employment Practices and Business Strategy* (New York: Oxford University Press).

Carnevale, A. P., and Porro, J. D. (1994), *Quality Education: School Reform for the New American Economy* (Washington, DC: US Department of Education).

Castells, M. (1992), 'Four Asian Tigers with a Dragons' Head: A Comparative Analysis of the State, Economy and Society in the Asian Pacific Rim', in R. Appelbaum and J. Henderson (eds.), *States and Development in the Asia Pacific Rim* (London: Sage).

—— (1994), 'The Information Economy and the New International Division of Labor', in M. Carnoy, M. Castells, S. Cohen, and F. H. Cardoso, *The New Global Economy in the Information Age* (University Park: Pennsylvania State University).

—— (1996), *The Information Age: Economy, Society and Culture*, i. *The Rise of the Network Society* (Oxford: Blackwell).

—— (1998), *The Information Age: Economy, Society and Culture*, iii. *End of Millennium* (Oxford: Blackwell).

CCE (Central Council on Education) (1996), *The Model for Japanese Education in the Perspective of the 21st Century*, First Report (Tokyo: Monbusho).

—— (1997), *The Model for Japanese Education in the Perspective of the 21st Century*, Second Report (Tokyo: Monbusho).

Chieh, H. C. (1999), 'What It Takes to Sustain Research and Development in a Small, Developed Nation in the 21st Century', in L. Low (ed.), *Singapore: Towards A Developed Status* (Singapore: Oxford University Press).

Cho, H., and Chang, P.-W. (1994) (eds.), 'Preface', *Gender Division of Labour in Korea*, Seoul, Korean Women's Institute series (Seoul: Ewha Woman's University Press).

Chua, B.-H. (1995), *Communitarian Ideology and Democracy in Singapore* (London: Routledge).

—— (1999), 'The Attendant Consumer Society of a Developed Singapore', in L. Low (ed.), *Singapore; Towards a Development Status* (Singapore: Oxford University Press).

Chusho Kigyo Cho (CKC) (1997), *Chusho Kigyo Hakusho* [White Paper on Small and Medium Enterprises of Japan] (Tokyo: Okurasho).

—— (1999), *Chusho Kigyo Hakusho* [White Paper on Small and Medium Enterprises of Japan] (Tokyo: Okurasho).

Clammer, J. (1993), 'The Establishment of a National Ideology', in G. Rodan (ed.), *Singapore Changes Guard: Social, Political and Economic Directions in the 1990s* (Melbourne: Longman).

Clark, B. (1962), *Education and the Expert Society* (San Francisco: Chandler).

Coffield, F. (1997) (ed.), *A National Strategy for Lifelong Learning* (Newcastle upon Tyne: Department of Education, University of Newcastle).

—— (2000*a*), 'Introduction: A Critical Analysis of the Concept of a Learning Society', in F. Coffield (ed.), *Differing Visions of a Learning Society*, i (Bristol: Policy Press).

Coffield, F. (2000*b*), 'The Three Stages of Lifelong Learning: Romance, Evidence and Implementation', in F. Coffield (ed.), *Differing Visions of a Learning Society*, ii (Bristol: Policy Press).

Coleman, J. (1997), 'Social Capital in the Creation of Human Capital', in A. H. Halsey et al. (eds.), *Education: Culture, Economy and Society* (Oxford: Oxford University Press).

Collins, A., Brown, J., and Newman, S. (1989), 'Cognitive Apprenticeship: Teaching the Crafts of Reading, Writing and Mathematics', in L. Resnick (ed.), *Knowing, Learning and Instruction* (Hillsdale, NJ: Erlbaum).

Collins, R. (1979), *The Credential Society: An Historical Sociology of Education and Stratification* (New York: Academic Press).

—— (1986), *Weberian Sociological Theory* (Cambridge: Cambridge University Press).

Committee on Singapore's Competitiveness (1998), Report, Ministry of Trade and Industry, Republic of Singapore.

Conradi, P., and Smith, D. (1999), 'From Business Miracle to Sick Man of Europe', in *Sunday Times*, 14 Mar.

Cooke, P., and Morgan, K. (1998), *The Associational Economy: Firms, Regions and Innovation* (Oxford: Oxford University Press).

Cortada, J. W. (1998) (ed.), *Rise of the Knowledge Worker* (Boston: Butterworth-Heinemann).

Cressey, P., and Kelleher, M. (1999), *Partnership and Investment in Europe: The Role of Social Dialogue in Human Resource Development*, LEONARDO Project, EUR/96/2/107/EA/III.2.a/FPC, Consolidation Report.

Crompton, R. (1999) (ed.), *Restructuring Gender Relations and Employment: The Decline of the Male Breadwinner* (Oxford: Oxford University Press).

—— and Sanderson, K. (1990), *Gendered Jobs and Social Change* (London: Unwin Hyman).

Crouch, C., and Streeck, W. (1997), *Political Economy of Modern Capitalism* (London: Sage).

—— Finegold, D., and Sako, M. (1999), *Are Skills the Answer?: The Political Economy of Skill Creation in Advanced Industrial Countries* (New York: Oxford University Press).

Culpepper, P. (1999), 'The Future of the High Skill Equilibrium in Germany', *Oxford Review of Economic Policy*, 15/1: 43–59.

Daly, A., Hitchens, D., and Wagner, K. (1985), 'Productivity, Machinery and Skills in a Sample of British and German Manufacturing Plants', *National Institute Economic Review*, May.

Dasgupta, P., and Serageldin, I. (2000), *Social Capital: A Multifaceted Perspective* (Washington DC: World Bank).

Davis, K., and Moore, W. E. (1945), 'Some Principles of Stratification', *American Sociological Review*, 10: 242–9.

Deardon, L., McIntosh, S., Myck, M., and Vignoles, A. (2000), *The Returns to Academic, Vocational and Basic Skills in Britain* (London: National Skills Task Force).

Dench, P., and Giles, L. (1998), *Employers' Perceptions of Key Skills*, Institute for Employment Studies Report 349, University of Sussex.

Dench, S. (1993), 'Employers' Provision of Continuous Training', Social Science Research Branch Working Paper No. 6 (London: Employment Department, mimeo).

—— Perryman, S., and Giles, L. (1998), 'Employers' Perceptions of Key Skills', IES Report 349, Institute of Employment Studies, Sussex.

Dennis, N., and Halsey, A. H. (1988), *English Ethical Socialism* (Oxford: Oxford University Press).

Department of Commerce (1999), *21st Century Skills for 21st Century Jobs* (Washington: US Government Printing Office). <http://vpskillsummit.gov>.

Department of Labor (1999), *Report on the American Workforce* (Washington, DC: US Department of Labor).

Dewey, J. (1916), *Democracy and Education* (New York: Macmillan).

DfEE (Department for Education and Employment) (1988), *National Adult Learning Survey* (London: DfEE).

—— (1998), *The Learning Age: A Renaissance for a New Britain* (London: HMSO).

—— (1999*a*), *Labour Market and Skills Trends 1998/1999* (London: DfEE),

—— (1999*b*), *Learning to Succeed: A New Framework for Post-16 Learning* (London: HMSO).

—— (2000), 'Skills for All: Proposals for a National Skills Agenda', *Final Report of the National Skills Task Force* (London: DfEE). <http://www.dfee.gov.uk/skillforce>.

Dore, R. (1986), *Flexible Rigidities: Industrial Policy and Structural Adjustment in the Japanese Economy 1970–1980* (London: Athlone Press).

—— (1998), 'Asian Crisis and the Future of the Japanese Model', *Cambridge Journal of Economics*, 22: 773–87.

—— (1999), 'Japan's Reform Debate: Patriotic Concern or Class Interest? Or Both', *Journal of Japanese Studies*, 25/1: 65–89.

—— (2000), *Stock Market Capitalism: Welfare Capitalism, Japan and Germany Versus the Anglo-Saxons* (Oxford: Oxford University Press).

—— and Sako, M. (1989) *How Japanese Learn to Work* (London: Routledge).

—— —— (1998), *How Japanese Learn to Work*, 2nd edn. (London: Routledge).

—— Lazonick, W., and O'Sullivan, M. (1999), 'Varieties of Capitalism in the Twentieth Century', *Oxford Review of Economic Policy*, 15/4: 102–20.

Doremus, P., Keller, W., Pauly, L., and Reich, S. (1998), *The Myth of the Global Corporation* (Princeton: Princeton University Press).

Drucker, P. (1993), *Post-Capitalist Society* (Oxford: Butterworth-Heinemann).

—— (1999*a*), *Management Challenges for the 21st Century* (Oxford: Butterworth-Heinemann).

—— (1999*b*), 'Putting the "Man" in Management', Interview with Simon Caulkin, *The Observer*, 9 May.

DTI (Department of Trade and Industry) (1997), *Competitiveness: Our Partnership with Business UK. A Benchmark for Business* (London: DTI).

—— (1998*a*), White Paper: *Our Competitive Future: Building the Knowledge-Driven Economy* (London: DTI).

—— (1998*b*), White Paper: *Our Competitive Future: Building the Knowledge-Driven Economy; Analysis Report* (London: DTI).

Due, J., Madsen, J., and Jensen, C. (1991), 'The Social Dimension: Convergence or Diversification of IR in the Single European Market?', *Industrial Relations Journal*, 22/2: 85–102.

Durand, J.-P., Stewart, P., and Castillo, J. (1999) (eds.), *Teamwork in the Automobile Industry: Radical Change or Passing Fashion?* (Basingstoke: Macmillan).

Durkheim, E. (1933), *The Division of Labour in Society*, trans. George Simpson (New York: Macmillan).

EC (European Commission) (1996), *Living and Working in the Information Society: People First Green Paper* (Luxembourg: European Commission). Reprinted as 'Employment in the Information Society', in W. Cortada James (1998) (ed.), *Rise of the Knowledge Worker* (Boston: Butterworth-Heinemann), 14–20.

—— (1999*a*), *Continuing Training in Enterprises: Facts and Figures* (Brussels: European Commission).

—— (1999*b*), *Employment in Europe, 1998* (Luxembourg: Office for Official Publications of the European Communities).

Economic Intelligence Unit (1998), Country Report: Germany, 3rd Quarter (London: EIU).

The Economist, 4 May, 2001.

EDB (Economic Development Board) (1998), *Singapore Economic Development Board Annual Report*, 1997/8.

Elger, T., and Smith, C. (1994), *Global Japanisation? The Transnational Transformation of the Labour Process* (London: Routledge).

Elliott, L., and Atkinson, D. (1998), *The Age of Insecurity* (London: Verso).

Eltis, W., and Fraser, D. (1992), 'The Contribution of Japanese Industrial Success to Britain and Europe', *Nat. West. Bank Quart Rev.* Nov.: 2–19.

EPA (Economic Planning Agency, Government of Japan) (1999), *Keizai Hakusho* [White Paper on Economy in Japan] (Tokyo: Okurasho Insatsu Kyoku).

Eraut, M. (1997), 'Perspectives on Defining "The Learning Society"', *Journal of Education Policy*, 12: 551–8.

Esping-Andersen, G. (1999), *Social Foundations of Postindustrial Economies* (Oxford: Oxford University Press).

Evans, K., and Heinz, W. (1994) (eds.), *Becoming Adult in England and Germany* (London: Anglo-German Foundation).

Fenby, J. (1999), 'They Reform Tiers, Don't They', *The Observer*, 2 May.

Fevre, R., Rees, G., and Gorrard, S. (1999), 'Some Sociological Alternatives to Human Capital Theory and their Implications for Research on Post-Compulsory Education and Training', *Journal of Education and Work*, 12: 117–40.

Finegold, D. (1999), 'Creating Self-Sustaining High Skill Ecosystems', *Oxford Review of Economic Policy*, 15/1: 60–81.

Finegold, D. and Soskice, S. (1988), 'The Failure of Training in Britain: Analysis and Prescription', *Oxford Review of Economic Policy*, 4/3: 21–53.

Foley, M. W., and Edwards, B. (1999), 'Is It Time to Disinvest in Social Capital?', *Journal of Public Policy*, 19/2: 141–73.

Fox, A. (1974), *Work, Power and Trust Relations* (London: Faber and Faber).

Frank, R., and Cook, P. (1996), *The Winner-Take-All Society* (London: Penguin).

Freeman, R. B. (1997), *When Earnings Diverge: Causes, Consequences, and Cures for the New Inequalities in the US* (Washington, DC: National Policy Association).

Freeman, R., and Schettkat, R. (1999), *Skill Compression, Wage Differentials and Employment: Germany vs the US*, paper presented at the Leverhulme Workshop, Sept., University of Essex.

Fryer, R. (1997), Report of the National Advisory Committee on Continuous Education and Lifelong Learning (London: DfEE).

Fukuyama, F. (1992), *The End of History and the Last Man* (London: Hamish Hamilton).

—— (1996), *Trust: The Social Virtues and the Creation of Prosperity* (London: Penguin).

Galbraith, J. K. (1977), *The Age of Uncertainty* (London: Andre Deutsch).

Gallie, D., and White, M. (1993), *Employee Commitment and the Skills Revolution* (London: Policy Studies Institute).

—— —— Cheng, Y., and Tomlinson, M. (1998), *Restructuring the Employment Relationship* (Oxford: Clarendon Press).

Gamble, J., Wilkinson, B., Humphrey, J., and Morris, J. (1998), *Integration and Segregation in China: Japanese and Korean Multinationals Compared*, paper presented to the APROS Colloquium, Pacific Paradigms: Organisation and Management in the Pacific rim, China Europe International Business School, Shanghai, China, 14–16 July.

Gardner, H. (1993), *Frames of Mind: The Theory of Multiple Intelligences* (London: Fontana).

Geroski, P., and Gregg, P. (1997), *Coping with Recession: UK Company Performance in Adversity* (Cambridge: Cambridge University Press).

Gershuny, J. (1978), *After Industrial Society: The Emerging Self-Service Economy* (London: Macmillan).

Gerth, H., and Mills, C. W. (1967) (eds.), *From Max Weber* (London: Routledge).

Giddens, A. (1991), *Modernity and Self-Identity: Self and Society in the Late Modern Age* (Cambridge: Polity).

Goleman, D. (1996), *Emotional Intelligence* (London: Bloomsbury).

Goodman, A., Johnson, P., and Webb, S. (1997), *Inequality in the United Kingdom* (Oxford: Oxford University Press).

Gopinathan, S. (1974), *Towards a National System of Education in Singapore, 1945–1973* (Singapore: Oxford University Press).

—— (1994), *Educational Development in a Strong-Developmentalist State: The Singapore Experience*, paper presented at the Australian Association for Research in Education Annual Conference.

—— (1999), 'Preparing for the Next Rung: Economic Restructuring and Educational Reform in Singapore', *Journal of Education and Work*, 12: 295–308.

Gott, S. (1989), 'Apprenticeship Instruction for Real Work Tasks: The Co-Ordination of Procedures, Mental Models and Strategies', in E. Rothhopf (ed.), *Review of Research in Education* (Washington, DC: American Educational Research Association).

Gough, I. (1999), 'Social Welfare Competitiveness: Social Versus System Integration', in I. Gough and G. Olofsson, *Capitalism and Social Cohesion: Essays on Exclusion and Integration* (Basingstoke: Macmillan).

Government of Singapore (1991), *Singapore: The Next Lap* (Singapore: Times Editions).

Granovetter, M., and Swedberg, R. (1992) (eds.), *The Sociology of Economic Life* (Boulder, Colo.: Westview).

Gray, J. (1997), *False Dawn: The Delusions of Global Capitalism* (London: Granta Books).

Great Britain (1996), *The Skills Audit Full Report: A Report from an Interdepartmental Group* (London: DfEE and the Cabinet Office).

Green, A. (1990), *Education and State Formation: The Rise of Education Systems in England, France and the USA* (London: Macmillan).

—— (1997*a*), *Education, Globalization and the Nation State* (Basingstoke: Macmillan).

—— (1997*b*), 'Educational Achievement in Centralized and Decentralized Systems', in A. H. Halsey et al., *Education: Culture, Economy and Society* (Oxford: Oxford University Press).

—— (1998), 'Core Skills, Key Skills and General Culture: In Search of the Common Foundations in Vocational Education', *Evaluation and Research in Education*, 12: 23–43.

—— (1999*a*), *Comparative Perspectives on Skills Formation in Japan, South Korea, Singapore and Germany*, High Skills Working Paper 5, Feb., Institute of Education, London.

—— (1999*b*), 'East Asian Skill Formation Systems and the Challenge of Globalisation', *Journal of Education and Work*, 12/3: 253–80.

—— (1999*c*), 'Education and Globalisation in Europe and East Asia: Convergent and Divergent Trends', *Journal of Education Policy*, 14/1: 55–71.

—— (2000*a*), 'Converging Paths or Ships Passing in the Night? An "English" Critique of Japanese School Reform', *Journal of Comparative Education* 36/2: 417–35.

—— (2000*b*), *Educational Achievement in Singapore: Outputs, Outcomes and Means*, Report to DfEE for International Benchmarking Study (London: Institute of Education).

—— and Steedman, H. (1997), *Into the Twenty First Century: An Assessment of British Skill Profiles and Prospects*, Special Report, Centre for Economic Performance, London School of Economics and Political Science.

Green, A., Ouston, J., and Sakamoto, A. (1999), *Comparing Japanese and English Schooling*, Working Paper Four, High Skills Project (London: Institute of Education).

——Wolf, A., and Leney, T. (1999), *Convergence and Divergence in European Education and Training Systems* (London: Institute of Education).

Greenhalgh, C. (1999), 'Adult Vocational Training and Government Policy in France and Britain', *Oxford Review of Economic Policy*, 15/1: 99–113.

Gregg, P., Harkness, S., and Machin, S. (1999), *Child Development and Family Income* (York: Joseph Rowntree).

Habermas, J. (1988), *Legitimation Crisis* (Cambridge: Polity).

Halsey, A. H., with Webb, J. (2000) (eds.), *British Social Trends: The Twentieth Century* (London: Macmillan).

——Heath, A., and Ridge, J. (1980), *Origins and Destinations: Family, Class and Education in Modern Britain* (Oxford: Clarendon Press).

Hampden-Turner, C., and Trompenaars, F. (1993), *The Seven Cultures of Capitalism* (London: Piatkus).

Harvey, D. (1989), *The Conditions of Post-Modernity* (Oxford: Blackwell).

Hasluck, C. (1999), *Employment Prospects and Skills Needs in Banking, Finance and Insurance Sector*, Skills Task Force Research Paper 9 (Sudbury: DfEE Publications).

Hassel, A., and Schulten, T. (1998), 'Globalisation and the Future of Central Collective Bargaining: The Example of the German Metal Industry', *Economy and Society*, 27/4: 486–522.

Hayek, F. A. (1944), *The Road of Serfdom* (Chicago: University of Chicago Press).

——(1960), *The Constitution of Liberty* (London: Routledge).

Healy, T. (1998), 'Counting Human Capital', *OECD Observer*, 212, June/July.

Heath, A., and McMahon, D. (1997), 'Education and Occupational Attainment: The Impact of Ethnic Orogins', in A. H. Halsey et al. (eds.), *Education: Culture, Economy and Society* (Oxford: Oxford University Press).

Heinz, W. (1999), 'Job-Entry Patterns in a Life Course Perspective', in W. Heinz (ed.), *From Education to Work: Cross National Perspectives* (Cambridge: Cambridge University Press).

Held, D., McGrew, A., Goldblatt, D., and Perraton, J. (1999), *Global Transformations: Politics, Economics and Culture* (Cambridge: Polity).

Hendry, C. (1999), *New Technology Industries*, Skills Task Force Research Paper 10 (Sudbury: DfEE Publications).

Herrnstein, R., and Murray, C. (1994), *The Bell Curve: Intelligence and Class Structure in American Life* (New York: Free Press).

Hickman, R. (1991), 'Art Education in a Newly Industrialized Country', *Journal of Art and Design Education*, 10/2: 170–89.

Higuchi, Y. (1997), 'Trends in Japanese Labour Markets', in M. Sako and H. Sato (eds.), *Japanese Labour and Management in Transition* (London: Routledge).

Hill, M., and Lian Kew Fee (1995), *The Politics of Nation Building and Citizenship in Singapore* (London: Routledge).

Hirsch, F. (1977), *The Social Limits to Growth* (London: Routledge).

HM Treasury (2000), *Productivity in the UK: The Evidence and the Government's Approach*, Budget Briefing Paper, Public Enquiry Unit, <http:/www. hm-treasury.gov.uk>.

Hobsbawm, E. J. (1977), *The Age of Capital, 1848–1875* (London: Abacus).

Hogarth, T., Bosworth, D., Wilson, R., and Shury, J. (2000), *The Extent, Causes and Implications of Skill Deficiencies: Survey Report*, Working Paper 24, Institute for Employment Research, Warwick University.

Holloway, S. D. (1988), 'Concepts of Ability and Effort in Japan and the United States', *Review of Education Research*, 58: 327–45.

Hood, N., and Young, S. (2000) (eds.), *The Globalization of Multinational Enterprise Activity and Economic Development* (Basingstoke: Macmillan).

Hutton, W. (1995), *The State We're In* (Kent: Mackays of Chatham).

—— (1997), *The State to Come* (London: Vintage).

—— (1998), 'So What Can Lead Us Out of this Mess?', *The Observer*, 6 Sept.

—— and Giddens, A. (2000) (eds.), *On the Edge: Living with Global Capitalism* (London: Jonathan Cape).

IBRD/WB (2000), *World Bank Atlas* (Washington, DC: World Bank).

ILO (International Labour Office) (1998), *World Employment Report 1998–99: Employability and the Global Economy, How Training Matters* (Geneva: ILO).

IMD (International Institute for Management Development) (1999), *World Corporation Yearbook* (Lausanne: IMD).

Inagami, T. (1999), 'Shin Nihon gata Keiei to Roshi Kankei no Saikouchiku' [Reconstruction of the Neo-Japanese Management and Employer–Employee Relationship], *Rodo Jiho*, Aug., Tokyo.

Inoki, T. (2000), 'Beikoku no Gijutsu teki Dokusen to Dou Tatakauka' [How Do We Confront the Technological Dominance of the US], *Chuo Koron*, Mar., Tokyo.

James, P., Veit, W., and Wright, S. (1997) (eds.), *Work of the Future: Global Perspectives* (St Leonards, NSW: Allen and Unwin).

Jasinowski, J. (1998) (ed.), *The Rising Tide* (New York: John Wiley).

Jayaweera, S. (1997), 'Women, Education and Empowerment in Asia', *Gender and Education*, 9/4: 411–23.

Jeong In-Soo (1996), 'Employment Structure Change in Korea', *Korean Economic Bulletin*, Apr.: 2–12.

Johnson, C. (1982), *MITI and the Japanese Miracle: The Growth of Industrial Policy 1925–1975* (Stanford, Calif.: Stanford University Press).

—— (1995), *Japan Who Governs? The Rise of the Developmental State* (New York: W. W. Norton).

—— (1998), 'Economic Crisis in East Asia: The Clash of Capitalisms', *Cambridge Journal of Economics*, 22: 653–61.

—— (2000), *Blowback: The Costs and Consequences of American Empire* (New York: Little Brown).

Johnson, P., and Reed, R. (1996), 'Intergenerational Mobility among the Rich and the Poor: Results from the National Child Development Survey', *Oxford Review of Economic Policy*, 12/1: 127–42.

Jones, B. (1997), *Forcing the Factory of the Future: Cybernation and Societal Institutions* (Cambridge: Cambridge University Press).

Jung, S.-H. (1999), *Defensive Europeanisation of Korean Consumer Electronics Firms: The Formation and Embeddedness of Korean Sales and Production Networks across the EU*, paper presented to the Regional Studies Association International Conference, Bilbao, Spain, Sept.

Kanter, R. M. (1998), 'Small Business and Economic Growth', in J. J. Jasinowski (ed.), *The Rising Tide* (New York: John Wiley & Son).

Keep, E. (1999), 'UK's VET Policy and the "Third Way": Following a High Skills Trajectory or Running up a Dead End Street?', *Journal of Education and Work*, 12/3: 323–46.

—— (2000), *Employer Attitudes to Training*, Skills Task Force Research Paper 15 (Sudbury: DfEE Publications).

—— and Mayhew, K. (1998), *Was Ratner Right? Product Market and Competitive Strategies and their Links with Skills and Knowledge*, Employment Policy Institute.

Kennedy, P. (1993), *Preparing for the Twenty-First Century* (London: Harper Collins).

Kern, H. (1998), 'Lack of Trust, Surfeit of Trust: Some Causes of the Innovation Crisis in German Industry', in C. Lane and R. Bachmann (eds.), *Trust within and between Organisations: Conceptual Issues and Empirical Applications* (Oxford: Oxford University Press).

Kerr, C., Dunlop, J., Harbison, F., and Myers, C. (1973), *Industrialism and Industrial Man* (Harmondsworth: Penguin).

Kim Byong-Sub (1994), 'Value Orientations and Sex-Gender Role Attitudes: On the Comparability of Attitudes of Koreans and Americans', in H. Cho and P.-W. Chang (eds.), *Gender Division of Labour in Korea*, Seoul, Korean Women's Institute series (Seoul: Ewha Woman's University Press).

Kitson, M., and Wilkinson, F. (1998), 'Employment Structure, Recruitment, Labour Turnover, Training and Labour Force Flexibility', in A. Cosh and A. Hughes (eds.), *Enterprise Britain: Growth, Innovation and Public Policy in the Small and Medium Sized Enterprise Sector, 1994–1997* (Cambridge: ESRC Centre for Business Research, University of Cambridge).

Klatt, R., and Richter-Witzgall, G. (2000), *Women in Future Occupations: Paths Related to Economic Equality of Opportunity for Women in Vocational Training*, Report to the Ministry for Women, Young People, Family and Health (Nordheim-Westfalen).

Klees, S. (1986), 'Planning and Policy Analysis in Education: What Can Economics Tell Us?', *Comparative Education Review*, 30/4: 574–607.

Knack, S. (2000), *Trust, Associational Life and Economic Performance in the OECD*, unpublished paper for HRDC–OECD International Symposium on

'The Contribution of Investment in Human and Social Capital to Sustained Economic Growth and Well Being', World Bank, Washington, DC.

—— and Keefer, P. (1997), 'Does Social Capital Have an Economy Payoff? A Cross-Country Investigation', *Quarterly Journal of Economics*, 112: 1251–88.

Knauss, J. (1998), 'Modular Mass Production: High Performance on the Low Road', *Politics and Society*, 26/2: 273–96.

Kobrin, S. (2000), 'Development After Industrialisation: Poor Countries in an Electronically Integrated Global Economy', in N. Hood and S. Young (eds.), *The Globalization of Multinational Enterprise Activity and Economic Development* (Basingstoke: Macmillan).

Kohn, M., and Schooler, C. (1983), *Work and Personality: An Inquiry into the Impact of Social Stratification* (Norwood, NJ: Ablex Publishing Company).

Koike, K. (1997), *Human Resource Development in Japanese Industry*, offprint.

—— and Inoki, T. (1990) (eds.), *Skill Formation in Japan and South East Asia* (Tokyo: University of Tokyo Press).

Korean Economic Bulletin (1999), May.

Krugman, P. (1996), 'Making Sense of the Competitiveness Debate', *Oxford Review of Economic Policy*, 12/3: 17–25.

—— (1999), *The Return to Depression Economics* (New York: W. W. Norton).

Kudomi, Y. (1999), 'Nihon no Gakko no Ikizumari to Saisei: Kyoso no Kyoiku no Hakyoku to Gakko Seido no Seitousei no Yuragi no Jidai ni yosete [Japanese Schools' Impasse and Revitalisation], in Hitotsubashi University (eds.), *The Society for the Study on Education and Society*, Studies on Education and Society 9, Murayama Insatsu, Tokyo.

Kumazawa, M. (1997), *Noryoku shugi to Kigyo Shakai* [Meritocracy and Industrial Society] (Tokyo: Iwanami).

Kuttner, R. (2000), 'The Role of Government in the Global Economy', in W. Hutton and A. Giddens (eds.), *On the Edge: Living with Global Capitalism* (London: Jonathan Cape).

Lam, A. (1992), *Women and Japanese Management: Discrimination and Reform* (London: Routledge).

Landes, D. (1998a), 'Homo faber, homo sapiens: Knowledge, Technology, Growth, and Development', in D. Neef (ed.), *The Knowledge Economy* (London: Butterworth-Heinemann).

—— (1998b), *The Wealth and Poverty of Nations* (London: Abacus).

Lane, C. (1998), 'European Companies between Globalization and Localisation: A Comparison of Internationalisation Strategies of British and German Multinational Companies', *Economy and Society*, 27/4: 462–85.

Lauder, H. (1999), 'Competitiveness and Low Skills Equilibria: A Comparative Analysis', *Journal of Education and Work*, 12/3: 281–94.

—— Hughes, D., and others (1999), *Trading in Futures* (Buckingham: Open University Press).

Lave, J., and Wenger, E. (1991), *Situated Learning* (New York: Cambridge).

Lazonick, W., and O'Sullivan, M. (2000), 'Maximizing Shareholder Value: A New Ideology for Corporate Governance', *Economy and Society*, 29/1: 13–35.

Leadbeater, C. (1999), *Living on Thin Air* (Harmondsworth: Penguin).

Lee Hye-Kyung (1994), 'Gender Division of Labour and the Authoritarian Development State', in H. Cho and P. W. Chang (eds.), *Gender Division of Labour in Korea*, Seoul, Korean Women's Institute Series (Seoul: Ewha Women's University Press).

Lee Tsau Yuan (1998), *The Financial Crisis: Impact on the Singapore Economy* (Singapore: Institute of Policy Studies).

Levin, H., and Kelly, C. (1997), 'Can Education Do It Alone?', in A. H. Halsey et al. (eds.), *Education: Culture, Economy and Society* (Oxford: Oxford University Press).

Lim Swee Say (1998), 'Constraints of Manpower Resources', in Arun Mahiznan and Lee Tsao Yuan (eds.), *Singapore: Re-Engineering Success*, Institute of Policy Strudies/Oxford University Press, Singapore.

Lim Tik En, David (1998), 'From Administrative State to Innovative Society', in A. Mahizhnan and Lee Tsao Yuan (eds.), *Singapore, Re-Engineering Success* (Singapore: Institute of Policy Studies/Oxford University Press).

Locke, R. (1989), *Management and Higher Education since 1940: The Influence of America and Japan on West Germany, Great Britain and France* (Cambridge: Cambridge University Press).

Loh, L. (1998), 'Technological Policy and National Competitiveness', in Toh Mun Heng and Tan Kong Yam (eds.), *Competitiveness of the Singapore Economy: A Strategic Perspective* (Singapore: Singapore University Press).

Low, L. (1998), *The Political Economy of a City-State: Government-Made Singapore* (Singapore: Oxford University Press).

—— and Liang, N. T. (1999), 'An Underclass among the Overclass', in L. Low (ed.), *Singapore: Towards A Developed Status* (Singapore: Oxford University Press).

—— and Ngiam Tee Liang (1999), 'An Underclass among the Overclass?', in L. Low (ed.), *Singapore: Towards a Developed Status* (Singapore: Oxford University Press).

—— Toh Mun Heng, Soon Teck Wong, Tan Kong Yam, and Hughes, H. (1993), *Challenge and Response: Thirty Years of the Economic Development Board* (Singapore: Times Academic Press).

Lundvall, B.-A. (1992), *National Systems of Innovation: Towards a Theory of Innovation and Interactive Learning* (London: Pinter).

Luttwak, E. (1999), *Turbo-Capitalism: Winners and Losers in the Global Economy* (London: Orion Business Books).

Mahbubani, K. (1998), *Can Asians Think?* (Singapore: Times Books International).

Mahizhnan, A., and Lee, T. Y. (1998) (eds.), *Singapore: Re-Engineering Success* (Oxford: Oxford University Press).

MCA (Management and Coordination Agency) (Statistics Bureau, Government of Japan) (1997), *Employment Status Survey* (Tokyo: Government of Japan).

—— (1998), *Monthly Statistics of Japan, August*, No. 446, Tokyo.

Marginson, S. (1993), *Education and Public Policy in Australia* (Cambridge: Cambridge University Press).

Marquand, D. (1988), *The Unprincipled Society* (London: Jonathan Cape).

Marsden, D., and Ryan, P. (1995), 'Work, Labour Markets and Vocational Preparation: Anglo German Comparisons of Training in Intermediate Skills', in L. Bash and A. Green (eds.), *World Yearbook of Education: Youth, Education and Work* (London: Kogan Page), 67–79.

Marshall, A. (1925), 'The Future of the Working Class (1873)', in A. C. Pigou (ed.), *Memorials of Alfred Marshall* (London: Macmillan).

—— (1961) [1890], *Principles of Economics*, i (New York: Macmillan).

Martin, H. P., and Schumann, H. (1997), *The Global Trap: Globalization and the Assault on Democracy and Prosperity* (New York: Zed Books).

Marx, K. (1976) [1867], *Capital*, i, trans. B. Fowkes (Harmondsworth: Penguin).

Mason, G. (1998), *Change and Diversity: The Challenges Facing Chemistry Higher Education*, Report by National Institute of Economic and Social Research to the Royal Society of Chemistry and the Council for Industry and Higher Education, National Institute of Economic and Social Research, London.

—— (1999), *Engineering Skills Formation in Britain: Cyclical and Structural Issues*, Skills Task Force Research Paper 7 (Sudbury: DfEE Publications).

—— (2000), 'Mix of Graduate and Intermediate Level Skills in Britain: What Should the Balance Be?', unpublished paper, National Institute of Economic and Social Research, London.

—— and van Ark, B. (1996), 'Productivity, Machinery and Skills: Engineering in Britain and the Netherlands', in D. Mayes (ed.), *Sources of Productivity and Growth* (Cambridge: Cambridge University Press).

—— and Wagner, K. (1998*a*), *High Level Skills, Knowledge Transfer and Industrial Performance: Electronics in Britain and Germany* (London: National Institute of Economic and Social Research).

—— and Wagner, K. (1998*b*), *Knowledge Transfer and Innovation in Britain and Germany: 'Intermediate Institution' Models of Knowledge Transfer Under Strain?* (London: National Institute of Economic and Social Research).

—— van Ark, B., and Wagner, K. (1996), 'Workforce Skills, Product Quality and Economic Performance', in A. Booth and D. Snower (eds.), *Acquiring Skills: Market Failures, their Symptoms and Policy Responses* (Cambridge: Cambridge University Press).

Mathews, J. (1998), 'Fashioning a New Korean Model Out of the Crisis: The Rebuilding of Institutional Capabilities', *Cambridge Journal of Economics*, 22: 747–59.

Maurice, M., Sellier, F., and Silvestre, J.-J. (1986), *The Social Foundations of Industrial Power: A Comparison of France and Germany* (Cambridge, Mass.: MIT Press).

Max Planck Institut (1998), Bericht der Kommission Mittestimmung at <http://www.mpi-fg-koeln.mpq.de/bericht/endbricht/anheng.htm>.

McKinsey Global Institute (1998), *Driving Productivity and Growth in the UK Economy* (London: McKinsey & Co.).

McNeill, D., and Bockman, H. (1998), 'Introduction' to Special Section on Viewpoints on the Asian Financial Crisis, *World Development*, 26/8: 1529–33.

Mehralizadeh, Y. (1999), 'The Relationship Between Schools and the Demands of Paid Work', Ph.D. thesis (University of Bath).

Merton, R. K. (1949), *Social Theory and Social Structure* (New York: Free Press).

Meyer-Larsen, W. (2000), *Germany Inc: The New German Juggernaut and its Challenge to World Business* (New York: Wiley).

Ministry of Education, Singapore (1998), *Learning to Think, Thinking to Learn: Towards Thinking Schools, Learning Nations* (Singapore: Ministry of Education).

Ministry of Manpower (MOM) (Government of Singapore) (1997), *Report on the Labour Force Survey of Singapore.*

—— (1998), *Report on the Labour Survey of Singapore.*

Miyauchi, Y., and Tahara, S. (1999), 'Shin Nihon Gata Keiei no Chosen' [The challenges of the Neo-Japanese Management System] (interview), *Chuo Koron*, Mar., Tokyo.

MOESSC (Ministry of Education, Science, Sports, and Culture) (1997), *Statistical Abstract of Education, Science, Sports and Culture in Japan* (Tokyo: Okurasho Insatsu Kyoku).

—— (1998*a*), *Statistical Abstracts of Education, Science, Sports and Culture* (Tokyo: Ministry of Education).

—— (1998*b*), *Wagakuni no Bunkyo Shisaku* [Guideline/Policy on Education in Japan] (Tokyo: Okurasho Insatsu Kyoku).

—— (1999), *Wagakuni no Bunkyo Shisaku* [guideline/Policy on Education in Japan] (Tokyo: Okurasho Insatsu Kyoku).

—— (2000), *Gakko Kihon Chosa* [School Survey] (Tokyo: MOESSC).

MOL (Ministry of Labour, Government of Japan) (1999*a*), *Rodo Hakusho* [White Paper on Labour in Japan] (Tokyo: Nihon Rodo Kiko).

—— (1999*b*), *Rodo Jiho* [Current News on Labour in Japan], Mar., July, Aug., Tokyo.

Moore, B., Jr. (1967), *Social Origins of Dictatorship and Democracy* (Boston: Beacon Press).

Moser, C. (1999), *A Fresh Start: Improving Literacy and Numeracy*, Report of the working group chaired by Sir Claus Moser, DfEE.

Munday, M., Morris, J., and Wilkinson, B. (1995), 'Factories or Warehouses? A Welsh Perspective on Japanese Transplant Manufacturing', *Regional Studies*, 29/1: 1–17.

—— Pickernell, D., and Roberts, A. (1999), *The Asian Crisis and Foreign Direct Investment: Evidence for Wales*, Welsh Economy Research Unit, Cardiff Business School, Cardiff University.

Murnane, R., and Levy, F. (1993), 'Why Today's High-School-Educated Males Earn Less that their Fathers Did: The Problem and Assessment of Responses', *Harvard Educational Review*, 63: 1–19.

—— —— (1996), *Teaching the New Basic Skills* (New York: Free Press).

Nakayama, A. (1999), 'Aratana Koyo Kanri Shisutemu no Sugata' [New Features of Human Management System (in Japan: the case study on the two Japanese companies)]' in MOL *Rodo Jiho*, July, Tokyo.

National Skills Task Force (1998), *Towards a National Skills Agenda: First Report* (London: DfEE).

—— (1999), *Delivering Skills for All: Second Report* (London: DfEE).

—— (2000*a*), *Skills For All: Research Report from the National Skills Task Force* (London: DfEE).

—— (2000*b*), *Tackling the Adult Skills Gap: Upskilling Adults and the Role of Workplace Learning: Third Report* (London, DfEE).

National Statistics Office (Republic of Korea) (1997) *Annual Report of the Economically Active Population Survey*, National Statistics Office, Seoul.

Neef, D. (1998) (ed.), *The Knowledge Economy* (Oxford: Butterworth-Heinemann).

Nelson, R. (1993) (ed.), *National Innovation Systems: A Comparative Analysis* (Cambridge: Cambridge University Press).

Nikkan Kogyo Shinbun Sha (1999), *Nikkan Kogyo Shinbun* [Daily Industry News Paper] 21 May, 1 June.

NIRA (National Institute for Research Advancement) (1994), *Mono-Zukuri Gijutsu Gino no Shorai Tenbo ni kansuru Chosa Kenkyu* [The Future of Technology and Technical Skills Needed by Manufacturing], NIRA Research Report No. 940038, NIRA, Tokyo.

Noble, D. F. (1977), *America by Design: Science, Technology and the Rise of Corporate Capitalism* (Oxford: Oxford University Press).

O'Mahoney, M. (1999), *Britain's Productivity Performance, 1956–96: An International Perspective* (London: NIESR).

O'Sullivan, M. (2000), *Contests for Corporate Control: Corporate Governance and Economic Performance in the United States and Germany* (Oxford: Oxford University Press).

OECD (1996), *Lifelong Learning for All* (Paris: OECD).

—— (1997*a*), *Education at a Glance* (Paris: OECD).

—— (1997*b*), *Science, Technology and Industry Scoreboard* (Paris: OECD).

—— (1998*a*), *Science, Technology and Industry Outlook* (Paris: OECD).

—— (1998*b*), *Human Capital Investment: An International Comparison* (Paris: OECD).

—— (1999), *Science, Technology and Industry Scoreboard* (Paris: OECD).

—— (2000*a*), *Education at a Glance* (Paris: OECD).

—— (2000*b*), *Poverty Dynamics in Six OECD Countries*, OECD Economic Studies, No. 30 2000/1, by H. Oxley, T. Than Dang, and P. Antolin (Paris: OECD).

—— (2000*c*), *Giving Young People a Good Start: The Experience of OECD Countries*, by N. Bowers, A. Sonnet, and L. Bardong (Paris: OECD).

OECD/Statistics Canada (1995), *Literacy, Economy and Society* (Paris: OECD).

Offe, C. (1976), *Industry and Inequality* (London: Edward Arnold).

Ohmae, K. (1990), *The Borderless World* (London: Collins).

—— (1995), *The End of the Nation State* (London: HarperCollins).

Ooi, G.-L., Tan, E.-S., and Koh, G. (1998), *Survey of State Society Relations: Social Indicators, Research Project Executive Summary Report*, IPS Working Papers, Institute of Policy Studies, Singapore.

Osborn, M., Rees, T., et al. (2000), *Science Policy in the European Union* (Brussels: European Commission).

Oulton, N. (1996), 'Workforce Skills and Export Competitiveness', in A. L. Booth and D. J. Snower (eds.), *Acquiring Skills: Market Failures, their Symptoms and Policy Responses* (Cambridge: Cambridge University Press).

Paik, S.-J. (1998), 'Educational Policy and Economic Development', in *Korean Perspectives on Educational Development* (Seoul: Korean Educational Development Institute).

Parsons, T. (1949), *The Structure of Social Action* (New York: Free Press).

—— (1959), 'The School as a Social System: Some of its Functions in American Society', *Harvard Educational Review*, 29: 297–318.

Patchell, J., and Hayter, R. (1995), 'Skill Formation and Japanese Production Systems', *Tijdschrift voor Economische en Sociale Geografie*, 86/4: 339–56.

Pearce, R. (1997), *Global Competition and Technology* (London: Macmillan).

Perkin, H. (1996), *The Third Revolution: Professional Ethics in the Modern World* (London: Routledge).

Peters, T., and Waterman, R. (1982), *In Search of Excellence* (New York: Harper and Row).

Pfau-Effinger, B. (1999), 'The Modernization of Family and Motherhood in Western Europe', in R. Crompton (ed.), *Restructuring Gender Relations and Employment: The Decline of the Male Breadwinner* (Oxford: Oxford University Press).

Piore, M., and Sabel, C. (1984), *The Second Industrial Divide: Possibilities for Prosperity* (New York: Basic Books).

Plender, J. (1998), 'Western Crony Capitalism', *Financial Times*, Weekend, 3–4 Oct.

Polanyi, K. (1944), *The Great Transformation* (New York: Rhinehart).

Porter, M. (1990), *The Competitive Advantage of Nations* (London: Macmillan).

—— Takeuchi, H., and Sakakibara, M. (2000), *Can Japan Compete?* (London: Macmillan).

Prais, S. J., and Wagner, K. (1985), 'Schooling Standards in England and Germany', *National Institute Economic Review*, No. 112.

—— Jarvis, V., and Wagner K. (1989), 'Productivity and Vocational Skills in Services in Britain and Germany: Hotels', *National Institute Economic Review*, Nov.

Prasad, E. (2000), *The Unbearable Stability of the German Wage Structure: Evidence and Interpretation*, IMF Working Paper WP/00/22, Washington, DC.

Presidential Committee for Quality-of-Life (2000), *DJ Welfarism: A New Paradigm for Productive Welfare in Korea*, Office of the President of the Republic of Korea.

Psacharopoulos, G. (1987) (ed.), *Economics of Education: Research and Studies* (Oxford: Pergamon).

PSB (Productivity and Standards Board) (1998), *CREST: Empowering People for the Knowledge Economy* (Singapore: PSB).

Purcell, J., and Purcell, K. (1998), 'In-sourcing, Outsourcing, and the Growth of Contingent Labour as Evidence of Flexible Employment Strategies', *European Journal of Work and Organizational Psychology*, 7/1: 39–59.

Putnam, R. (1993), *Making Democracy Work: Civic Traditions in Modern Italy* (Princeton: Princeton University Press).

Quack, S., O'Reilly, J., and Hildebrandt, S. (1995), 'Structuring Change: Recruitment, and Training in Retail Banking in Germany, Britain and France', *International Journal of Human Resource Management*, 6/4: 759–94.

Rasher, D., and Brown, C. (1997), *The Competitive Semi-Conductor Human Resources Project: Second Interim Report* (Berkeley: Institute of Industrial Relations).

Rees, G., Fevre, R., Furlong, J., and Gorrard, S. (1997), 'History, Place and the Learning Society: Towards a Sociology of Lifetime Learning', *Journal of Education Policy*, 12/6: 485–97.

Rees, T. (1998), *Mainstreaming Equality in the European Union* (London: Routledge).

Regini, M. (1995), 'Firms and Institutions: The Demand for Skills and their Social Production in Europe', *European Journal of Industrial Relations*, 1/2: 191–202.

Reich, R. (1991), *The Work of Nations: A Blueprint for the Future* (London: Simon and Schuster).

Research and Statistics Department (Singapore Ministry of Labour) (1998), *Report on the Labour Force Survey of Singapore* (Singapore: Government Printing Office).

Rifkin, J. (1996), *The End of Work* (New York: Tarcher/Putnam).

Rodan, G. (1989), *The Political Economy of Singapore's Industrialisation* (London: Macmillan).

—— (1993), 'Preserving the One-Party State in Contemporary Singapore', in K. Hewison, R. Robinson, and G. Rodan (eds.), *Southeast Asia in the 1990s: Authoritarianism, Democracy and Capitalism* (St Leonards, NSW: Allen and Unwin).

Rogoff, J., and Lave, J. (1984), *Everyday Cognition: Its Development in Social Context* (Cambridge, Mass.: Harvard University Press).

Romer, P. M. (1994), 'Economic Growth and Investment in Children', *Daedalus*, Fall: 141–54.

Rose, N. (1989), *Governing the Soul: The Shape of the Private Self* (London: Routledge).

Rosecrance, R. (1998), 'The Rise of the Virtual State', in D. Neef (ed.), *The Knowledge Economy* (Boston: Butterworth-Heinemann).

Rosecrance, R. (1999), *The Rise of the Virtual State: Wealth and Power in the Coming Century* (New York: Basic Books).

Rosenbaum, J. (1999), 'Institutional Networks and Informal Strategies for Improving Work Entry for Youths', in W. Heinz (ed.), *From Education to Work: Cross National Perspectives* (Cambridge: Cambridge University Press).

Sabel, C. (1982), *Work and Politics: The Division of Labour in Industry* (Cambridge: Cambridge University Press).

Sakamoto, A., Green, A., Brown, P., and Lauder, H. (1998), *Japan's Human Resource Response to the Challenges of the 1990s*, Working Paper 1, High Skills Project (London: Institute of Education).

Sako, M., and Sato, H. (1997) (eds.), *Japanese Labour and Management in Transition* (London: Routledge).

Scarpetta, S., et al. (2000), *Economic Growth in the OECD Area: Recent Trends at the Aggregate and Sectoral Level*, OECD Working Paper 8 (32) (Paris: OECD).

Schein, E. (1996), *Strategic Pragmatism: The Culture of Singapore's Economic Development Board* (Cambridge, Mass.: MIT Press).

Schement, J. R., and Curtis, T. (1998), 'The New Industrial Society', in J. W. Cortada (ed.), *Rise of the Knowledge Worker* (Boston: Butterworth-Heinemann).

Schulz, T. W. (1971), *Investment in Human Capital: The Role of Education and Research* (New York: Free Press).

Schumpeter, J. (1934), *The Theory of Economic Development: An Inquiry into Profits, Capital, Credit, Interest and the Business Cycle* (Cambridge, Mass.: Harvard University Press).

—— (1961), *The Theory of Economic Development* (New York: Oxford University Press).

—— (1976), *Capitalism, Socialism and Democracy* (London: Allen and Unwin).

Seki, M., and Ukai, S. (1992), *Hitode Busoku to Chusho Kigyo* [Labour Shortage and Small and Medium Enterprises] (Tokyo: Shin Pyo Ron).

Sennett, R. (1998), *The Corrosion of Character: The Personal Consequences of Work in the New Capitalism* (New York: Norton).

—— and Cobb, J. (1977), *The Hidden Injuries of Class* (Cambridge: Cambridge University Press).

Shils, E. (1965), 'Charisma, Order and Status', *American Sociological Review*, 30: 199–213.

—— (1968), 'Charisma', *International Encyclopaedia of the Social Sciences*, ii. 286–90.

Singapore Government (1991), *The Next Lap* (Singapore: Times Editions Pte Ltd).

Skills Research Group (2000), *Research Report*, National Skills Task Force.

Smith, A. (1976) [1776], *An Inquiry into the Nature and Causes of the Wealth of Nations*, ed. R. H. Campbell and W. B. Todd (Oxford: Clarendon Press).

Soros, G. (1998), *The Crises of Global Capitalism: Open Society Endangered* (London: Little, Brown and Company).

Soskice, D. (1993), 'Social Skills from Mass Higher Education: Rethinking the Company-Based Training Paradigm', *Oxford Review of Economic Policy*, 9/3: 101–13.

Spring, J. (1998), *Education and the Rise of the Global Economy* (Mahwah, NJ: L. Erlbaum Associates).

Stasz, C. (1997), 'Do Employers Need the Skills They Want? Evidence from Technical Work', *Journal of Education and Work*, 10/3: 205–24.

Steedman, H. (1999*a*), 'Intermediate Skills and Productivity—How the UK Compares', in C. Lloyd and H. Steedman, *Intermediate Level Skills—How Are They Changing*, Skills Task Force Research Paper 4 (Sudbury: DfEE Publications).

—— (1999*b*), *Looking into the 'Black Box': What Can International Surveys Tell Us about Basic Competence?*, Centre for Economic Performance, London School of Economics.

—— and Green, A. (1996), *International Comparisons of Skills Supply and Demand*, Report to DfEE, London School of Economics.

—— and Wagner, K. (1987), 'A Second Look at Productivity, Machinery and Skills in Britain and Germany', *National Institute Economic Review*, Nov.

—— —— (1989), 'Productivity, Machinery and Skills: Clothing Manufacture in Britain and Germany', *National Institute Economic Review*, May.

—— Vignoles, A., Bruniaux, C., Wagner, K., and Hansen, K. (2000), *International Comparisons of HE Quality: Engineering and Computer Science: Summary Report* (London: London School of Economics and Political Science).

Streeck, W. (1989), 'Skills and the Limits of Neo-Liberalism: The Enterprise of the Future as a Place of Learning', *Work, Employment and Society*, 3/1: 89–104.

—— (1992), *Social Institutions and Economic Performance* (London: Sage).

—— (1996), 'Lean Production in the German Automobile Industry: A Test Case for Convergence Theory', in S. Berger and R. Dore (sds.), *National Diversity and Global Capitalism* (New York: Cornell University Press), 138–70.

—— (1997), 'German Capitalism: Does It Exist? Can It Survive?', *New Political Economy*, 2/2: 237–56.

—— and Schmitter, P. (1991), 'From National Corporatism to Transnational Pluralism: Organized Interests in the Single European Market', *Politics and Society*, 19/2: 133–64.

Swedberg, R. (1996) (ed.), *Economic Sociology* (Cheltenham: Edward Elgar).

Takeuchi, H., and Nonaka, I. (1995), *Chishiki Sozo Kigyo* [The Knowledge Creating Company: How Japanese Companies Create the Dynamics of Innovation] (Tokyo: Toyo Keizai Shinpo Sha).

Tamney, J. B. (1994), *The Struggle over Singapore's Soul: Western Modernization and Asian Culture* (New York: Walter de Gruyter).

Tan, J., Gopinathan, S., and Ho, W. K. (1997) (eds.), *Education in Singapore: A Book of Readings* (Singapore: Prentice Hall).

Tan Kong Yam, and Toh Mun Heng (1998), 'The Macro-Economic Perspectives of Competitiveness', in Toh Mun Heng and Tan Kong Yam (eds.), *The*

Competitiveness of the Singapore Economy: A Strategic Perspective (Singapore: Singapore University Press).

Terashima, J. (2000), 'Seigi no Keizai Gaku no Fukken' [The Reinstatement of Economics for Justice], *Chuo Koron*, Mar., Tokyo.

Thompson, E. P. (1968), *The Making of the English Working Class* (Harmondsworth: Penguin).

Thurly, K., and Lam, A. (1990), 'Skill Formation of Electronic Engineers: Comparing the Learning Behaviour of British and Japanese Engineers', *Comparative Industrial Relations*, Discussion Paper Series, 90/211.

Thurow, L. (1993), *Head-to-Head: The Coming Economic Battle among Japan, Europe and America* (London: Nicholas Brealey).

—— (1996), *The Future of Capitalism* (London: Nicholas Brealey Publishing).

—— (1999), *Building Wealth: The New Rules for Individuals, Companies, and Nations in a Knowledge-Based Economy* (New York: HarperCollins).

Tobin, J. (1999), 'Method and Meaning in Comparative Classroom Ethnography', in R. Alexander, P. Broadfoot, and D. Phillips (eds.), *Learning from Comparing*, i. *Contexts, Classrooms and Outcomes* (Wallingford: Symposium Books).

Toh Mun Heng, and Tan Kong Yam (1998) (eds.), *Competitiveness of the Singapore Economy: A Strategic Perspective* (Singapore: Singapore University Press).

Toh, S., and Yeo Soek Lee (1995), 'Trends in Mean Years of Schooling', in *Statistics Singapore Newsletter*.

Tremewan, P. (1994), *The Political Economy of Social Control in Singapore* (Basingstoke: Macmillan).

UK Office of National Statistics (1998), *Labour Market Trends*, Oct. (London: HMSO).

UNCTAD (1996), *Transnational Corporations and World Development* (London: Thomson Business Press).

Vygotsky, L. (1978), *Mind in Society: The Development of Higher Psychological Processes* (Cambridge, Mass.: Harvard University Press).

Wade, R. (1990), *Governing the Market, Economic Theory and the Role of Government in East Asian Industrialisation* (Princeton: Princeton University Press).

—— (1998), 'From *Miracle* to *Cronyism*: Explaining the Great Asian Slump', *Cambridge Journal of Economics*, 22: 693–706.

—— and Veneroso, F. (1998), 'The Asian Crisis: The High Debt Model Versus the Wall Street–Treasury–IMF Complex', *New Left Review*, 228: 3–23.

Wagner, K. (1999), 'The German Apprentice System under Strain', in P. Culpepper and D. Finegold (eds.), *The German Skills Machine* (New York: Berghahn Books).

Wakisaka, A. (1997), 'Women at Work', in M. Sako and H. Sato (eds.), *Japanese Labour and Management in Transition* (London: Routledge).

Waterson, P., Clegg, C., Boulden, R., Pepper, K., Warr, P., and Wall, T. (1999), 'The Use and Effectiveness of Modern Manufacturing Practices: A Survey of U.K. Industry', *International Journal of Production Research*, 37: 2271–92.

Werner, Rudolf (2000), *30,000 Contracts in Apprenticeships in New Skills*, in-house paper for BIBB. The data cited by Werner are taken from the BIBB Vocational Training Reports 30 Sept. 1998 and 1999 (Bonn: BIBB).

Whittaker, D. H., and Kurosawa, Y. (1998), 'Japan's Crisis: Evolution and Implications', *Cambridge Journal of Economics*, 22: 761–71.

Wilkinson, R. (1996), *Unhealthy Societies: The Afflictions of Inequality* (London: Routledge).

Willms, J. D. (1999), 'Inequalities in Literacy Skills among Youth in Canada and the United States', *International Adult Literacy Survey* (Ottawa: Statistics Canada).

Witte, J., and Kalleberg, A. (1995), 'Matching Training and Jobs: The Fit between Vocational Education and Employment in the German Labour Market', *European Sociological Review*, 11/3: 293–317.

Wong, Soon Teck (1988), *Education Reform for Economic Development*, Institute of East Asian Studies.

—— (1992), *Development of Human Resources and Technological Capability in Singapore*, Working Paper, the Economic Development Institute of the World Bank.

Woo, C. (1998), 'Human Capital and the Economic Development of Korea: New Challenges and New Vision', Korea Development Institute, Working Paper No. 9801, Feb., Seoul.

—— and Lee, J.-H. (1999), 'The Efficiency of Korean Education: Myth and Mission', Korea Development Institute, Working Paper No. 9906, Apr., Seoul.

Wood, A. (1994), *North–South Trade, Employment and Inequality: Changing Fortunes in a Skill-Driven World* (Oxford: Clarendon Press).

Woodhall, M. (1997), 'Human Capital Concepts', in A. H. Halsey et al. (eds.), *Education: Culture, Economy and Society* (Oxford: Oxford University Press).

Woolcock, S. (1996), 'Competition amongst Forms of Corporate Governance in the European Community: The Case of Britain', in S. Berger and R. Doer (eds.), *National Diversity and Global Capitalism* (New York: Cornell University Press).

World Bank (1993), *The East Asian Miracle: Economic Growth and Public Policy* (New York: Oxford University Press).

—— (2000), *Entering the Twenty-First Century: World Development Report 1999/2000* (New York: Oxford University Press).

World Economic Forum (1997), *The Global Competitiveness Report* (Oxford: Oxford University Press).

WTO (World Trade Organisation) (1997), *WTO Annual Report: International Trade Statistics* (Geneva: WTO).

Yeandle, S. (1999), 'Women, Men and Non-Standard Employment: Bread-winning and Caregiving in Germany, Italy and the United Kingdom', in R. Crompton (ed.), *Restructuring Gender Relations and Employment: The Decline of the Male Breadwinner* (Oxford: Oxford University Press).

Yergin, D., and Stanislaw, J. (1998), *The Commanding Heights* (New York: Simon and Schuster).

Yip, Soon Kwong, John, Eng Soo Peck, and Jay Yap Ye Chin (1997), '25 Years of Educational Reform', in J. Tan, S. Gopinathan, and Ho Wah Kam (eds.), *Education in Singapore* (Singapore: Prentice Hall).

Young, M. (1998), *The Curriculum of the Future* (London: Falmer).

Zuboff, S. (1988), *In the Age of the Smart Machine: The Future of Work and Power* (New York: Basic Books).

AUTHOR INDEX

SUBJECT INDEX